EXERCISES IN SPATIAL THINKING

This book is one of a series of studies in Spatial Economic Analysis stimulated by theoretical and applied research conducted within the Netherlands Economic Institute, Rotterdam, and published by Gower. Titles in the series are:

J.H.P. Paelinck (ed.), *La Structure Urbaine en Europe Occidentale/ Urban Structure in Western Europe*

J.H.P. Paelinck and P. Nijkamp, *Operational Theory and Method in Regional Economics*

L.H. Klaassen, J.H.P. Paelinck and Sj. Wagenaar, *Spatial Systems: A General Introduction*

J.H.P. Paelinck and L.H. Klaassen (with J.P. Ancot, A.C.P. Verster and Sj. Wagenaar), *Spatial Econometrics*

W. Molle (with B. van Holst and H. Smit), *Regional Disparity and Economic Development in the European Community*

N. Vanhove and L.H. Klaassen, *Regional Policy: A European Approach*

L.H. Klaassen, J. Bourdrez and J. Volmuller, *Transport and Re-urbanisation*

L.H. Klaassen, W. Molle and J.H.P. Paelinck (eds), *Dynamics of Urban Development*

J.H.P. Paelinck (with J-P. Ancot and H. Kuiper), *Formal Spatial Economic Analysis*

W. Molle and L.H. Klaassen (eds), *Industrial Mobility and Migration in the European Community*

W. Molle, *Industrial Location and Regional Development in the European Community: the FLEUR model*

W. Molle and E. Wever, *Oil Refineries and Petrochemical Industries in Western Europe*

J.H.P. Paelinck (ed.), *Human Behaviour in Geographical Space*

Leo van den Berg, *Urban Systems in a Dynamic Society*

Leo van den Berg, Leland S. Burns and Leo H. Klaassen (eds), *Spatial Cycles*

L.H. Klaassen, *Exercises in Spatial Thinking*

Exercises in Spatial Thinking

Case Studies of Regional Development Issues

LEO H. KLAASSEN

Avebury
Aldershot · Brookfield USA · Hong Kong · Singapore · Sydney

Published by
Avebury
Gower Publishing Company Limited
Gower House, Croft Road
Aldershot, Hants GU11 3HR
England

Gower Publishing Company
Old Post Road
Brookfield, Vermont 05036
USA

British Library Cataloguing in Publication Data

Klaassen, Leo H. (Leo Hendrik), 1920–
Exercises in spatial thinking: case studies of
regional development issues.
1. Economics. Spatial analysis
I. Title
330'.724

Library of Congress Cataloging-in-Publication Data

Klaassen, Leo H. (Leo Hendrik), 1920–
Exercises in spatial thinking: case studies of
regional development issues / Leo H. Klaassen.
p. cm.
Includes index.
1. Regional economics – Case studies. 2. Space
in economics – Case studies. 3. Regional planning –
Case studies. I. Title.
HT388.K54 1988
338.9 – dc19

ISBN 0 566 05710 7

Printed and bound in Great Britain by
Athenaeum Press Limited, Newcastle upon Tyne

Contents

Preface

Some time ago, some Polish scholars came to me with the request that I compile a volume from articles already published by me or together with co-authors concerning the contribution of the space concept to economic science. The idea was to illustrate that the addition of this spatial dimension not only makes economic arguments more realistic, but is even essential to the proper understanding of what economics is about.

After the Polish edition had appeared, to prepare an English version seemed right and proper, and hence the present volume. It differs in some respects from the Polish edition: for one thing, more recent work has been inserted, and for another, views have changed, even in the short period of two years separating the two editions. It is hoped that this book may be helpful to the study of spatial problems on the various levels it addresses: methodology, urban problems, transport, the environment, welfare theory, government policy and futurology.

Thanks are due to the publishers of the original articles and to co-authors for their consent to have their papers included in this book. Thanks are also due to Mrs A.C.A. Elderson for her excellent translations, and to Mrs S. Kleyngeld for her immaculate typing.

Leo H. Klaassen

1 Introduction

1.1 On regional science

Introduction

The penetration of economics into the geographer's thinking was one phenomenon that, through economic geography, logically led to regional economics. But it has by no means been the only factor, for regional economics is quite as much a branch of general economics. At least, that is the view of many general economists; spatial economists prefer to think of it as a tributary which has made general economics even more general.

Macro-economics and regional economy

A logical conclusion from the fact that all economic phenomena proceed in space is that their study requires the delimitation of that space, if only to allow proper measurement of the phenomena to be studied.

There is no denying that macro-economics has tended strongly to consider the national territory eminently suitable as a spatial framework for economic analyses. Almost all macro models are concerned with the economic relations within a national territory, referring to other areas only in their export and import departments. Actually they split up the world into two regions, the domestic nation and the rest of the world.

Such an approach has two implications. The first is that builders of macro models evidently respect the political or administrative boundaries of the national territory. The second is that some macro models refer to small, even tiny, nations and others to large, even huge, ones. That cannot be helped so long as there are small and large countries and macro-economists go on looking on national territories as relevant areas.

But are administrative borders at all relevant for the definition of regions as objects of economic analysis? Apart from the practical advantage that statistical data, easy to obtain for administrative regions, are hardly if at all available for regions otherwise delimited, there is in fact only one convincing argument, namely that in administrative regions there is always a responsible authority (national or regional government) which can or wants to influence developments in general, and economic ones in particular. If economic analysis is supposed to provide a foundation for policy-making in a given administrative area, understandably it will be confined to that area, recommendations being derived from it for the actions of the responsible authorities. Whether such policy recommendations will have optimum influence on the administrative area's development remains to be seen. If the area (by whatever criterion) forms part of a larger economic system, the effect of the recommended policy, pursued for its benefit by, say, the national authorities, might remain below expectations; they might have been better had the analysis covered a larger area in the first place, and other regional authorities than those of the region directly involved been consulted.

To give an example: nation-oriented economic analysis could never have revealed that Bavaria, Austria, Switzerland, Baden Württemberg, Haute Savoie, the French Riviera and part of northern Italy form one large coherent area; in fact the Alpine region shows clear signs of being a potential prosperity region. A regional-economic approach to European development, however, might have revealed to the five national governments involved that in parts of their national territories evolutions are proceeding which are amply worth their support.

On the other hand, for certain analyses the area envisaged might also be too large. Indeed the overall averages and totals feeding models which cover very large regions, such as large countries, do no justice to the widely varied endowment of subregions, while the deviation from national averages is the very source of the problems many countries are contending with. If important regional differences within a national economy are left out of consideration, the country's essential problems tend to be overlooked and its economic policy runs the risk of being based on an average that has no real significance.

Two opposite points of view can be taken. From the macro point of view, macro developments, being most important to the nation, are the most likely objects of analysis; indeed their analysis provides the national government with instruments to influence these developments most effectively. From the regional point of view, on the contrary, the nation's boundaries, being determined by historical, political and military factors, have no economic relevance; indeed economic phenomena and processes tend to become more and more independent from national frontiers. For the adequate study of these processes, their *relevant* region would be the proper framework, and only by pure chance would it coincide with national frontiers.

The results of the so-called FLEUR project (Molle, 1980) carried out at the Netherlands Economic Institute several years ago, by which the economic developments in a hundred West European regions since 1950 were investigated, show that in every region progress is influenced by general, supranational factors as well as national and regional ones. Even if their economic structures are comparable, some West European countries have, in nearly all their regions, significantly higher growth rates than other countries. On the other hand, within the same national territory some regions show significantly better economic results than others in similar circumstances. Evidently, there is every reason to recognise that national and regional components, as well as the general one, are relevant to economic development. Which of the three is the most important, can be determined only through further analysis; the outcome will probably vary from country to country and from case to case.

Sectoral considerations

One of the most important features of an economic activity is the extension of its relevant region, roughly defined as the region beyond whose boundaries there are no significant exports or imports of the goods and/or services produced by or through that activity (Vanhove and Klaassen, 1987). Typical activities with vast relevant regions are oil refineries, steel production, production of agrarian bulk products, etc. Examples of activities with small relevant regions are: retail trade, various forms of services, repair activities and production of highly perishable goods. The dichotomy of basic (driving) and non-basic (providing) activities common in the older regional economic literature can never be unequivocal, as may be clear from the foregoing; whether an activity boosts the economy or provides for the population depends on the extension of the region studied. An activity with a motor function for a municipality may be of the providing kind for a province (a regional hospital).

Obviously if regions are understood as parts of a larger economic entity, the regional component is highly important to activities with a relatively small relevant region. For in that case their developments are fully determined by, among other things, the income level and the population volume of the region involved. Where the relevant region coincides with the national territory, then we may speak of a national activity. However, as may be derived from our earlier argument, a national activity is not the same for a large and for a small country. The development of activities with a very extensive relevant region, of which we have given some examples above, is governed by international factors.

The logical implication is that the extent to which a region's development is governed by international, national and regional factors, depends on its economic structure. Little can be said about that, a priori, especially because individual sectors naturally do not develop in isolation. National sectors, for instance, are bound to have some connection with both international and regional sectors.

Intersectoral and interregional relations

In macro models the relations among sectors are expressed in national input–output tables. However, these tables have lost much of their informative value through the summation over regions. Regionally disaggregated, they would indicate not only the relations among sectors, but also the interregional relations within supraregional sectors, thus underlining that the nation is not in fact one single region, but a system of coherent regions, which also functions as such. When that is recognised and when the national economy, the sum total of all regional economies, is no longer supposed to represent all that goes on in individual regions, but it is recognised as a system of mutually influential sectoral and regional variables, then the views of the regional economist will have been generally accepted. Regional economy describes and analyses the developments in a country or part of the world as a system of regional and sectoral interdependences. Obviously the variables referring to the regions of one country will add up to the corresponding national variable.

The foregoing clearly refutes the opinion that regional economics is not much else but a disaggregated form of macro-economics, which after dividing the national territory into regions, carries out an analysis comparable to macro-analysis on the regional level, which in the eyes of many is inferior to the national level. We have set out to prove that practising regional economics is not just a matter of dividing the national economy into smaller ones. The essential idea is that economic developments within the national territory are resultant in the developments within a coherent system of regions and sectors, in which foreign regions, too, can play an important part. The most important determinant of the cohesion within the system is the communication among regions. Should the communication costs among regions play no role at all – which implies that the distances among regions should be irrelevant to economic evolution – then the macro treatment might be justified. However, that is not so, and to understand macro developments, we need to understand the links among regions. That is why the notion of communication costs (including generalised transportation costs, composed of money and time sacrifices and transportation efforts) is so essential to regional economics.

Regional economics and regional science

In the previous section we have argued that regional economics has a very special relation to macro-economics, often erroneously called general economics. However, that does not fully account for the position of regional economics. Indeed the regional approach has given rise to a variety of other developments and has, in particular, contributed to the interdisciplinary treatment of regional problems.

The first important new factor to be studied was the relations that regions maintain among themselves. We have already mentioned communication costs (including transportation costs) as one item of the costs involved in the regions' functioning as a coherent system, or to put it differently, the frictions influencing the intensity of interaction among regions. The level of these costs, or frictions, determines both the internal coherence and the efficient functioning of the regional system. Both depend on the quality of the technical infrastructure linking the regions together, the physical distance separating them and the psychological distance that may keep them apart. The study of a system of regions logically entails the study of the quality and nature of infrastructural provisions, the level of generalised transportation costs, the length of psychological distances and their influence on the interregional relations. Therefore, research into the distance behaviour of family and production households is central to regional economics. In general economics it is a little known area of research, although the accessibility of workplaces and facilities are generally recognised as an essential part of the individual household's prosperity.

The regional approach to economic problems also leads more or less as a matter of course to the study of problems of strong regional relevance. One of the most important is the conservation of the environment. Environmental pollution is a typical regional phenomenon, likely to inspire mostly regional reactions. Several investigations have shown that differences in environmental quality and scenery have contributed significantly to the recent migration behaviour of family households – a phenomenon that is, in turn, important for the quality of the labour supply in the regions. The steep decline of the large towns' population share, and the growing inclination to live in small towns and rural parts at a respectful distance from the large towns, also springs from dissatisfaction with the environment, the lack of space and bad access to natural beauty which mark the large towns. To describe regional developments in an adequate fashion, regional economists are naturally apt to take an interest in environmental problems and thus to co-operate with disciplines concerned with those problems for other reasons.

An area traditionally favoured with the interest of regional economists is that of people's spatial behaviour, their shopping habits, leisure activities, etc., as functions of their residence and the spatial spread of shopping and leisure centres, the available infra- and superstructures and their variable willingness to bridge distances for making various kinds of purchase and filling their leisure time. To know people's fundamental behaviour is becoming more and more important too, because together with shopping and leisure conditions, it determines the actual shopping and leisure-time flows. Why do different socio-economic groups behave differently? Does fundamental behaviour change through time? And can it be influenced? Such are the questions posed in spatial investigations, and the answers to them are needed for smooth and efficient planning. Co-operation with experts of economic psychology suggests itself; hopefully, it will be intensified and extended to other areas. The collective analysis of time budgets in conjunction with money budgets appears a fertile field of co-operation.

From the awareness that in successful spatial planning an understanding of spatial behaviour is essential springs the insight that town development and regional science have essential interests in common and cannot in fact be practised independently. The regional economist needs to have a feeling for and an insight into the principles of town building as much as the town planner, to fulfil his task adequately, and must not overlook spatial behaviour patterns. Fundamental changes in the structure of urban economies as discovered in the CURB (Costs of Urban Growth) project (van den Berg *et al.*, 1982), in which 14 countries participated, and which, as far as Holland is concerned, was a collective effort of Erasmus University (Department of Regional and Socio-economic Research) and the Netherlands Economic Institute (continued in 1980 as PURDY – Project Urban Dynamics), are of the greatest importance to town planners anxious to find adequate answers to questions about the future planning of towns – and answers that are essential to the regional researcher who, in turn, finds himself faced with the question of how the town planner's response can curb, perhaps turn, dynamic trends.

Many more examples could be mentioned of the scientific field linked with that of regional economics. Those given may suffice, however, to demonstrate how the researcher's concern with the spatial element in the economy may compel him to operate far above, as well as far below, the national level and also – quite as important – often far outside his original discipline. Perhaps that last possibility is what makes regional science so fascinating? The regional element turns research into an attempt to penetrate into the fundamental behaviour of firms, people and households; to examine the ways in which society functions, especially in space; and the ways in which households adjust to new conditions while themselves, through their altered behaviour, causing new developments, both spatial and non-spatial. The environment of ordinary men and women and the way they fend for themselves in that environment and, at the same time, influence it become the the objects of analysis. Being close to human-kind is what makes many sciences, regional science not the least among them, so attractive.

An afterthought

Our description of the birth of a new science has not been a mono-disciplinary tale. In fact it describes how originally separate disciplines, overlapping but practised more or less in isolation, have been melted into one new, more general discipline, which by the natural annexation of peripheral areas has grown to be a science with the ambition to penetrate to the basic determinants of human beings in their spatial habitat. Human behaviour on the labour market, in shops and in free-time activities, in short, all actions forming part of the total spatial behaviour of households and individuals, have become objects of regional science.

Probably, the process of incorporating new disciplines has not yet gone far enough. That what makes a region special with its own culture, its own language (recognised as such and no longer despised as mere 'dialect'), its own religion, regional customs and habits and all those matters so essential to a region's prosperity and well-being, have up till now been neglected by regional research, even though they have been gaining in political significance. Presumably, as has all too often happened in economics, they have been neglected because they are difficult to measure. Hopefully, the renascence of regional cultures (Petrella, 1978) will change that, too, adding another old geographic theme to regional science. That continuous expansion will go on fascinating and inspiring its scholars. A better guarantee for its survival can hardly be imagined.

References

van den Berg, L., Drewett, R., Klaassen, L.H., Rossi, A. and Vijverberg, C.H.T. (1982), *Urban Europe: A Study of Growth and Decline*, Oxford: Pergamon.

Molle, W.T.M. (1980), *Regional Disparity and Economic Development in the European Community*, Farnborough: Saxon House.

Petrella, R. (1978), *La Renaissance des cultures regionales en Europe*, Paris: Editions Entente.

Vanhove, Norbert and Klaassen, L.H. (1987), *Regional Policy: A European Approach*, Aldershot: Gower.

2 Methodology

2.1 Asymmetry in shift-and-share analysis*

The problem

Suppose g_i is the rate of growth of the economy of region i and g_j that of region j ($i, j = 1, 2, \ldots, r$). By definition:

$$g_i = \sum_k g_{ik} f_{ik} \tag{2.1}$$

and accordingly:

$$g_j = \sum_k g_{jk} f_{jk} \quad (k = 1, 2, \ldots, s)$$

in which $g_{ik} \cdot g_{jk}$ are the rates of growth of sector k in i and j respectively, and $f_{ik} \cdot f_{jk}$ are the fractions of sector k in the total economy of i and j respectively.

Obviously the difference between g_i and g_j is caused by two effects, namely (a) the differences in growth rates per sector (g_{ik} and g_{jk}), and (b) the difference in structure of the two economies (f_{ik} and f_{jk}). Effect (a) will be called the growth effect, and (b) the structural effect. Shift-and-share analysis tries to define the difference in growth

*See L.H. Klaassen and J.H.P. Paelinck, *Regional and Urban Economics*, Amsterdam: North-Holland, 1972.

between the regions i and j as the sum of these two effects. It will be clear, however, that there are two ways to do this, i.e. either by weighting the differences in growth with the structure of region i or with the structure of region j as far as the growth effect is concerned, and by either weighting the differences in structure with the growth rates of region i or with those of region j as far as the structural effect is concerned. Applying one of the two methods implies that by definition the difference between g_i and g_j is composed of different structural and growth effects than that between g_j and g_i.

This phenomenon can be expressed in symbols as follows:

$$\begin{aligned} g_i - g_j &= \sum_k g_{ik} f_{ik} - \sum_k g_{jk} f_{jk} \\ &= \sum_k g_{ik} f_{ik} - \sum_k g_{ik} f_{jk} + \sum_k g_{ik} f_{jk} - \sum_k g_{jk} f_{jk} \\ &= \sum_k g_{ik} (f_{ik} - f_{jk}) + \sum_k (g_{ik} - g_{jk}) f_{jk} \qquad (2.2) \end{aligned}$$

In this expression the structural effect is measured as a weighted sum of the differences in structure. The weights applied are the growth rates of i. The weights in the growth effects are the structural fractions of j. However, we could also have written:

$$\begin{aligned} g_i - g_j &= \sum_k g_{ik} f_{ik} - \sum_k g_{jk} f_{jk} \\ &= \sum_k g_{ik} f_{ik} - \sum_k g_{jk} f_{ik} + \sum_k g_{jk} f_{ik} - \sum_k g_{jk} f_{jk} \\ &= \sum_k (g_{ik} - g_{jk}) f_{ik} + \sum_k g_{jk} (f_{ik} - f_{jk}) \qquad (2.3) \end{aligned}$$

In expression (2.3) the structural differences are weighted with the growth rates of j and the differences in growth rates with the structure of i. The two approaches give evidently different results, meaning that there are two ways of defining structural and growth effects depending on the method chosen.

Matrix presentation

This asymmetry can be expressed more elegantly in the following way. Write F for the $r \times s$ matrix of the fractions of the different sectors in all the regions. An element f_{ik} indicates the fraction of sector k in the economy of region i.

Write G for the $r \times s$ matrix of growth rates; g_{ik} is the growth rate of sector k in region i.

An element of the product of the two matrices F and G' expresses the growth rates that would apply to a region i if it had had the structure of region j. The elements of the main diagonal therefore express the actual growth rates of the r regions. Now define:

$$gi' = \bar{G} = \begin{bmatrix} \bar{g}_{11} & \bar{g}_{11} & \cdots & \bar{g}_{11} \\ \bar{g}_{22} & \bar{g}_{22} & \cdots & \bar{g}_{22} \\ '' & '' & & '' \\ '' & '' & & '' \\ \bar{g}_{rr} & \bar{g}_{rr} & \cdots & \bar{g}_{rr} \end{bmatrix} \tag{2.4}$$

in which g is the vector of actual growth rates. We then write:

$$D_S = \bar{G} - FG' \tag{2.5}$$

In D_S all *structural* effects are represented. The elements on the main diagonal are zero. The element ij represents the difference in the actual growth rate of region i and the growth rate this region would have had if its structure had been identical to that of region j.

The *growth* effects evidently are represented by the matrix:

$$D_G = FG' - \bar{G}' \tag{2.6}$$

The sums of both effects equal the differences between the actual growth rates:

$$D = D_S + D_G = (\bar{G} - FG') + (FG' - \bar{G}') - \bar{G} - \bar{G}' \tag{2.7}$$

Since:

$$D' = \bar{G}' - \bar{G} = -D \tag{2.8}$$

D is negatively symmetrical.

This result is identical to the one obtained in the previous section where we stated that the difference between two growth rates can be defined in two different ways:

$$D = D_S + D_G = (\bar{G} - FG') + (FG' - \bar{G}') \tag{2.9}$$

and:

$$D = -D' = -D'_S - D'_G = (GF' - \bar{G}') + (\bar{G} - GF') \qquad (2.10)$$

We thus have two structural effects: $(\bar{G} - FG')$ and $(\bar{G}' - GF')$; and two growth effects: $(FG' - \bar{G}')$ and $(GF' - \bar{G})$.

Possible solutions

Averaging out In order to overcome this asymmetry we can write:

$$D = \tfrac{1}{2}(D - D') = \tfrac{1}{2}(D_S + D_G) - \tfrac{1}{2}(D'_S + D'_G) = \tfrac{1}{2}(D_S - D'_S)$$

$$+ \tfrac{1}{2}(D_G - D'_G) = \tfrac{1}{2}(\bar{G} - FG' + GF' - \bar{G}')$$

$$+ \tfrac{1}{2}(\bar{G} - GF' + FG' - \bar{G}') = D_S^N + D_G^N \qquad (2.11)$$

In expression (2.11) both D_S^N and D_G^N are negatively symmetrical. This means that this expression fulfils the condition that the structural effect, as well as the growth effect, between i and j are equal to those between j and i with a negative sign. In Σ notation we may write:

$$D_S^N = D_S - D'_S = \sum_k (g_{ik} - g_{jk}) \tfrac{1}{2}(f_{ik} + f_{jk})$$

and: (2.12)

$$D_G^N = D_G - D'_G = \sum_k (f_{ik} - f_{jk}) \tfrac{1}{2}(g_{ik} + g_{jk})$$

Differences in growth between regions i and j are thus weighted with the average structure of i and j. Differences in structure are weighted with the average growth rates of sectors in both regions.

Keeping the asymmetry Another view of the asymmetry mentioned might be the following:

$$g_i - g_j = \sum_k (g_{ig} - g_{jk})f_{jk} + \sum_k (f_{ik} - f_{jk})g_{jk}$$
$$+ [(g_i + g_j) - (g_{ij} + g_{ji})] \qquad (2.13)$$

where:

$$g_{ij} = \sum_k f_{jk} g_{ik}$$

$$g_{ji} = \sum_k f_{ik} g_{jk}$$

or:

$$g_i - g_j = (\Delta^g_{ij})_j + (\Delta^f_{ij})_j + \Delta^s \qquad (2.14)$$

The first two terms in equation (2.14) are the expression of what we might want to measure, i.e. the difference in growth rates between region i and j supposing on the one hand that region i had the structure of region j (but its own growth rates), and on the other hand that region i had the growth rates of region j (but its own structure).

The remaining term is symmetrical and may be interpreted as the joint contribution (positive or negative) to overall growth which might have been due to a complete switch in the respective 'roles' of the regions, the rates of growth of one region being applied to the structure of the other, and vice versa.

As this last term is obviously the same for both regions and of second-order magnitude as compared to the asymmetrical terms, comparison of the shift-and-share parts as defined in expressions (2.13) and (2.14) makes sense.

An example might clarify this. Take $g_i - g_j$ as 0.20 and compare the following situations:

$$g_i - g_j = 0.20 = -0.10 \text{ (structure)} + 0.28 \text{ (growth)} + 0.02$$

$$= -(g_j - g_i) = 0.2 \text{ (structure)} - 0.024 \text{ (growth)} - 0.02.$$

Obviously giving region i the dynamism of region j would pay, whereas a structural shift would only worsen matters: region j could benefit both by getting region i's structure and dynamism.

2.2 Some indicators of regional labour market equilibrium*

Introduction

The need for a new measure for labour market equilibrium emerged from the discussion around a fundamental study of labour and the labour market, carried out by the Netherlands Economic Institute (Heijke, Klaassen and Offereins, 1975). It became clear during this discussion that the traditional indicators of the situation on the labour market, such as unemployment, open demand, etc., are insufficiently precise in describing the actual situation; the reasons for this will be given below.

Labour market equilibrium is generally defined in terms of demand

*See L.H. Klaassen and J.A.M. Heijke, *Economie appliquée*, Archives de l'ISMEA, Tome XXVIII-1975, Librairie Droz, Geneva, 1975.

for and supply of positions. The condition for equilibrium is then D = S (demand for labour (supply of positions) equals supply of labour (demand for positions): equilibrium *ex ante*), or D = S = E (demand and supply equal the number of filled positions; in other words, there is no unemployment and there are no vacancies: equilibrium *ex post*). The degree to which the actual situation on the labour market deviates from the equilibrium position is usually expressed in a percentage of the working population.

When these figures are handled on a very high level of aggregation (e.g. the national level) it appears extremely difficult to get a good insight into the actual situation of the labour market. This can be improved by differentiation of the indicators according to regions, sectors, professions or other separate markets. Seasonal and frictional elements are then still left out of consideration, but maybe more important is the problem that even after disaggregation, the figures indicate *registered* supply and *registered* demand rather than actual supply and actual demand. Particularly as far as the supply of positions is concerned, these figures may deviate very considerably from reality. To come nearer to reality, the concepts of 'disguised unemployment' and 'disguised vacancies' have been introduced, rightly so, though these concepts seem very difficult to estimate. Furthermore, additional insight into the regional situation may be gained from figures about commuting and migration, though it should not be forgotten that these volumes of commuting and migration are also determined by other factors than the employment situation, and cannot therefore be looked upon as indicators of the deviation from the equilibrium situation of the labour market.

But even when all the above considerations have been accounted for, it is still questionable if such factors as 'vacancies' and 'unemployment' cover all the elements that play an essential role in the situation of a specific labour market. In the conventional equilibrium concepts, factors like commuting distance, wage levels, work conditions and labour performance are left out of consideration, yet they relate directly to the labour and production situations, and an understanding of the tensions existing in connection with them is essential in appreciating whether or not the actual situation is one of equilibrium.

Some fundamental considerations

It seems appropriate to start the search for a proper measure of labour market equilibrium from the basic concept of well-being (Menger, 1986; Klaassen and Botterweg, 1974). Our well-being rests not only on the goods we possess and can effectively enjoy, but also (and especially) on the ratio between them and all the goods that we feel could contribute to our well-being. In other words, it is not the quantity of goods in our possession, but that quantity seen *in relation to* the quantity we desire, that determines our degree of well-being. The degree of well-being is the ratio between the goods we have to satisfy our needs and those needs themselves, or formulated in yet another way, it is the degree to which our needs can be satisfied by the goods that are available to us.

A similar definition is given by Pigou (1951): 'A man's welfare then consists in his satisfactions. But what does satisfaction mean? . . . It might seem that, when his desire attitude is given, his satisfaction depends straightforwardly on the extent to which his desires are fulfilled.'

To translate this definition of well-being in terms of labour and the labour market, it seems useful to define the labour market somewhat more precisely than (as is usually done) as the functional place where labour is supplied and demanded. Within the framework of welfare economics the following definition might be more appropriate: 'The labour market contains everything relevant to the efforts of workers and entrepreneurs to satisfy their needs as far as these needs can be satisfied through labour efforts.' This definition implies that the degree to which needs are satisfied, i.e. the relative tension between the desired and the actual situation, forms together with the possibility to reduce this tension for both workers and entrepreneurs by adjusting either the desires or the work conditions, the central problem of the labour market. Essential, though difficult to measure, are the preference functions of individual workers with respect to the various aspects of positions to be filled, such as income to be earned, profession to be carried on and circumstances under which the work is to be performed, as well as the preference function of the entrepreneurs with regard to the number and nature of the positions to be created, the wages they are prepared to pay and the working conditions they are prepared to offer. The confrontation of these functions with the actual situation constitute the essence of the labour market problem.

Two discrepancies may now be distinguished in relation to those demanding positions and those supplying positions:

1 The ratio (or the difference) between the desires of the workers and the actual situation as far as it is relevant to them with regard to e.g. income, profession and journey-to-work distance.
2 The ratio (or the difference) between the desires of the entrepreneurs and the actual situation as far as it is relevant to them with regard to e.g. wages to be paid and work performance.

If the needs of workers (or potential workers) are indicated by P_s and the actual situation by R, the discrepancy ad 1 can be written as:

$$T_s = P_s - R$$

the discrepancy ad 2, analogously, equals:

$$T_d = P_d - R^*$$

The greater the 'distance' between the needs or desires and the actual situation, the less satisfactory these situations are. Workers and entrepreneurs are fully satisfied only if both $T_s = 0$ and $T_d = 0$.

It may be assumed that the above-mentioned discrepancies will cause both workers and entrepreneurs to try to adjust R in order to reach a more satisfactory situation. An attempt to improve the situation could be that workers start negotiations with entrepreneurs to accomplish an adjustment. A worker could also try to improve his relative position by looking for work with another firm. The discrepancies can become so great in certain cases that workers start looking for positions with a character completely different from that of the one they are holding, that is, for a different profession. The remaining discrepancy may give rise to a number of phenomena such as training and re-training, sickness, frustration and decreased work performance.

Entrepreneurs might seek to improve the situation by decreasing the number of positions to be filled (by means of mechanisation or otherwise), adjusting the nature of positions in such a way that they can be filled by workers who are actually available, and so on. For those demanding labour the situation will never become quite satisfactory either.

Although we shall return to this point later, it seems appropriate to indicate here that the situation of the parties on the labour market seen from the angle set out above is completely similar to the position of an individual in welfare theory, who is also trying to improve his relative position, but will never be completely satisfied.

J. Kornai indicates that the equilibrium concept is closely connected with the concept of 'rest'. He defines an economic equilibrium as a situation in which none of the participants in the economic process is interested in changing his behaviour and consequently destroying the equilibrium situation (Kornai, 1981). Applying this definition to the labour market with respect to both workers and

*Obviously these discrepancies can also be expressed as ratios. In that case, they are, respectively: $T_s = P_s/R$, and $T_d = P_d/R$.

entrepreneurs, equilibrium will exist if there is no discrepancy either for workers or for entrepreneurs. That means that $T_s = 0$, and $T_d = 0$; then:

$$P_s = P_d = R$$

will hold. In fact, in practice, there will never be a situation of equilibrium in this sense. For that reason, we will rather concentrate on the search for a measure that indicates the *deviation from equilibrium*, and the way in which that deviation can be decreased. Obviously this measure will be of a complex nature, and will have to be built up gradually to become operational in labour market policy.

A measure of discrepancy

The spatial element in equilibrium We will start the construction of a discrepancy coefficient by considering the spatial element in the labour market.

Denote the attractiveness of a position in region i for a *worker* living in h by a_{hi}. Assume that the attractiveness of this position is a decreasing function of the distance between h and i (d_{hi}). We may then write:

$$a_{hi} = \exp(-a d_{hi}) \qquad (2.15)$$

The coefficient a represents the degree to which the attractiveness of the position decreases with distance. Since this distance has to be interpreted as generalised transportation costs (money costs, time and effort), its value depends among other things on the means of transportation available to the worker.

Obviously the minimum value of a_{hi} equals 0. This value is reached for $d_{hi} \rightarrow \infty$. The maximum value of the attractiveness of the position, *ceteris paribus*, of course, equals unity (for $d_{hi} = 0$).

In principle, the coefficient will be different for different individuals. It will, however, be possible to define social groups (social positions, age-groups, sex) within which the as differ relatively little. It will be assumed in the following that a is equal for all individuals.

The supply discrepancy can now be defined as the ratio between the ideal situation and the actual situation. If the actual situation is indicated by a_{hi}, reached for a distance d_{hi}, the discrepancy coefficient for an individual in this case equals:

$$T_h^s = \frac{(a_{hi})_{max}}{a_{hi}} \qquad (2.16)$$

Since $(a_{hi})_{max} = I$ (commuting distance zero), the supply-discrepancy coefficient equals:

$$T_h^s = \frac{I}{a_{hi}} = \exp(ad_{hi}) \tag{2.17}$$

a_{hi} thus represents the partial welfare position of an individual living in h and working in i, that is the degree of satisfaction he gains from his present position in relation to his ideal position. Considering that policy-makers do not aim at an ideal labour situation but focus their policy on feasible objectives, one might envisage discrepancy coefficients in which $(a_{hi})_{max}$ is replaced with $(a_{hi})_{acceptable}$. In what follows we shall not pursue this idea, however.

If the number of people living in h who are willing to fill a position is indicated by S_h (working population), the total attractiveness of the existing situation to this group equals:

$$S_h a_h$$

If from this group E_{hi} individuals work in i, then the total attraction felt by workers in h towards filling positions in all regions equals:

$$\sum_i E_{hi} a_{hi} = \sum_i E_{hi} \exp(ad_{hi}) \tag{2.18}$$

The remaining part of the population is unemployed (U_h). To express their situation mathematically, it is assumed that their work is located at an infinite distance from h. Total attractiveness of work for residents in h willing to work is thus:

$$\begin{aligned} S_h a_h &= \sum_i S_{hi} \exp(-ad_{hi}) = \sum_i \{U_h . 0 + E_{hi} \exp(-ad_{hi})\} \\ &= \sum_i E_{hi} \exp(-ad_{hi}) \end{aligned} \tag{2.19}$$

Since $(S_h a_h)_{max} = S_h$, and $T_h^s = \frac{(S_h a_h)_{max}}{S_h a_h}$, it follows that:

$$T_h^s = \frac{I}{a_h} = \frac{S_h}{\Sigma E_{hi} \exp(-ad_{hi})} = \frac{U_h + \sum_i E_{hi}}{\sum_i E_{hi} \exp(-ad_{hi})} \tag{2.20}$$

Similarly, for the whole labour market (all regions h), it may be stated that:

$$T^s = \frac{\sum_h S_h}{\sum_h \sum_i E_{hi} \exp(-ad_{hi})} = \frac{\sum_h U_h + \sum_h \sum_i E_{hi}}{\sum_h \sum_i E_{hi} \exp(-ad_{hi})} \tag{2.21}$$

Obviously the discrepancy T^s increases with increasing distances, and reaches a minimum value when all $d_{hi} = 0$ and all $U_h = 0$. In this case, everybody willing to work finds employment in his immediate neighbourhood; T^s then equals unity. If the measure for the discrepancy between *supply equilibrium* and the actual situation is defined in such a way that it reaches a zero value in case of equilibrium, we may write:

$$\Upsilon^s = I - \frac{I}{T^s} \tag{2.22}$$

It may be assumed that *entrepreneurs* are indifferent to the commuting distances of their workers as long as these do not influence their work performance. Under this assumption we may derive the demand discrepancy as follows.

The attractiveness of the labour market situation will reach a maximum for the entrepreneur in i when all positions offered (D_i) are occupied. The actual attractiveness can be derived from the actual number of positions filled ($\sum_h E_{hi}$) if the attractiveness of unfilled positions is put at zero. The demand discrepancy with regard to region i can then be written as:

$$T_i^d = \frac{D_i}{\sum_h E_{hi}} = \frac{V_i + \sum_h E_{hi}}{\sum_h E_{hi}} \tag{2.23}$$

in which V_i indicates the number of vacancies. T_i^d will decrease when the number of positions actually filled in respect of the supply of positions increases. The minimum value is reached when $V_i = 0$; T_i^d then equals unity.

Similarly, for the whole labour market we obtain:

$$T^d = \frac{\sum_i D_i}{\sum_i \sum_h E_{hi}} \tag{2.24}$$

As a measure for the discrepancy between *demand equilibrium* and the actual situation we may define, analogously to the discrepancy relating to supply equilibrium:

$$\Upsilon^d = I - \frac{I}{T^d} \tag{2.25}$$

The discrepancy between a state of equilibrium and the actual situation on the labour market as a whole equals:

$$\Upsilon = w_d \Upsilon^d + w_s \Upsilon^s \tag{2.26}$$

in which w_d and w_s represent the weights given to the demand side and the supply side of the labour market ($w_d + w_s = I$).

The professional element in equilibrium The preceding section was limited to the spatial aspects of the labour market. In this section the professional element will be introduced. It will be shown that basically the same approach is possible after the introduction of the concept of 'distance' between professions. It is difficult to give a precise definition of this concept; we shall use as a preliminary definition that the distance between two professions represents the reciprocal of the propensity to shift from one profession to another, all other things being equal.

The distance between professions j and m can be written as δ^s_{jm}, in which the superscript s indicates that the distance is considered from the workers' point of view:

$$a^{jm} = \exp(-\delta^s_{jm}) \tag{2.27}$$

where a^{jm} represents the attractiveness of working in profession m for somebody skilled in profession j. Since the distance between professions has not, a priori, a definite dimension, no coefficient need be introduced. Obviously the value of a^{jm} lies between zero and unity.

Combining the two aspects of space and profession, we may write:

$$a^{jm}_{hi} = \exp(-a d_{hi}) \cdot \exp(-\delta^s_{jm}) = \exp\left(-a \left\{\frac{\delta^s_{jm}}{a} + d_{hi}\right\}\right) \tag{2.28}$$

The term $\frac{\delta^s_{jm}}{a} + d_{hi}$ is the sum of the elements $\frac{\delta^s_{jm}}{a}$ and physical distance. This implies that $\frac{\delta^s_{jm}}{a}$ had the dimension of physical distance.

The supply discrepancy for region h and profession m is now defined as:

$$(T^s)^m_h = \frac{S^m_h}{\sum_j \sum_i E^{jm} \exp(-a d_{hi} - \delta^s_{jm})} = \frac{U^m_h + \sum_j \sum_i E^{jm}_h}{\sum_j \sum_i E^{jm}_{hi} \exp(-a d_{hi} - \delta^s_{jm})} \tag{2.29}$$

Supply equilibrium is defined as the situation in which $d_{hi} = 0$, $\delta^s_{jm} = 0$ and $U^m_h = 0$. In this case, everybody working in profession m and living in region h finds work in their own profession and in their own region.

The supply discrepancy for all professions m in region h equals:

$$T_h^s = \frac{S_h}{\sum_m \sum_j \sum_i E_{hi}^{jm} \exp(-ad_{hi} - \delta_{jm}^s)} \qquad (2.30)$$

Consequently total supply discrepancy equals:

$$T^s = \frac{\sum_h S_h}{\sum_h \sum_m \sum_j \sum_i E_{hi}^{jm} \exp(-ad_{hi} - \delta_{jm}^s)} \qquad (2.31)$$

For the demand for labour a similar function can be written. Like before, the commuting distance will not play a role, but the distance between the profession required and the actual profession of the worker will. Indicating the attractiveness of this situation for an entrepreneur in i by c_i^{jm}, we may write:

$$c_i^{jm} = \exp(-\delta_{jm}^d) \qquad (2.32)$$

This time the distance has a superscript d indicating that the distance between professions j and m is judged from the point of view of the entrepreneur.

The demand discrepancy for profession m in region i can thus be written as:

$$(T^d)_i^m = \frac{D_i^m}{\sum_j \sum_h E_{hi}^{jm} \exp(-\delta_{jm}^d)} \qquad (2.33)$$

For the sake of simplicity, no distinction is made between sectors. Total demand discrepancy can be written, analogously to total supply discrepancy:

$$T^d = \frac{\sum_i D_i}{\sum_i \sum_m \sum_j \sum_h E_{hi}^{jm} \exp(-\delta_{jm}^d)} \qquad (2.34)$$

The significance of the results The significance of the foregoing results is to be found in the fact that the formulas express tensions existing on the labour market that are not reflected in the conventional definitions of labour-market equilibrium. They show that considerable discrepancies in terms of either commuting distances or profession distances may exist even in a situation where there is a formal equilibrium on the labour market (no unemployment, no vacancies). It appears that the new approach has considerable advantages over the conventional ones, since the latter's definitions will never contribute to the explanation of the adaptation processes that result from the discrepancies. As such we have already mentioned migration, training and retraining; we may add that failure to adapt may lead to sickness and frustration. It seems that the definitions of employed, unemployed and vacancies leave too much undefined that is of basic importance for the explanation of actual behaviour of participants in the labour market.

Empirical verification of the functions

The authors realise that measuring the coefficients as well as the variables themselves in the functions indicated above will be extremely difficult. In the following some suggestions will be made, which are no more than pointers in a certain direction, waiting to be elaborated further.

The basic assumption is that the attractiveness of a given movement or shift manifests itself in the relative number of movements or shifts from one position to another.

The attractiveness for a person living in *h* skilled in profession *j* of working in *i* in profession *m* was given by:

$$a_{hi}^{jm} = \exp(-\delta_{jm}^{s} - a d_{hi}) \qquad (2.35)$$

Since d_{hi} is known, we need estimates of a and δ_{jm}^{s} in order to be able to estimate a_{hi}^{jm}, the basic element of the supply discrepancy. Once all a_{hi}^{jm} are known, the supply discrepancy can be calculated. Now assume:

$$n_{jm} = n_j n_m \exp(-\delta_{jm}^{s}) \qquad (2.36)$$

where n_{jm} is the number of people shifting from profession j to profession m, n_j the number of workers in profession j at the beginning of the period and n_m the number of workers in profession m at the same point in time. As the scale by which δ_{jm}^{s} is measured is irrelevant, expression (2.36) is presented without a scale coefficient:

$$\frac{n_{jm}}{n_j} = n_m \exp(-\delta_{jm}^{s})$$

or:

$$\gamma_{jm} = n_m \exp(-\delta^s_{jm})$$
$$\delta^s_{jm} = \ln n_m - \ln \gamma_{jm} \tag{2.37}$$

In this equation n_m is supposed to be known; γ_{jm} can be derived from the transition matrix Γ in:

$$n_{t+1} = \Gamma n_t \tag{2.38}$$

which represents the fractions of the number of workers in one profession shifting to another during the period to which the matrix applies. Provided adequate information is available, it would be best to base oneself on professional shifts within one single region, so as to minimise the disturbing effect of differences in commuting distance.

The foregoing leads to an estimate of δ^s_{jm}. The estimation of a might proceed as follows. Assume:

$$n_{hi} = \frac{A_{hi}\exp(-ad_{hi})}{\sum_i A_{hi}\exp(-ad_{hi})} n_h \tag{2.39}$$

in which n_{hi} is the number of people commuting from h to i, A_{hi} is the attractiveness of the labour market in i for workers in h, to be calculated on the basis of the knowledge of all δ^s_{jm}'s gathered in the first stage. Similarly, we may write:

$$n_{ki} = \frac{A_{ki}\exp(-ad_{ki})}{\sum_i A_{ki}\exp(-ad_{ki})} n_k \tag{2.40}$$

From expressions (2.39) and (2.40) we can derive:

$$\frac{n_{hi}}{n_{ki}} = \frac{A_{hi}}{A_{ki}}\exp(-ad_{hi} - d_{ki})\frac{n_h}{n_k} \tag{2.41}$$

from which a can be estimated.

It appears that the method is relatively simple and straightforward. However, the search for a better method, in which the δ^s's and a are estimated simultaneously, should continue.

For the demand side the situation is in fact simpler, though probably more difficult to measure from general data. Surveys within firms will very likely have to provide the necessary data. Theoretically, however, the procedure is quite simple. If:

$$\frac{\partial \phi}{\partial n_{jj}} = p_{jj} \tag{2.42}$$

is the marginal productivity of a worker skilled in profession j and working in the same profession, and:

$$\frac{\partial \phi}{\partial n_{mj}} = p_{mj} \tag{2.43}$$

is the productivity of a worker skilled in profession m but working in profession j, then the attractiveness of employing the latter rather than the former is:

$$\frac{\partial \phi}{\partial n_{mj}} \Big/ \frac{\partial \phi}{\partial n_{jj}} = p_{mj}/p_{jj} \tag{2.44}$$

Since the attractiveness of employing an m-worker in a j-profession has been defined as:

$$c_{mj} = \exp(-\delta^d_{mj}) \tag{2.45}$$

we easily find:

$$\delta^d_{mj} = -\ln \frac{p_{mj}}{p_{jj}} \tag{2.46}$$

A final remark

It is not unlikely that there are differences between the values that a and even the δ's take for different social groups, and it seems, a priori, important to focus studies on these differences. Age-groups, and the worker's sex, will also have to be taken into account.

Moreover, though the two factors covered in the preceding sections will constitute the body of the analysis, it may be assumed that other factors, too, are of importance. The two authors will in the near future be involved in studies in these fields which they feel might give some insight into labour market problems, problems that seem more important now than ever before.

2.3 A note on behavioural changes and the concept of mobility*

During the Eighth ECMT (European Conference of Ministers of Transport) Symposium, held in Istanbul in September 1979, one of the topics of discussion was the definition of mobility. The discussion arose from the presentation of two papers. The main title of both papers was 'Behavioural changes, passenger transport: mobility and lifestyle'. The subtitle of the paper presented by W. Brög (1979), the Manager of Socialdata Institute for Empirical Social Research in Munich was: 'Sociological aspects', and of that presented by Professor H. Schuster from the University of Linz: 'Economic aspects'.

In his paper, Brög defines 'personal mobility' as 'the number and kind of changes in location made by an individual (p. 1). On the same page, it is said that (in the first instance), 'measures only affect marginal behavioural situations and altered transport conditions arise only as the sum of the subjective changes in the behaviour of individuals in response to altered marginal conditions'. And further that: 'This average daily mobility per inhabitant is a combination of two basic parameters: 'the proportion [of people] who are in fact mobile; the number of journeys made by these mobile people'. And also, on the same page, 'An improved definition of personal mobility should therefore – in the transport planning field as well – include not leaving the house' (p. 11). It is obvious that Brög's definition of mobility is the one often used in transportation and physical planning publications where mobility is in fact held to be equal to the number of actual movements.

In Schuster's paper a different definition appears to be used. In the ECMT publication he defines it as 'the ability to overcome or to "bridge" space' (p. 69). This ability is determined, in his opinion, by transport supply and the possibility of using it: 'The most important determinants on the transport supply side are such familiar factors as speed, frequency, fares, comfort, etc. The possibility of using the transport supply depends mainly on income, available time and the availability of a car'.

Although this definition is different as far as the wording is concerned, it is in fact identical to Brög's definition. If the supply of transport facilities together with the possibility of using these facilities defined as income, available time, etc. determine mobility, then mobility is obviously to be understood as number and character

*See L.H. Klaassen, 'A Note on Behavioural Changes and the Concept of Mobility', Netherlands Economic Institute, Rotterdam, FEER 1979/17.

of movements. If conditions on the supply side change, for instance, because a new road is opened up, or if income changes, mobility changes too and so does the pattern of trips made. The latter expressions are then used as synonymous.

There is no need to determine whether the definitions of mobility used, among others, by the two rapporteurs, are right or wrong, for any author is entitled to his own definition. The only thing that counts is that their definitions are efficient in a paper concerned with behavioural changes, and consistent with other definitions used in the paper.

In considering the elements that determine how many movements an individual makes, we shall confine ourselves to one motive: shopping; and also to one shopping centre. By 'movements' is understood the trips of one individual to that shopping centre. The generalised costs of transportation from the individual's place of residence to the shopping centre determine the resistance factors to be overcome in making the trips. The relative attractiveness of the shopping centre determines the strength of the individual's motive to go there; a number of other factors (among which is the level of income which determines whether it is possible for him/her to make the trip).

In (somewhat simplified) mathematical form we may write:

$$n_{ij}^{s} = \psi(\mathbf{a}^{s}, \mathbf{c}, y) \tag{2.47}$$

where n_{ij}^{s} = number of shopping trips from i to j;
$\mathbf{a}^{s}$ = vector of the level of attraction of all shopping centres among which a_j^s ;
$\mathbf{c}$ = level of all generalised costs of transportation from i to all js;
y = individual's income.

In other words, this formula represents the *movements* of the individual as a function of the strength of the *motives* (attractiveness of the different shopping centres), the *barriers* (generalised transportation costs) and the *possibility* to move (income).

All the elements indicated by Professor Schuster are therefore present in expression (2.47). However, it is evident that knowledge of $\mathbf{a}^{s}$, $\mathbf{c}$ and y does not enable us to determine n_{ij}^{s} unless we are informed about the mathematical specification of ψ and the numerical values of its coefficients. Together they represent *the degree to which* an individual reacts to changes in $\mathbf{a}^{s}$, $\mathbf{c}$ and y. They indicate the *propensity* to move (*Geneigtheit zur Bewegung*) which is very different from the *ability* to move (*Fähigkeit zur Bewegung*). If the propensity to move is high, then small changes in one of the explaining variables suffice to cause considerable changes in the number of movements. If the propensity to move is low, then even considerable changes in the explaining variables cannot change to any noticeable extent the number of trips. In the former case, we call the individual *mobile* in the sense of 'quickly responding to any stimulus; easily moved', *Webster's Dictionary* aptly formulates; in the latter case, we call him *immobile*. So, given the mathematical form of the reaction function ψ, the numerical values of the coefficients determine the individual's level of *mobility*. We thus get the structure as shown in Figure 2.1.

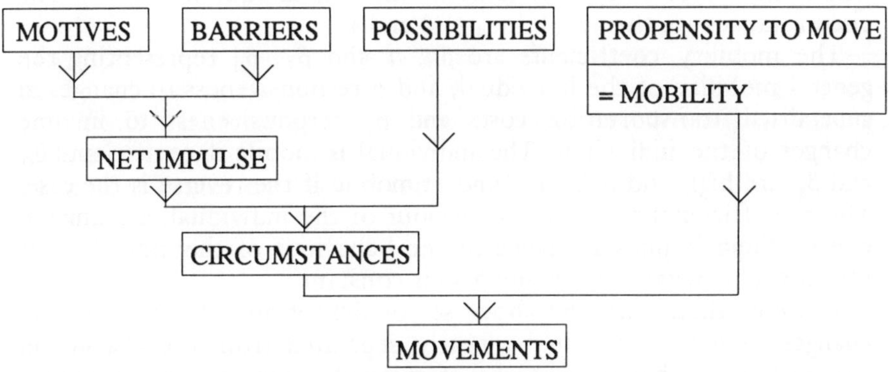

Figure 2.1 Determinants of movement

How, then, should behaviour be defined in an efficient way? We could define the individual's behaviour as the pattern of his movements, but that would mean defining any change in this pattern as a change in behaviour. However, in the foregoing we have made it clear that the pattern of an individual's movements results from the values of explaining variables and the size of coefficients in the reaction functions; it can hardly be efficient to regard the influences of a change in an explanatory variable as well as of one in the coefficient both as changes in behaviour; it seems far more appropriate to regard only the latter influence as a behavioural change that would result in a different pattern of movements even if everything else remained the same (to cite, once again, *Webster's Dictionary*: '2. Behaviour is the way in which an organisation, organ, or substance acts, esp. in response to a stimulus'). A change in the other factors merely represents a change in the circumstances under which the fundamental behaviour materialises, not a change in behaviour itself. Proceeding along these lines, we arrive at the conclusion that a change in behaviour implies a change in mobility, the structure of the latter being defined as the set of reaction coefficients in the equation explaining the movements.

The foregoing can be illustrated by a practical example. Write, as in expression (2.47):

$$n^s_{ij} = \beta_0 \frac{a^s_j \exp(-ac_{ij})}{\sum_j a^s_j \exp(-ac_{ij})} y^{\beta_1} \tag{2.48}$$

where the symbols have the same meaning as in equation (2.47). The circumstances are then $a^s_j\ (V_j)$, $c_{ij}\ (V_j)$ and y.

The mobility coefficients are β_0, a and β_1, β_0 representing the general mobility of the individual, and a responsiveness to changes in generalised transportation costs and β_1 responsiveness to income changes of the individual. The individual is mobile if coefficients β_0 and β_1 are high and a is low, and immobile if the reverse is the case. These coefficients reflect the behaviour of the individual; a change in one of them implies a change in the behaviour of the individual. If they are all constant, behaviour also is constant.

It seems that, with the above set of definitions, the fundamental changes in behaviour can be neatly separated from the changes in circumstances. That seems to be of particular importance for government policy and especially for transportation policy, a government's policy always implying a change in *circumstances* (e.g. in case of an improvement in infrastructure, a change in c_{ij}). The effect of such a change, the reaction to it, is the expected result of the policy and determines its efficiency. The size of this effect can be estimated only if the size of the reaction coefficient is known. If this coefficient is very low, even considerable changes (for instance, in the rates for public transport) will not produce the desired results. Knowing these coefficients is, therefore, essential for transport politicians.

The separation of the different elements in the preceding arguments also seems to suggest a nice division (of work) between economists and sociologists. The economist is probably best suited to *estimate* the values of behavioural coefficients, their changes through time and the differences between social groups of the population. It would be for the sociologist to *explain* these differences between groups and changes through time by more fundamental psychological and sociological factors.

2.4 The use of discount rates*

Introduction

The Commission for Policy Analysis (COBA) in the Netherlands has up till now favoured the application of the same discount rate for evaluating the benefits and costs of all projects, on the assumption that it reasonably reflects both the capital supplier's time preference and the capital demander's marginal return in an equilibrium situation, and that the use of such an 'equilibrium rate' will result in the optimum allocation of the production factor 'capital'.

Is that assumption correct? To provoke a discussion, we set out here to question the wisdom of the procedure so far favoured and actually applied.

For the sake of the argument, let us ignore for the moment that projects may have negative external effects apart from costing money†, and yield, besides benefits counted in money, others that count for much in social terms. Indeed to the building of a cathedral other criteria apply than to the construction of a peppermint factory or an establishment turning out plastic garden gnomes.

Principles

Discount rates (fixed or otherwise) express the conviction that a certain amount of money will (to a certain extent) be worth less in the future than it is now, a conviction that most individuals will share. To possess 100 guilders now is preferable to acquiring the same sum a year hence, if only because, if saved, they will have grown to more than 100 in a year's time. But is it also true that *f*100 now are worth more to one individual than they will be worth to someone else next year? Given the choice, the former individuals will prefer the *f*100 to be given to themselves; the latter obviously will rather have *f*100 next year than see them going to someone else now. The point is, however, that the individual of the next generation has no way of making their preferences known, either because they have not yet been born, or because they are still living in happy ignorance of such matters. *And yet, projects undertaken for the very long term are planned as if their benefits fall to those who are now making the investment decisions.* An example may illustrate what may happen as a consequence.

Take a long-term project which requires an investment of 100 for

*See L.H. Klaassen, R. Iwema and J.H.P. Paelinck, 'The Use of Discount Rates', Netherlands Economic Institute, Rotterdam, FEER 1981-6.
†But see final section.

25 years without yielding any profit during that period; in the 26th year the project starts to yield benefits. If these benefits amount to 983 a year and go on for an infinite period, the B–C ratio will be equal to one at a discount rate of 10 per cent.

Now compare this project with a scheme consisting of 25 smaller projects each requiring a total investment of 100 and started at one-year intervals, so that, again, 100 will be invested every year during a period of 25 years. Each of the small projects after one year begins to give an infinite series of annual returns of 10; total benefits will then be 10 in the second year, 20 in the third, etc., until in year 25 the benefits amount to 240, to remain constant at 250 in subsequent years. At a discount rate of 10 per cent, the B–C ratio of this scheme of projects is of course also equal to 1.

In the latter case, profits start early but rise no more than 250 above those of the first year, against 983 in the former case; on the other hand, the big project yields nothing at all until a quarter of a century has elapsed.

From a contemporary point of view, both projects are equally attractive; from the point of view of 25 years hence, the large project provides an income nearly four times that of the 25 small projects taken together and is therefore the more attractive by far. An income in the initial year of 1,000 will have grown to 1983 after 25 years if the large project is undertaken, to 1,250 with the small ones; average (fictitious or implicit) income growth in these 25 years will thus be 2.70 per cent in the former and 0.9 per cent in the latter case. Obviously the long-term project, on a par with the short-term project from a contemporary point of view, has a far greater positive effect on long-term growth, to be paid for by short-term sacrifices.

We have worked out the example for a 10 per cent discount rate, but the arguments hold for any rate chosen; indeed it is not the height of the discount rate that is essential, but the fact that profitable long-term projects, though giving less economic growth at short delay than equally profitable short-term projects, *make for far more growth in the long run*. Indeed, the choice between equally profitable long-term and short-term projects depends on the *weights attached to long-term and short-term growth*. Naturally the difference between the benefits to be reaped now and in the far future will be greater as the discount rate one applies is higher.

There is another factor to be taken into account, namely flexibility. In the first 25 years it is easier for decision-makers to choose between investing and not investing, and to profit from new possibilities if the small-project scheme has been undertaken, but later on the large project, with its greater returns, offers the better opportunities. So decision-makers have to weigh up not only the benefits accruing to successive generations, but also the flexibility these generations have in their decisions.

And don't let us forget that we are now reaping the benefits of sacrifices made by our ancestors; should they have undertaken only short-time projects, our income would probably be considerably less than it is now. (Cases in point are land reclamations, the New Waterway connecting Rotterdam with the sea and the Deltaworks protecting a number of islands against it.)

That two projects by current B–C calculations should emerge as equally profitable, although one of them after a couple of years yields by far the higher income, points to a deficiency in the calculation method. Indeed, as stated at the beginning of this section, the present method treats even very long-term projects as if their benefits accrue to the individuals who are now deciding on the investments involved. It relies on the fiction that all individuals are immortal, or that all generations love one another as themselves; while acknowledging a 'time preference', it ignores the 'generation preference'. But there *is* such a preference, and therefore the usual B–C calculation is suitable only for weighing up projects that are accomplished within one generation (i.e. projects that benefit the generation that makes the sacrifices for it. To weigh up several projects extending beyond the span of one generation, or to weigh such a project against a scheme spanning only one generation, a 'generation-preference rate' should be added to the usual discount rate; in the following example an easy way to do so is shown.

An example

Suppose a project yields a yearly benefit R from the year t_0 onward; in the period of the present generation, τ, it will give a total benefit $R\tau$, the present value of which at time t_0 is equal to:

$$R/r\ [1 - \exp(-r\tau)] \qquad (2.49)$$

where r is the rate of interest. The present value of the benefits to be enjoyed by the next generation during the period $\tau - 2\tau$, reduced to the point in time $t_0 + \tau$ relevant to that generation, is the same; the same holds, with the relevant adaptations, for subsequent generations.

If at time t_0, the initial point in time of the present generation, we have to evaluate the total project, we shall have to weight the benefits accruing to a future generation in respect to benefits falling to our own generation; to that end, let us assume that each generation values the interests of the next at γ times their own, where γ is a positive figure which normally lies between 0 and 1 but may be larger than 1 in certain cases.

The benefits of the project summated over all generations are then valued at:

$$R/r\,[1 - \exp(-r\tau)] + \gamma R/r\,[1 - \exp(-r\tau)]$$
$$+ \gamma^2 R/r\,[1 - \exp(-r\tau)] + \ldots = \frac{R}{r(1-\gamma)}\,[1 - \exp(-r\tau)] \qquad (2.50)$$

The implicit discount rate ρ can be computed from:

$$\frac{1}{\rho} = \frac{1}{r(1-\gamma)}\,[1 - \exp(-r\tau)] \qquad (2.51)$$

giving:

$$\rho = \frac{r(1-\gamma)}{1 - \exp(-r\tau)} \qquad (2.52)$$

The following conclusions may, then, be drawn.

1 For $\gamma = \exp(-r\tau)$, $\rho = r$; in other words, the usual discount rate applies if a generation values the interests of the next at $\exp(-r\tau)$ its own; at $\tau = 25$ and $r = 10$ per cent, the present generation would have to consider its own benefits more than 12 times more important than those of the next generation.

2 For short-term projects (of, say, less than 25 years), γ is irrelevant and the usual discount rate applies.

3 Putting $r = 0.1$ and $\tau = 25$, we get:

$$\rho = 0.109\,(1 - \gamma) \qquad (2.53)$$

For $\gamma = 1$, that is if the present generation considers the interests of the next one as important as its own, the implicit discount rate ρ is equal to 0; if the next generation is considered totally unimportant, the implicit discount rate is 10.9 per cent; and should the next generation be thought of as half as important as the present one, the discount rate becomes 5.45 per cent.

4 An implicit discount rate equal to zero means that, for a project extending for an infinite number of years, the benefits are infinite too, such a project should be preferred to all others. Large-scale environmental projects, such as keeping the world's

oceans clean, maintaining the world's oxygen supply (tropical woods) or safeguarding, say, the Netherlands against floods come into this category.

If γ is larger than 1, the implicit discount rate becomes negative; a common case in the individual sphere, where parents tend to put their children's interests before their own.

To apply a discount rate that is inferior to the rate of interest means that an implicit subsidy is accorded to the project involved. Introduction of ρ implies that the benefits, which at the (financial) interest rate would be no more than R/r, are set at R/ρ. The subsidy thus accorded by the present generation to the project – or better, formulated, the present generation's transfer to all generations to come – then can be computed as:

$$R/\rho - R/r = \frac{R}{r(1-\gamma)} [1 - \exp(-r\tau)] - R/r = \tag{2.54a}$$

$$R/r \left[\frac{1 - \exp(-r\tau)}{1-\gamma} - 1\right] \tag{2.54b}$$

For $\gamma = \exp(-r\tau)$, this implicit subsidy accorded to the project is of course equal to 0.

Conclusion

We suggest, then, to replace the monetary rate of interest with the implicit rate of interest, a function of the former, equal to it only in a particular case.

The same method applies to cases more complicated than the one described in the previous section; ρ then becomes a function of time, to be calculated from:

$$\exp(-\rho[t]\, t = f(r, t, \gamma) \tag{2.55}$$

where f is, for a given point in time, the 'choice discount function'. If, for instance, equation (2.50) (p. 32) is applied to the second generation after the present, the above function will be equal to:

$$f(r, t, \gamma) = \frac{\gamma^2}{r} (1 - \exp[-r]) \tag{2.56}$$

Finally, spatial effects (externalities) and group (income) effects are easy to include in the model; for example, R_t, the (non-constant) benefits in period t, are equal to:

$$R_t^{\Delta} = \sum_i \sum_g (B_{tig} - K_{tig})$$

where B_{tig} is the benefits falling to group g in region i at time t, and K_{tig} is the corresponding costs.

References

Brög, W. (1979), 'Behavioural change, passenger transport: mobility and lifestyle: economic aspects', paper presented at the European Conference of Ministers of Transport, Istanbul, September.

Heijke, J.A.M., Klaassen, L.H. and Offereins, C.J. (1975), *Naar een arbeidsmarktmodel*, Groningen: H.D. Tjeenk Willink.

Klaassen, L.H. and Botterweg, T.H. (1974), *Prosperity and Well-Being: A Plea for Attainable Ends*, Foundations of Empirical Economic Research series, Netherlands Economic Institute, Rotterdam, 1974/18.

Kornai, J. (1971), *Anti-Equilibrium. On Economic Systems Theory and the Tasks of Research*, Amsterdam/London, pp. 24, 25.

Menger, K. (1968), *Grundsätze der Volkswirtschaft*, London: London School of Economics and Political Science, Series of reprints, nos 17–20.

Pigou, A.C. (1951), 'Some aspects of welfare economics', *American Economic Review*, vol. XLI (June), p. 288.

3 Urban developments in Europe

3.1 Disurbanisation and re-urbanisation in Western Europe

Disurbanisation

City centres have been losing population since around the turn of the century. The inner cities were then among the most densely populated areas with the oldest houses – and presumably even in those days traffic – and, in particular, the organic external effects of horse power was not conducive to undisturbed enjoyment of the urban beauties. As soon as their income permitted it, people therefore left the innermost quarters for newer ones around the centre. In those days most people's financial vaulting-pole did not yet allow them to jump further afield to join the really rich families, who for many decades already had lived quietly and pleasantly in the rural parts encircling the cities, far from the noise and bustle of the town.

Yet that first leap was found beneficial. The environment was more enjoyable, and the beauties of nature had come within easier reach. Being that much further away from the centre was rather a nuisance, but one cannot be in two places at once, and first things must come first.

It was unfortunate, though, that the outward movement was strengthened and extended. The town's outskirts moved further and further away from its centre, and with motor-cars becoming more and more popular, it became possible to go and live in adjoining semi-agrarian municipalities. The migrants still were not too concerned about being at some distance from the city centre, but they became aware of the fact that to stay close to nature, they had to remain on the move. Indeed every individual decision to move out towards nature had the effect of pushing it away from earlier settlers. It was not a very fast process, each new settler taking up only a small area, but there were so many of them that in the course of the years the situation deteriorated perceptibly. The town was spreading and sprawling, eating into the countryside. To describe the phenomenon in a concise manner, the word 'suburbanisation' was coined.

Meanwhile keen businessmen were quick to perceive that many people were leaving the town, and that those people were well-to-do. Service companies always ready to serve those with money to spend, decided to move out also, and that movement, too, soon gathered strength.

It would be a mistake to suppose that the city centres were left empty; that happened only in American towns. In European towns, with their cultural traditions of long standing, vacant lots were soon occupied by huge and sometimes even impressive office buildings. When there were enough of them side by side, whole streets of large buildings came into being, which were apt to be called 'avenues' or 'allées' with some word in front or behind to indicate whether it belonged to a kingdom or to a republic.

The building fever was contagious; indeed every self-respecting bank or insurance company felt compelled to set up a massive building in a city centre, just to prove to their clients that they had a few millions to throw about. Status apart, there was not much need for them to settle in city centres. What with letters and telephone calls, to say nothing of telegrams and telex communications, they could function just as efficiently and effectively elsewhere. And it was rather unfortunate that these companies employed so many people, who were all expected to work the same hours. That did not seem a handicap to those driving a car, nor to those who would soon be able to afford one, incomes rising faster than car prices. However, when almost everybody began to commute to town by car, there was not enough space to park them all during the day; the disappointing issue was a new phenomenon, called congestion.

Local authorities, loath to dispense with the financial advantage of selling land to offices at high prices, kept high by the steady demand, sought to solve congestion problems by introducing means of transport designed to convey masses of people from their homes in pleasurable surroundings to their workplaces in or near to city centres, trying at the same time to convince everybody of the salutary effects as far as the environment was concerned. There were indeed enough passengers for public transport, but unfortunately the demand was concentrated in a few hours of the day, and thus it became very difficult to exploit the means of public transport without incurring heavy losses; indeed the deficits of public transport increased progressively.

To an economist the logical result would be a very high price for a tram or bus ticket. But the authorities reasoned otherwise: because it is first and foremost the people in the lower-income brackets who travel by public transport, people who cannot afford to pay a high price for their ticket, public transport will have to be financed with the help of taxes to be imposed on people with higher incomes who, after all, can go on driving their cars as long as all the others take the bus or the tram.

Gradually it became clear, however, that it is not only the direct money price that counts with those in need of transport, but also the (dis)comfort experienced and the time spent in changing vehicles and waiting. So it dawned on local authorities that most people, counting the generalised costs, decided to stay in their cars. These authorities, having insisted on the creation of enormous concentrations of employment at nearly inaccessible places, were not pleased with the way things developed, and proceeded to drastic measures: they ordered the construction of underground railways, or, more precisely, metropolitan railways, running underground where land is expensive, and surfacing where it is cheap. Of course, railway viaducts do not enhance the beauty of a town more than motorways, but any murmurings to that effect were soon silenced and the construction was started.

It is true that underground railways have an enormous passenger capacity, but they require enormous investments and the costs are huge. With taxes already raised to the sky, the only way to make ends meet was to attract more passengers. In that reasoning it was good sense to attract even more employment to the city centres, to create residential concentrations as far as possible from that employment, and then to connect the two by public transport. The demand for transportation thus created would, in the expectation of those responsible, bring grist to the mill of the public-transport companies.

But will it? The latest developments seem to point in another direction. For suburbanisation is now passing into disurbanisation. In the Netherlands, in particular, many people have come to the conclusion that just one more move will take them nearer to nature as well as to an urban centre while relieving them of pollution and congestion. Indeed they can have all the benefits and none of the drawbacks of town life with the beauties of nature thrown in, by settling in a medium sized town.

Migration to medium-sized towns has its counterpart in the depopulation of the larger agglomerations; some of the latter, finding their population decreasing by some 2 per cent per year, are busily planning for decline, while medium-sized towns are growing lustily and enjoying increasing incomes.

It is too soon to predict where the present dynamic process of re-finding an equilibrium will lead. If the present trend continues, we are on our way towards a new situation in which the large towns have become smaller and the small ones larger, so that the difference between the two categories dwindles and may even disappear. Western Europe will then be a region dotted with towns of comparable size with equally polluted environments and equal congestion.

But will the national population go on growing? After all, with technology proceeding, we may well have to reckon with a decreasing national population in a few years' time. If by then the equalisation process just described is completed, all agglomerations will have to plan for decline. Admittedly, with families tending to be smaller, the demand for houses may continue to grow for some time, but in the end the time will come for the physical contraction of our towns. How far the population will shrink is not for us to say; the human race is not likely to die out – perhaps the day will come when fertility pills are distributed on the National Health? But don't let us look so far ahead, and rather limit ourselves to the imminent period of disurbanisation and equalisation, of planning for decline in large towns and planning for growth in smaller ones, a period of development towards the equal spatial distribution of all things good and bad.

Re-urbanisation

For the sake of a vivid picture, we have so far taken abstraction from any reactions to the phenomena of disurbanisation. It is easier to extrapolate a trend than to analyse a complicated process, which is the reason why the former is mostly done in practice, and why most forecasts fail. However, the previous section was not meant as a forecast, but – like perhaps the majority of current 'forecasts' – as an attempt to picture the fearsome issue of a certain process in the hope of awakening counter-forces able to turn the tide; as a 'self-destroying prophecy', so to speak. By such counter-forces we do not understand the actions often expected of governments 'to do something' about certain unwanted situations or phenomena, but rather counter-forces that work in society, forces that the government should try to guide and control rather than fight, which indeed it cannot fight, for even the most tenacious government must give in when the political and financial price of fighting on becomes too high.

Such societal forces spring, traditionally, from the towns. It is there that some people begin to have misgivings as they see how the central function of city cores are being eroded, how their residential function is dwindling, how the level of provisions is falling, while on the other hand offices are getting the upper hand, with their massive employment, more and more space being taken up by infrastructure for public and private transport, for which purpose houses are sacrificed, so that once more the residential function is violated, and so on and so forth. The misgivings of the few become the nightmares of many, who foresee a future of utter drabness, with the economic centres of the community going to wrack and ruin, and losing their cultural and social functions in the process. Voices are raised in favour of two concrete, logical conclusions. The first, virtually uncontested, is that traffic should be reduced; the important thing to be noticed is that no difference is made between private and public transport because the truth is dawning that instead of meeting the crave for transport by creating means of mass conveyance, we should try to change the urban spatial structure in a way that reduces transport demand. The second conclusion is directly concerned with that spatial structure. There is a growing conviction that the residential function of inner cities ought to be restored and the office function reduced because, in that way, new impulses can be given to city centres, purchasing power attracted, shops revived and the traffic situation improved. Indeed this second conclusion is fully consistent with, and complementary to, the first: there will be less traffic, and of a more favourable structure, in core cities *because* they are restored to their residential function.

With that argument we are reversing the reasoning in the opening lines of this article. It was the failing residential function and the concentration of employment in city centres that caused our present traffic problems; so relief is now expected from strengthening the residential function and reducing employment.

That seems sound reasoning, but it must be recalled that the whole process started with people being sick and tired of living in cities and yearning for nature. Who would want to live in the cities now?

It is on that score that there is perhaps a manifest difference between America and Europe. On both continents people are becoming environment conscious, but only in Europe are people becoming aware of urban beauty and the qualities of the intimate architectural structure of past centures; there is hardly anything of that kind to be found in America. Admittedly Europeans, too, are still very active in destroying beautiful city centres and erecting gigantic office buildings; Paris, Brussels and Frankfurt are deplorable examples. There are so-called promotion companies who thrive on the business, sharing their profits with municipal governments.

But such activities will be of a temporary nature; the original structures will be more and more preferred and attempts will be made to rehabilitate them. Rehabilitation rather than reconstruction is going to determine the image of our old inner cities; large-scale razing will come to an end.

Nor are environmental considerations and love of urban beauty the only reasons to save and restore our towns. It is evident that reconstruction and razing, carried out for the purpose of making the town more liveable, have indeed led to the massive destruction of social structures. Such structures are often invisible or, at any rate, less visible than the state of technical disrepair of the premises within which they exist; that may be the reason why until a short time ago technical considerations were the only ones that counted in town reconstruction plans. Things are changing gradually, in the sense that nowadays rehabilitation should respect the social structures. The building industry, accustomed in past decades to massive demolition and large-scale reconstruction, is now facing quite a different task, but a task that is much more gratifying, being concerned with re-urbanisation instead of disurbanisation.

The process thus set going is one of turning degenerated urban patches once more into towns with living cores, fulfilling a real economic, social and cultural function, a process of re-urbanisation. Its ultimate fascinating objective is the revival of the town, fascinating to many individuals who have learned in hard practice that living near to nature means mowing the lawn every week, driving to town in long queues in the morning, and driving out of town in long queues in the evening, that a suburban home means buying wives a second car, so that they may flee the periphery, etc. The more people realise all this, the less they will want to leave the inner city if they are still there, and the stronger will become the desire to live just there, leading a modern life in an old town full of atmosphere.

An acceptable equilibrium?

The developments we have indicated by disurbanisation lead to the urban cake being crumbled and spread until the whole country is covered with a layer of very nearly equal thickness. By the developments called re-urbanisation the town will once more absorb its surroundings and its core will be restored to its old glory. In the latter case, the centripetal forces get the better of the centrifugal ones that are at work in disurbanisation.

Is there an equilibrium to be found anywhere? Is it possible to predict where we are really going? Can something be said of the direction in which the societal forces will lead us and the authorities?

Let us start from the assumption that an individual is always right whatever location he prefers. A man who says, 'I prefer living in the centre of a large town and am prepared to take a longer drive into the country', is right, and so is the one who claims to prefer a one-family home with a garden close to nature. He who migrates to a smaller town is also right, for a variety of reasons. Realising this, we must conclude that everybody must have the opportunity to find his or her own happiness through free choice of residence. But we do have to take care that while striving for their own kind of happiness, these people do not hinder one another; the external effects of their aspirations, as far as they are negative, should be limited to the utmost.

Conditions should be created such that anybody who wants to decide on one of the main directions indicated above, may do so within the limits set by the external effects. What are these effects and how important are they?

People who leave a large town for a smaller one will cause negative external effects in the latter, but reduce such effects in the town they have left to a greater extent; they give no difficulty. Those who move from the suburbs to the inner city, and those who decide not to leave it because of improvements hoped for, help to reduce the traffic volume and to improve its structure (making it easier for those living in the suburbs to reach their workplaces in town); that holds for both private and public transport. The behaviour of these two groups will thus lead to an improvement in the general situation by:

(a) improvement of the traffic structure;
(b) reduction of the traffic volume;
(c) strengthening of the functions of the urban centres.

It is otherwise with the third group, the group of those who want to live outside the town, for they contribute to the deterioration of the traffic structure, the increase of traffic volume and the weakening of the functions of urban centres. This group really spoils the picture somewhat, but we have stated that everybody is right, so we must abide by that, perhaps trying to determine a bit more accurately the position of this group. We are welcoming every individual who wants to come and live in the inner city, because as the situation is, every bit of traffic going the other way means a relief and an improvement; however, should everybody want to live in the city, then we should be glad of every move to a suburb.

What we want most is an equilibrium, and for that reason an

instrument that helps to establish it. Such an instrument is the traditional price mechanism, loved by many, but with a reputation in urban economies that is far from immaculate. However, that reputation is due to the fact that in large towns the external effects of any development can be so huge that they dwarf any internal effects that *can* be discounted in the prices.

It will now be clear that for the price mechanism to be effective in urban economies, two effects have to be internalised: (a) the negative external effects on traffic and city life that tend to bring to town only employment-creating activities; and (b) the positive external effects in traffic and city life that strengthen the residental function of the inner city. Capitalisation of these effects would lead to the conclusion that land should be allotted to, say, offices, at extremely high prices, but at relatively low prices for building houses in the inner city.

The system is attractive because it will tend towards an equilibrium situation. Living in the inner city becomes attractive through lower rents, but only as long as there are indeed positive external effects. As soon as there are so many inhabitants in the centre as to cause negative effects and thus higher land prices (and hence higher rents), the enthusiasm for living there will be dampened, and suburbs will once more become an attractive proposition. In that way, a reasonable equilibrium can establish itself, and there will be no need to prevent anybody by physical means from being happy in his own way.

But will such a system be accepted? What municipality would not prefer in the end a wide boulevard with impressive banks to a network of intimate small streets. In Brussels one may observe how drastic intervention has done away with the Brussels of tradition, a pleasant intimate town; now everything is becoming large and impressive. Not beautiful, not human in scale, but who should want that nowadays? And, above all, who can make money out of it? No, it will not be easy to turn the tide. And there is another thing. The large metropolitan railway systems may perhaps turn out to be no longer needed so much, for one thing because far less capacity will suffice in the peak hours and for another because the car once more comes into its own as the road infrastructure is used in a more balanced way. An unwelcome development for many people, for once an underground railway is there, its use should be maximised and not minimised. Minimisation may be satisfactory for private cars and, perhaps, for municipal buses, but not for the underground, for it would then run at even greater losses. And it should not be forgotten that many towns possess land in their centres, part of which could soar in price, but which as far as destined for housebuilding, or suitable for maintaining the residential function, would experience a sudden fall in prices. Moreover, it could be that the rise to be charged for office buildings could be so steep, even for offices already in use, that the land would no longer be sold for that purpose, so that the 'profit' cannot be cashed. Not an alluring prospect for the municipalities concerned; they are not likely to be enthusiastic, nor, perhaps, are their municipal boards.

It might well be that the proposed system for all its benefits to welfare and its ability to create an equilibrium between extreme re-urbanisation and extreme disurbanisation will prove unacceptable on account of its lack of advantages for municipal finance. Would a system of congestion taxes on traffic be better? With such a system, everybody pays according to the time and the direction of his/her participation in traffic; indeed a system that puts the charges where they belong and where they are most effective. But also a system with the political disadvantage of laying the burden also on the humble worker who lives in a suburb quarter. Even if that were fully justified from the point of view of economic theory, the man will be supported in his protest by his political party, going on about the effects of congestion tax on the purchasing power of the humble.

And that is the essence of the problem. Rent differentiation which reinstates an equilibrium violates the municipal finances, congestion tax meets political resistance because of the alleged effect on the income of simple workers. That is why probably we shall not be able to achieve a balanced system, and why we keep sliding down towards disurbanisation. We may have observed with joy that the government cannot accomplish what society does not want, but we may have to admit that the government can fail to do what society wants. Very likely the development of the European towns will be disappointing, even if the statistics record a further rise of income per head.

3.2 Urban planning and its impact on the quality of life in West European cities*

Introduction

Writing about the quality of life in European cities means dealing with the question of what makes a city a *European* city, or at least on which common feature of European cities could a paper be focused? The only common feature, at least at first sight, is that European cities are those cities which are located within the European territory. This is about as meaningful as defining a human being as a living thing

*In A. Kuklinski (ed.), *Social Issues in Regional Policy and Regional Planning*, The Hague/Paris: Mouton, 1977.

that is neither a plant nor an animal! Venice and Glasgow, Estoril and Moscow and Dubrovnik and Hammerfest are all European cities, but they have as little in common as Bangkok and Scranton, Pennsylvania.

Still, there is a common feature that could serve as a background for our considerations. Let us describe the European cities as cities that are located on a continent that in the economic as well as the historical sense takes a place between the USA, on the one hand, with its high income level and relatively short history, and the rest of the world, on the other hand, with its low income level and ancient cultures that still are manifest in many places but with remnants gradually becoming more or less foreign elements in the societies that have developed. Europe has not reached the US income level and cannot boast a culture older than the Greek. But it has, maybe for this very reason, remained conscious of that culture that expresses itself in a multitude of ways in its society in general, and its urban life in particular. Perhaps this explains why social elements in European societies play a role that seems more pronounced than in the two other societies. In the USA, as well as in the Third World, economic considerations seem to be weighted higher than in Europe where the culture is old enough to place social objectives high on the list of objectives, and income is high enough to allow governments to pursue these objectives more or less successfully. Although we should be careful not to generalise too easily the view expressed above might serve as a vague background for considering the European city and its developments.

Some general considerations

I do not consider it my task to go very deeply into the historical developments that made urban life in Europe what it is today. But it might be useful to elaborate somewhat on developments that explain some of its main characteristics when comparing it with that in a country like the USA.

One of the principal and very essential points is of course that Europe consists today, and always has consisted, of a large number of independent nations with their own policies, languages, religions and cultural backgrounds that are reflected in urban life. The frontiers between those nations were not fixed, but have changed considerably over time as a consequence of wars and unification of smaller nations into larger ones as well as division of larger nations into smaller ones. Over the last centuries the map of Europe has changed continuously and the effects of this on urban life and the distribution of urban activities have been considerable.

A few examples might elucidate this point. When comparing the spatial distribution of cities over France with that of Germany, it immediately becomes obvious that the very high degree of centralisation of the French governmental system resulted in a heavy concentration of activities in Paris as compared to other cities in France. In Germany, on the contrary, the present nation developed out of the unification of a number of independent states with their own governments and their own capital. This original position reflects itself clearly in the present equal size distribution of cities over the country where not one city is nearly as large as Paris. To a certain extent, London and Vienna underwent the reverse development. Both were capitals of large empires which gradually broke down leaving hardly anything but the national territory. Vienna, the capital of a country some 300 miles in extent, is now situated at the extreme edge of that country, 20 miles from the Czechoslovakian border!

Recent developments have again altered the picture of European urban life. The wartime destruction of cities in Germany and German-occupied territories in a large number of cases considerably influenced the quality as well as the structure of life in those cities. Coventry, Belgrade, Rotterdam and Warsaw are just four examples outside Germany where almost complete renewal resulted in structures quite different from those before the war. The war influenced urban life in two other ways as well. The first, the division of Europe into capitalist and socialist countries, is most evident in the countries on which borders the two systems meet. West German urban development has concentrated most heavily in the cities of its western and southern regions. Large areas in the east need special financial support to maintain an acceptable standard of living. The almost absolute border pressed economic activities westward, where the main Western developments took place and, consequently, urban growth manifested itself most clearly.

A second development that is to a certain extent linked with the former is the building of economic blocks in Europe. The Common Market (EC) and the European Free Trade Area (EFTA) in the West, and Comecon (the economic association of Communist countries) in the East, are developing and beginning to influence urban life in Europe. The most important effect is the gradual disappearance of customs barriers between countries. The map of Europe still shows clearly the influence of the frontiers on the degree of economic development of frontier regions. Except for areas endowed with raw materials, border regions show only limited economic activities, partly for understandable economic reasons and partly due to the awareness that border areas are where frontiers are most likely to change, giving entrepreneurs a feeling of uncertainty about the risks to their firms if such a change occurred.

Devoted members of the European movement believe that abolition of economic barriers will result in a rapid unification of Europe. Apart from the question of whether a completely unified Europe is preferable to a 'Europe of Nations' in which each individual country preserves its most precious characteristics, this opinion may be somewhat utopian. European countries are separated not only by custom barriers, but even more so by differences in languages, religion, history, educational systems, political structures, etc. which do not disappear with the removal of import restrictions.

One study has made this point clear: see Klaassen and Wagenaar (1971). On the basis of data on the number of telephone calls between districts in Belgium, the authors measured the influence of telephone density, distance between the regions as well as the language difference on the intensity of communication by telephone between those districts. It appeared that language differences had a considerable influence. This influence was expressed as a multiplicative factor of actual physical distance. The result was that the density of communication by telephone between two districts where different languages were spoken was equal to the density of communication between two districts speaking the same language but located at a distance 2.6 times as large. The same level of communication as between two districts speaking the same language will thus be found between two districts speaking different languages only if the distance between those two regions is 60 per cent smaller. The research into the phenomena of psychological distance is being pursued at the Netherlands Economic Institute. Application at a much more general level, starting from more general hypotheses, might allow us also to get more insight into communication within cities between different social groups.

Finally, there is undoubtedly a general tendency towards a European integration on a higher macro level between the EC, EFTA and Comecon. This is, however, more an outlook on the longer term, at least as far as Comecon is concerned. The only important point is that cultural and scientific communication is rapidly increasing and even more open relations may be expected to establish themselves in the near future.

The foregoing shows that a European urban or regional policy does not exist. To a certain extent, there exists an EC regional policy focusing on measures to promote the growth of depressed regions in the EC countries. A large part of the funds made available for this programme are allocated to the development of the Mezzogiorno in Italy.* After the entrance of the UK, considerable attention is also paid to Scotland and Wales.

*This region shows that considerable differences in income level might persist between regions even if there were no custom barriers or differences in language or religion.

Considerations concerning the quality of life

In order to find well-defined regional and/or urban policies we will have to descend to the national level. However, before doing so, it seems useful to consider in some detail a definition of the quality of life. Let us suggest a terminology that will be used throughout this section and that seems to be efficient for the subject at hand. By efficiency, I mean concepts that have operational value and can be applied in practical research. Undoubtedly, there is ample room for other definitions, especially those that are far more general.

First, let us assume that the quality of life has four dimensions. These are social, economic, environmental and cultural. Consequently the quality of life is determined by:

1 The presence of social institutions, the social context of individuals, including the density of their relations with other groups, as well as the framework of social legislation within which they live.
2 The income level of individuals, the quality of their work, their job opportunities (implicitly including the degree of freedom to move from one region to another and from one job to another).
3 The quality of the environment, including the degree of pollution of air and water, congestion and noise as well as the availability of recreational facilities.
4 The presence of cultural institutions as well as the general cultural level of the community in which the individual lives.

The quality of life of the individual is not necessarily determined in a unique and positive way by all these factors. Given the level and structure of the demands of the individual, the actual supply might be above as well as below his/her aspirations. In both cases, the quality of his/her life might be lower than if supply could just satisfy the individual's demands. This means that the level of satisfaction in the community is maximal if the structure of the supply is such that it enables each individual to satisfy his/her demand at the level which corresponds to his/her ambitions. This will be the case if all amenities are available at each level. Apart from the ubiquitous components of the quality of urban life, the social legislation, the political climate of the country, and its cultural and economic level, the quality of life of the individual with a given position living in a given place is largely determined by the distances of the different elements from his/her living and working place. This means that the quality of life is not determined by the presence in the individual's country of certain recreational elements, schools or hospitals, but rather more by the distance to be covered to reach these elements. If they are readily accessible from the individual's living place, he/she may satisfy life quality demands easily. On the contrary, if he/she has to cover large distances to reach them, he/she not only will have to pay a high price for transportation and effort, but also will require much time to consume the services. This last point means that, given the limited time daily available, the individual will restrict his/her potential consumption. If this means that he/she cannot satisfy their demand, the quality of life will be lower than if all or most of the services are readily accessible.

These considerations imply that it is not justified to speak of *the* quality of life if we do not define simultaneously the spatial context considered. For this reason, we will consider separately the quality of life in a regional context, in an urban context and in the narrowest context of all, the neighbourhood of the city in which the individual lives. Obviously such a separate treatment of the different levels of the quality of life implies considering policies at different administrative levels. Let us formalise this point in the following way:

1 Denote an amenity with a high-distance elasticity of demand as an amenity of low order and one with a low-distance elasticity as one of high order. By this definition, a university is a high-order amenity and a kindergarten a low-order amenity. In general, the number of low-order amenities is high. The number of higher-order amenities decreases with the order of the amenity.
2 Denote further an authority of high level as an authority covering a large territory, and consequently an authority of low level as an authority covering a small territory. A national government is a government of high order, a county or municipal government is one of low order.

We then may make the following assumptions:

(a) a decision considering a given element, or amenity, will have to be taken at the lowest possible level in such a sense that the order of the government by which the decision is made is no lower than the order of the element concerned;
(b) if the differences in order between the government making the decision and the order of the element itself is large, the part of the population immediately concerned should have a large say in that decision. This means that the population of a neighbourhood in a large city should be enabled to exert a considerable influence on decisions of that order which corresponds to the size of their neighbourhood.

Both points imply that at least on these grounds the number of governmental levels should be relatively large. Their number will have to be limited considerably, however, for reasons of co-ordination. The size of the co-ordination problem increases more than proportionally with the number of governmental levels. In practice, the number of levels is historically determined but current discussions in Holland show that a major change in the governmental structure is possible and may even be highly desirable. In a dynamic, changing society also the governmental system should adjust itself regularly to social developments in order to reach a better correspondence between the order of decisions and the order of governmental bodies.

The foregoing means that the quality of life of the individual is influenced by governmental decisions at different levels. In order to discuss these influences properly we should consider them separately in the proper context.

Regional policies

The first level to be discussed is the national level at which the decisions for a regional policy are taken.

The main objective of regional policy is to obtain a better spatial equilibrium between population and economic activities in the country. In most countries this distribution is characterised by a high concentration of both population and economic activities in a relatively few cities. This means that most countries are faced with all the problems connected with a high degree of urbanisation as well as with an unequal distribution of income between the urbanised and the non-urbanised parts of the country. Recent developments have shown that this problem is aggravated by the unfavourable development of a number of stagnating sectors such as textiles, mining, shipbuilding, and even iron and steel production. Long-run developments in the competitive position of those sectors have brought distress to a number of formerly flourishing cities and regions. By this a new dimension has been added to our regional problems. Classifying the regions according to two economic criteria, level of income and potential growth of income, one might arrive then at the position shown in Table 3.1.

To each of the groups a different sort of regional policy should apply. The first group, economically prosperous because high income level as well as high income growth characterise the larger cities with a favourable economic structure. The nature of problems of regions in this group is social and environmental (air and noise pollution and traffic congestion) rather than economic. Although their typical urban structural problems will be considered later, it should be

Table 3.1 Classification of regions according to economic criteria

		Income growth compared to average national growth	
		high	low
Income level compared to average national income level	High	(1) Prosperous areas	(3) Potential distressed areas
	Low	(2) Potential prosperity areas	(4) Distressed areas

mentioned here that decentralisation as a result of motorisation is also one of their main problems. In Europe it is common practice to limit further growth of urban areas of this type by imposing restrictions on the locations of new activities (London and Paris) or by levying special taxes on capital investments (as are currently contemplated in Stockholm and the Dutch Rimcity). Although the policies in London and Paris have met with a certain degree of success as far as the *number* of new locations or extensions of existing firms is concerned, there is some doubt about the influence of such measures on the degree to which new, valuable initiations of more than local importance have been suppressed. For both cities there is awareness of the fact that large urban areas serve as breeding places for innovations that spread from the cities to the rest of the country. The consequences of policies which suppress urban growth, and with it innovations, should be considered generally with care, and particularly if they have long-run consequences. Promoting growth elsewhere might be a much more effective policy than suppressing it in the prosperity regions.

Group 2 contains the potential prosperity areas with income levels below and growth rates above the national average. From a purely economic point of view those regions are worth investing in, but no policy in Europe is directed towards promoting the growth of this type of area. The reason for this is clearly that regional policies are in fact more social than economic. Still, long experience with regional policies in Europe makes it clear that promotion of the growth of those regions or cities might be preferred very much over the existing policies of promoting the growth of areas in distress. Distressed areas could be aided more effectively by assisting the growth of the potential prosperity areas (and thus assisting indirectly the distressed areas) than by jumping directly from the prosperity regions to the regions in distress. In France regional policy is directed at promoting the growth of the so-called 'metropoles d'équilibre', larger cities in France which show the most favourable potential for growth, at least compared to the distressed regions. In Holland it is obvious that the cities peripheral to the Rimcity at a distance of some 50–70 miles show the highest growth potentials, although their growth has never been supported by public development measures. There is, however, the possibility that their growth will be promoted by the government as part of future regional policy. In fact the new towns in the UK are based on the same principle, i.e. that communities with the highest growth potentials are located at a reasonable distance from the main urban centres. If this proves to be true, and it seems that there is some evidence now available, this would mean that a decentralisation policy is effective in reaching its objectives of both gradually decreasing the growth of the main urban centres and promoting the growth of distressed peripheral areas. If the policy is to be successful, it should be carried out in two stages, namely:

Stage I: Promotion of potential growth centres at acceptable distances from the main urban areas.

Stage II: Promotion, after having successfully completed stage I, of new growth centres at acceptable distances from the first ones.

A regional policy of this nature would do justice to natural tendencies and simultaneously reach the policy objectives even more rapidly than by direct promotion of distressed regions in distress, particularly when evidence on programmes of this nature shows only limited success.

Group 3 consists of potentially distressed regions. The group is characterised particularly by the older textile centres, mining towns and other single industry mono-structured cities. They are characterised as well by obsolete housing stocks, unattractive centres, a mixing of industries and residential neighbourhoods as well as lop-sided economic and social structures.

The policy called for is one of economic restructuring, eventually supplemented with a policy of subsidised outmigration if stagnation of the economy fails to provide sufficient job opportunities for the labourforce. Typical regions of this type in Europe are the Ruhr area, the textile areas all over the western part of the continent, the Borinage in Belgium, the Sarre, and the Newcastle–Sunderland area in the UK.

Perhaps the social problems in these cities are even greater than the economic. The cities are environmentally unattractive, and the labour and firms who can afford it financially are inclined to leave. This is particularly evident in the Ruhr area where the pace of outmigration of German workers exceeds that of the decline in the traditional sectors to such an extent that large numbers of foreign workers, principally from the Mediterranean countries have to be 'imported' to do the work the Germans themselves have abandoned, in an environment the Germans have left behind. These cases demonstrate the usefulness of social indicators that could show the influence of such developments on the quality of life in these areas both for domestic and foreign workers. Government policies have not taken these developments into account, nor have governments been kept informed of the interaction between economic and social developments in these areas.

Without strong and effective government intervention, these cities and regions will soon belong to group 4, the distressed areas. Even more than for the group 3 areas, the distressed areas need a powerful policy providing for complete economic restructuring, migration and retraining. For agricultural areas, this combination of policies and programmes has been rather successful but to date the degree of success in urban areas has been modest. To make these policies more effective, we may again point at the phasing principle of regional policy, mentioned earlier. The areas in greatest distress are frequently a nation's peripheral areas. A gradual relocation of activities from the main urban centres outwards eventually will reach the periphery of the country. This will take time but apparently less time than would be the case if present policies are maintained.

Regional policies differ from country to country and are changing within countries in Europe. Germany has no formal migration policy. Sweden heavily subsidises migration to its main urban centres of Stockholm, Göteborg and Malmö. The UK, France and Holland subsidise some movements to development centres (growth poles) in distressed areas, but not to the prosperous urban areas. Most countries base their policy on the 'growth-pole' principle, promoting growth in a relatively small number of cities and towns rather than dispersing it over developing areas as in the UK model. Most countries adopting the growth-pole principle, have subsequently yielded to too many designated growth points. Holland counts 50 growth poles and the Federal Republic of Germany over 300!

The overall picture is as interesting as it is confusing. For the student of regional economics and regional policy, Europe is a laboratory where nearly all possible experiments have become reality. A severe difficulty of making an effective use of the laboratory is the fact, however, that a regional policy is basically a long-run policy. In practice, policies change rather frequently, leaving the student to determine which part of what actually happened should be attributed to the old policy (or no policy), which part to the new and which part to autonomous developments. So far attempts to measure the effectiveness of regional policies in Europe are limited to very few countries and periods (a good example is Vanhove, 1961). An overall evaluation of the policies after the Second World War could not only inform us systematically about the evolution of the thinking on these matters, but teach us a great deal about the degree to which different policies have contributed to national objectives.

Urban policies

The second level for consideration is the urban level. Since urban policy is defined as the use of the set of instruments that influence the development of urban areas, it is mainly a policy of local authorities. Consequently the variety of forms of urban policy found in Europe is even larger than is the case of regional policies. Yet there is one common feature that narrows down the range of major problems and thus policies in urban areas, i.e. motorisation and its impact on urban development. Traffic problems, as well as pollution, congestion and urban sprawl, are among the most discussed topics at conferences all over Western Europe. They are also entering into the discussions in Eastern Europe where motorisation is beginning to have its impact on urban development.

The structure of the problem is well known and can be summarised as follows:

1 Most cities are mononuclear in structure with the central business district (CBD) representing the main attraction centre as both a working and shopping place.
2 Motorisation enables people formerly living in the urban core to move out to more pleasant places which combine the nearness of urban amenities with the advantages of a house in 'the green'.
3 The increased traffic flows resulting from these moves endanger the chances of survival of the CBD and induce activities to decentralisation to places on the outskirts of the city.
4 Space in the CBD becoming available by this process is rapidly occupied by offices and banks, worsening again traffic problems.
5 As a result of this process, the quality of life in the urban cores deteriorates rapidly, stimulating further downward trends.
6 The principal solution proposed by local government is improvement of public transport and restriction of private car traffic in certain areas of the CBD.

Although these developments are certainly not the only ones

influencing the quality of urban life, their importance is vital and justifies a broader treatment.

When considering these problems, we will do well to focus attention much more on the traffic problem as a whole than only on the problem of auto traffic. The solution to be found is not how to divert people from automobiles to public transport, but how to influence the behaviour of people such that the result is optimal both for the individual and for the urban society as a whole. Broadly speaking, measures to be taken (and partly already taken) should be considered for their effect on:

(a) the volume of traffic;
(b) the spatial structure of traffic;
(c) the temporal structure of traffic.

In discussing the measures in more detail, it will be assumed that they will not adversely affect the quality or the volume of communication in a broader sense.

The very large number of measures taken* forces a categorisation into three large groups, namely measures influencing the demand for traffic, those influencing the supply of infrastructure and public means of transportation and those influencing the modal split.

Concerning the measures influencing *the demand for traffic*, it is useful to distinguish between two subcategories, decentralisation policies and measures of timing. The idea behind decentralisation policy is that the heavy concentration of employment in the CBDs forces large numbers of people to commute to this district during the morning hours, using only half the infrastructure and moving out of the centre after work using the other half. This implies not only an extremely inefficient use of existing infrastructure over time, but also spatially, and causing heavy congestion in one direction during a few hours and the need to provide large-capacity public transport during the same limited number of hours in the same direction. The phenomenon that causes congestion of private traffic is the same that leads to heavy deficits for the public means of transportation. Obviously measures promoting the evolution of the mononuclear structures of our cities into multinuclear structures, simultaneously strengthening the residential function of the inner urban core, could not only influence favourably the volume of traffic as a whole, but also its spatial and temporal structure.

A simple example illustrates this point. The inner city of

*See, among others, the papers presented at the IG Metall Meeting (1972). Contributions on traffic problems came from Beesley (1972); Busch (1972); Rittel (1972); Schuck (1972); and Klaassen (1972).

Rotterdam, which was completely rebuilt after the Second World War, is though limited in size rather varied in structure. Moreover, its importance as a residential area has the advantage that people living in the centre, where attractive apartments are available, either work in the centre or work outside. In either case, the influence of their location is favourable. If they work in the centre, the volume of traffic they generate for the journey to work as well as for other motives (shopping, concerts, theatre, etc.) is considerably smaller than would be the case if they all lived outside the centre. In the second case, those who work outside the centre use off-peak capacity of public transportation. Any policy that works in the other direction – and unfortunately there are many such policies in Europe, notably in Germany, Holland and France – aggravates the traffic problem, and in so doing, worsens the quality of urban life.

Basically the policy proposed is similar to that followed in the regional context. Also there the aim is improvement of the quality of life through a more equal distribution of population and activities albeit on a regional basis. In the proposed urban policy this is translated to the urban scale.

Obviously a large number of problems are posed in the implementation of this policy. The first problem is how to make the centre of our cities attractive places to live in. Recent trends in Europe have shown that young people, in particular, appreciate living in town centres and the more they do so the more intimate the atmosphere in the centre is. Old towns like Cologne, Munich and Amsterdam offer splendid opportunities for living in historical places in the middle of everything that a city of some size and character has to offer. By living there, they themselves contribute to the atmosphere of the city. By demanding amenities available in the urban core, they stimulate the typical centre activities, they make the city more attractive by their mere presence after working hours and, above all, they prevent the city from being 'bought' by bankers and insurance companies who would build enormous so-called representative offices in the city centre and turn the area into a dead and unpleasant place during most of the day. Frankfurt is a unique example of the quick death of a beautiful centre as a result of this very process, and Paris is going rapidly in the same direction (see also *NRC-Handelsblad*, 1972).

The very fact that actual developments are going in this unhappy direction reflects the public indifference to the lack of governing power matter of urban land use allocation. Many European countries have precise rules concerning land zoning in new areas. Manufacturing firms are strictly forbidden in residential areas, and residential construction is not permitted in recreational areas, etc. But there is no law that enables city councils to forbid a large bank from occupying the most valuable land in the city core. Clearly much study will have to be completed before we can propose an optimal land use system in the whole of our urban areas but local authorities should at least have the power to halt developments under way in order to have time to think through questions about basic spatial structures. If this time is properly used, it should result in proper zoning ordinances for the inner cores of the cities. These should enable the authorities to redirect activities with very low visitor–worker ratios to places with high accessibility (activities which no longer belong in city centres), thus considerably decreasing the demand for land in the urban centres. This autonomous decrease in demand will favourably affect land prices and make the centres more attractive for residential purposes as well as for activities with high visitor–worker ratios such as theatres, shops, cafés and restaurants, and all the small but extremely important activities that make a city centre an attractive place – a place for people rather than for prestige buildings.

As the situation is now, even shopping activities are leaving the cities. An article in *The Economist* (15 April 1972, p. 60) includes a map which shows the growth of hypermarkets in Europe, and particularly in Germany and Belgium. The fear is great that these developments, which are mainly induced by motorisation, will seriously affect the shopping facilities in existing towns and cities. The article states for Britain:

> Pressure from retailers for out-of-town planning permission is bound to mount. But will Britain be overrun with hypermarkets a decade or two from now? Wheatsheaf/Carrefour forecasts 37 hypermarkets in Britain by 1973, turning over 200 million a year – still a minute proportion of what is estimated will be a total retail turnover of £15 billion. More pessimistic forecasters say that Britain cannot comfortably support more than 20 hypermarkets without serious damage to existing shopping facilities.
>
> This would be fewer than a country as small as Belgium has now, but, if it should be true, then planning decisions should not be left to individual local authorities to take according to their own priorities. The government would do well to follow the industry's little Neddy's suggestion for a strategic plan drawn up on a regional basis; but there is nothing to suggest that the Department of the Environment is thinking that way. (*The Economist*, 15 April 1972, p. 61)

We find here a typical example of decisions of an order higher than the order made by the (local) governments. Municipalities or countries around the urban areas might make decisions that heavily influence the urban cores without even contemplating the effects of such decisions on the quality of life in the region as a whole.

What is lacking in Europe generally is basic thinking about future structures of towns and cities. Present thinking is anti-car and pro-public transport. In the meantime developments are taking place rapidly in a direction that nobody really considers desirable. A proper setting of objectives might change this rigid thinking and replace it by the study of instruments to be used to reach the objectives. Only this could save European cities from becoming characterless suburban rings around city centres consisting of dead office buildings.

A second group of measures that influence the *level of demand* for traffic facilities concerns measures of timing. There are three possibilities:

(a) flexible working hours;
(b) staggered opening and closing times of offices and shops;
(c) shift work.

Obviously working in shifts might have serious social drawbacks that can hardly be compensated by higher wages. Therefore it seems appropriate to concentrate more on (a) and (b). Flexible working hours in shops and offices do not decrease the overall volume of traffic. They do, however, decrease considerably the size of the peak and thus the temporal structure of traffic. Flexible working hours are now rapidly being introduced, especially in Germany and gradually in the Netherlands. By enabling the worker, within certain limits, to adjust his/her working hours to personal preferences, he/she contributes not only to the solution of the traffic problem, but also to the satisfaction he/she finds in his/her work. Flexible opening and closing times for shops have the same effect for the workers in shops but simultaneously improve the 'temporal accessibility' of the shop for workers in all branches. In Europe shops still close at about the same hours as offices providing their customers with little or no time to do their shopping other than on Saturday (in Germany and Austria until noon only).

The measures on the *supply side* of the traffic market may be divided in four groups:

1 increasing the efficiency of existing means of transportation;
2 introducing new means of transportation;
3 integrating transportation systems;
4 more efficient utilisation of the private car by increasing the number of riders per car (car-pooling).

Although new and revolutionary systems of transportation could contribute to the preservation of present city structures, their environmental impact may be considerable. This holds even for extensions of conventional railway systems in urban areas. Particularly in cities where underground railway systems cannot be built without destroying construction above the ground, a rigorous extension of such a system could ruin the character of the city just as effectively as could a freeway through the city. Still, particularly in new cities, or cities where large-scale urban renewal is programmed, new technologies might be introduced profitably. Their number is, however, at least in Europe, rather limited.

The final type of measure concerns the *modal split*. Here we have two groups: first, those directed at influencing the relative advantages and disadvantages of using private vs public means of transportation through a policy of pricing and quality improvement (comfort); and secondly, those which impose quantitative restrictions on private transportation in city centres. The first group comprises:

(a) a system of differentiated road pricing (Beesley, 1972);
(b) subsidies for public transport including subsidies to the transport companies for improving the quality of their services;
(c) the introduction of parking fees.

It seems correct to assume, as has Professor Beesley, that the simultaneous use of all instruments could prove to be the most effective. The importance of a zero price for public transportation should not be overestimated. First, the total volume of traffic increases. Secondly, the price of public transportation, at least in relation to the value attached by the user of a private car to the difference in time and comfort, is so high that a decrease of the fare even to zero would hardly influence his decision. Experience in Rome, where a zero-price experiment was recently conducted, indicates that a zero price considerably influences the volume of public transport riders but hardly affects the number of cars on roads. For this reason, the scheme of road pricing introduced by British transport economists where the road user is charged for the marginal congestion costs on the road he uses seems to be much more sensible. This pricing policy decreases the volume of traffic and charges the car user with the true costs of his use of the road.

The second group of measures concerned with modal split comprises the quantitative restrictions. These involve: (a) limited access to centres for private cars; and (b) parking restrictions.

The limited accessibility of the centre to private cars should be implemented in such a way that it does not impose upon those who live in the centre, nor upon those with whom these persons have social contacts. Severely limiting accessibility should not make the city centre less attractive as a place to live or the policy will conflict with an objective of higher order, i.e. the desired structure of the city centre.

It cannot be denied that urban and regional measures are often taken without proper study of the way the measures *should* be taken and even less of the consequences to be expected. It still is not generally recognised, for instance, that long-parking restrictions in the city centres in the short run increase the peak in public transport but decrease the use of the car during the off-peak hours. These measures thus unfavourably influence the deficits of the public transport system by increasing the peak and decreasing the volume of traffic in the off-peak hours. It is not that measures of this kind should not be taken, but rather that authorities should be aware of the consequences and take them into account before deciding when, how and where to introduce the measures.

It seems useful to consider briefly the general impact of the measures proposed on the quality of urban life. We will consider all four elements of this quality and the impact of all measures mentioned on these elements. The elements are:

1	The environment	(ENV)
2	The economy	(ECO)
3	Social life	(SOC)
4	Cultural life	(CUL)

The variables concerned may be listed as follows:

1 *Demand side*
(a) decentralisation; (D)
(b) timing. (T)

2 *Supply side*
(a) efficiency improvement (E)

3 *Modal split*
(a) competitive position; (C)
(b) quantitative restrictions. (Q)

We may now state:

1 All measures proposed have a positive influence on the environment.
2 All measures proposed have a positive effect on the effectiveness of the economy with the possible exception of quantitative restrictions, the influence of which is uncertain.
3 The influence of the instruments on the quality of social life is

much less clear. They have been studied much less than the influences on ENV and ECO. However it seems justified to state that the influence of D is uncertain and influences of all other variables are zero. In general, it can be expected that there will be hardly any influence of the measures proposed on the quality of social life in our cities.

4 The effects on cultural life of T, E and C are probably zero. Quantitative restrictions will likely have a negative influence on cultural life, and the influence of decentralisation is doubtful.

We may summarise the foregoing as in Table 3.2.

Table 3.2 Summary of effects

								Measures	Term
ENV		+	+	+	+	+	D		Long
ECO	=	+	+	+	+	+	T	Demand side	Medium
SOC		±	0	0	0	0	E	Supply side	
CUL		±	0	0	0	–	C	Modal split	Short
							Q		

In general, the effects of the measures proposed are positive or neutral. Only some effects on cultural life might be negative. As for the term, the recommendations are:

(a) in the short term: measures concerning the modal split (C and Q);
(b) in the medium term: measures concerning the improvement of efficiency (E) and timing (T);
(c) in the long term: decentralisation (D).

It is rather difficult to list which measures are taken where in Europe. It might be clear from the foregoing that road pricing is most likely to be introduced in the UK first. This is probably the most promising development in urban transportation policy. Otherwise rather conventional thinking prevails. Not even experiences in US cities have penetrated to many European cities. Those who try to introduce more new thinking, more constructive planning methods and do not condemn the car and favour public transportation should anticipate that their proposals will be regarded with suspicion.

The foregoing considerations have focused basically on the trends in our cities evolving from increasing income levels and motorisation of the population. It is true that these considerations fail to cover the whole field of urban development, but their importance is so overwhelming that it seemed justified to devote so many words to them.

Neighbourhood planning

The planning of neighbourhoods is a critically important part of the work of the physical planners of cities and towns. Other than the planners who are responsible for the physical structure of the city as a whole, their task concentrates on typical neighbourhood activities to be carried out in agreeable residential surroundings. Primary and sports facilities comprise the most important of these activities. It is the task of the city planner to plan the overall structure and to indicate the framework into which the neighbourhood should fit. The task of the neighbourhood planner is to make the neighbourhood a pleasant place to live, to create a micro-structure that promotes social contacts and creates optimal conditions for the young to grow up in and for the elderly to enjoy living in. This task is not easier than that of the planner of the city as a whole. It is just different in nature. Many examples all over Europe show how easy it is to do a bad job, to build monotonous residential deserts devoid of any character or intimacy.

Bad planning does not restrict itself to new neighbourhoods. Urban renewal projects plans in older parts of our cities are characterised by ruthless destruction of existing communities without any respect for informal social structures of the communities of those areas. Many renewal plans are based upon such technical criteria as age of the dwellings and facilities in the houses. Proper sociological studies of social structures and living patterns in those neighbourhoods are rarely carried out properly and even less often taken into account. All too often it is forgotten that the city is there for the people living in it, and that they are more important than the technical qualities of the physical structures in which they live. For the people to decide whether or not the place where they live is agreeable or not goes far beyond technical criteria. It is certainly true that very old houses should be modernised but it is certainly not true that the best way to bring a neighbourhood up to modern standards is replacing that whole neighbourhood by a new one. This *might* be true but is not necessarily so. Examples in the Netherlands, such as Amersfoort, prove that a careful policy of restoration and interior renovation of old houses may yield far better results than ruthless, so-called renewal. Europe seems to be the ideal place to show how careful adjustment policies in older neighbourhoods with proper financing might not just conserve what is valuable from an architectural point of view, but also keep those important parts of our cities alive. Action groups in many European cities where urban renewal plans are contemplated demonstrate that the populations of those areas often have completely different views on what should be done than do the public authorities with their rigid beliefs about what is good for them. They should be listened to, it is their neighbourhood. Authorities should keep in mind that the order of the decision might be too low to be taken by the city council. The weight of the opinions on the appropriate level should be in accordance with the importance of the decision for the very population involved.

A reconsideration of some principles

City planning is a long-run activity. It is planning a place for people to live and to work for the future as well as the present. Many European cities still have basically the same physical structure that was designed centuries ago. Most Italian and Spanish cities and many French, German, Belgian and Dutch cities and towns remain as examples of brilliant architecture in the micro as well as the macro sense. What principles did the builders of these cities have in mind? Were the cities built with the intention that they remain forever? Were the builders of Rome or Salzburg constructing something for the enjoyment of all future generations? Or were they maximising a discounted cash flow? We apply the latter criterion using a discount rate of 10 per cent which means that everything after 20 years from now no longer counts. But is this compatible with the fact that what we build now, with some exceptions, will still be there in another 100 years? Were not large parts of the inner cores of present-day European cities built during the Middle Ages? Since then, over a period of 700 or 800 years, people enjoyed living in and looking at these cities. The more famous examples drew millions of tourists from all over the world. But all this joy during all these centuries would not have been, had a discount rate of 10 per cent been applied in the planning! Then only benefits during the first few years would have counted.

It is in fact a strange procedure that we apply. Our decisions are perhaps too much influenced by financial constraints and conditions. The interest rate is essentially a purely financial factor that certainly is influenced by the average or marginal returns on capital. But the real question is what the contribution of a given investment is to the society as a whole, now and in the future. We are beginning to understand that urban renewal, for instance, might be highly profitable if we calculate on a purely financial basis, i.e. if we just count the price we paid for the land and the old structures on it and do not incorporate in our decisions the social structures that are being destroyed, the damage done to the overall image of the city, the impact on traffic conditions, and so on. But if we would incorporate into our calculations all of these adverse effects, would then our return on capital be as high? Maybe we would not even earn 2 per cent as the true rate of return.

It seems that a first conclusion can be drawn from these considerations. That conclusion is that city planning is not only to be left to private developers who are understandably forced to calculate in purely financial terms. If they are omitted from city building, they should only participate in planning and building under very strict rules set by local authorities, in the hope of course that those rules are sensible and wise. In other words, we should shift from decisions giving attractive financial rates of return on capital to decisions giving an attractive rate of return considering the society as a whole. Whether this is done by shadow pricing or by more qualitative methods is basically irrelevant. The main thing is that we ought to start from a welfare function as older economists used to do as the only way to make correct decisions and not from one element of that welfare function, the financial part only.

The second conclusion is linked to the former and concerns the discount rate to be used in the decision to carry out/not to carry out a given project. If we argue that the rate of return should be based on the contribution of the particular project to the welfare of the society as a whole, then we must also argue that *all* projects should be judged on this basis. But this means that the discount rate with which we compare the rate of return of an individual project has to be considerably lower, too, than the financial rate of return on the isolated projects. If, to state the criterion formally, we could force the individual project developer to 'pay' for the social damage – to the environment, to other economic subjects in our society, in other words, for all the social, economic, cultural and environmental external effects – then a large number of projects would not have been profitable at all. And this is nothing else than saying that the average rate of return reflected in the interest rate is a bad criterion for the selection of investment projects.

The conclusion from both statements is that the individual project probably has a much lower real rate of return than usually is assumed by developers, but that also the discount rate to be applied will be lower than the prevailing rate of interest. Since urban projects have relatively many and important external effects compared to industrial projects, for example, the corrected rate of return on urban projects will decrease by this correction more than the overall rate of return. This implies that the relative attractiveness of urban renewal projects for developers will decrease considerably if they are charged for all external effects of their projects, and even more if they must guarantee that there will be no external disbenefits at all.

This group of problems is closely linked with the timing procedure in city planning. In many European countries the conventional planning procedure calls for preparing a plan in 1970 for the city in the year 1980. In 1980 the plan is revised and a new plan for 1990 is made, and so on. It is basically *point planning*.

First, this procedure implies a planning period, in the case at hand, of 10 years. This is saying nothing but that the periods after the planning period are ignored. And this is basically the same as applying an interest rate of some 15 per cent. Applying a rate of, say, 5 per cent would mean that a much longer period would have to be taken into account. Suppose for a moment that we would do this. Then the period would extend from 1970 to, say, the year 2000. The planning for the year 1980, then, will be basically different from the first one, in which the year 1980 was considered as the final year. In the new procedure the plan for 1980 has to be such that it fits into the development up to the year 2000. Arriving in the year 1980, the plan for 1990 will have to fit into the plan for the year 2010, etc. This planning period in this procedure may be determined by an optimisation process in which the discount rate, as well as the costs of continuous adjustment and the lifetime of the buildings, play a role. It goes without saying that this discount rate should be corrected for *all* external effects of construction and demolition.

The procedure proposed yields, at least to a reasonable extent, the possibility of real long-term planning where due regard is paid to social and cultural factors that all too often are neglected by modern city planners.

These considerations lead us directly to the final point. That point is that city planning is basically an interdisciplinary activity in which economists, engineers, sociologists, architects, traffic experts and ecologists should take part. It is not the task of *a* professional city planner. In fact such a profession should not exist at all. What should be done is to charge a team of experts to draw up, in close co-operation, a city plan in which all interests are in balance. There is no guarantee that they always will succeed in building a city in which everybody is happy but the chances that they will *not* be happy are at least considerably smaller than often is the case when applying conventional procedures.

There remains still much to be done in European city planning. The interest shown in the subject nowadays and the revived interest in the values of the past give us the hope that the cities of the future will become better places to live in than the cities of the present. It is the duty of students in this field to assist governments in this enormous but fascinating task.

3.3 The future of the larger European towns*

Introduction

How European towns will develop in future depends largely on the changes in Europe's economic and political structure. Before embarking on a detailed discussion of European towns, we must therefore try to understand broadly how Europe as a whole is evolving. However, the totality of European development and the development of towns are increasingly hard to separate, for on the continent of Europe such a large proportion of the total population is now living in towns that it is difficult to analyse the two types of development separately. Nevertheless, as we shall see, such separate analysis is still meaningful.

World scenarios

We can picture several future structures of the world economy, one of which is to assume that the Pacific region is the growth area of the future. Recent developments in that region, notably in Japan but lately also in Taiwan, Korea and Hong Kong, suggest that the so-called Pacific scenario is the most probable of all the scenarios one could envisage. There are signs that other countries are also developing faster than could initially be expected: Brasil and India are cases in point. Their growth is not likely to detract much from the supposed leadership of the Pacific region; indeed, the rise of China and Indonesia, countries which also give signs of accelerated development, is consolidating the position of the Pacific. The evolution in China may well make a particularly heavy impact on the world's economic development: remember that China has four times as many people as either the USA or the EC, so that the effect of a certain increase

*See L.H. Klaassen, 'The Donald Robertson Memorial Lecture, 1968', *Urban Studies*, Centre for Regional and Urban Research, Glasgow, 1987.

in income per head of population there is twice that of the same increase in the USA and the EC together. Economic growth is known to add more to international than to national trade, and the statistics confirm that tendency: international trade has clearly grown faster in the Pacific than in the Atlantic region.

Despite this, we need not despair of the future of Europe or the USA, but we do need to follow world developments closely, and learn from them. While on the one hand we should rejoice in the favourable development of countries in the Far East, on the other hand we can realise that the western part of the USA may well develop differently from the eastern part. Although the whole of the USA undoubtedly belonged for quite a while to the Atlantic region, states in the West are naturally tending more to the Pacific than to the Atlantic region not only because of its geographical situation, but also owing to the very high concentration of Asiatics to be found there, for instance, in universities and high-grade professions. But unlike Thailand and Malaysia, the western parts of Central and South America will not so readily be integrated in the fast-growing Pacific region.

As such, the rapid growth of such an extensive region as the Pacific is a favourable phenomenon, profitable to many. Nevertheless, this growth, if continued, could cause worldwide problems, e.g. in respect of energy. Energy supply was a serious concern for some time. Extensive saving measures after the 1973 and 1978 crises had to be undertaken, and extremely high energy prices caused inflation which plunged many consumers of energy into financial distress. On the other hand, high prices greatly stimulated exploration, which since 1978 has yielded remarkable results. At the moment, energy supply seems to be relatively stable, the Organisation of Petroleum Exporting Countries (OPEC) apparently having lost much of its power, and given present prices, the situation does not look too bad. But what is going to happen if one-third of world population – for that is what the Pacific region stands for – suddenly find that their income allows them to pass from self-sufficiency with energy from agrarian sources to the consumption of more modern types of energy? That seems the more likely as the region's economic evolution will be attended by accelerated urbanisation, favouring a further increase in the consumption of fossil fuels. Such a development might provoke a further rise in the price of energy and revive programmes for energy saving which are now lying all but forgotten in bottom drawers.

Macro-economic structures

While until a short time ago the economic world hegemony of Europe and the USA was taken for granted, present world developments render it far less secure. Many developing countries are not following the neat pattern that had theoretically been expected, and Europe has sorely felt the consequences. Shipyards have felt the effects of relatively low wages and Western economies, in general, have felt the effects of the undeniable technical genius in such developing countries as Korea and Taiwan. Such effects were foreseeable, however, and we must accept them with good grace. Thus if we contribute, by our development aid, to a country's industrial evolution, we must be prepared to admit to our markets the goods which it produces as a result. Nevertheless, that is not the real problem.

For a long time those parts of the world which we were wont to call the West took the lead in technological progress. All innovations were hatched there, and it was believed that the West was so far ahead of the developing countries that it had to find alternative, labour-intensive techniques corresponding to the scarce capital and low wages prevailing in those countries. But Japan, Hong Kong and Taiwan did not fit that conception at all; on the contrary, they began to perfect the techniques used in the West, and proved so good at it that after a short while they introduced techniques that were superior, even in the eyes of the West. Innovatory products incorporating new technology began to push the products of European and American industry from their own markets and the East seemed to be fast becoming more modern than the West.

In economics competition from outside is the surest incentive to innovation, and it is fair to say that the efforts which Europe and the USA have made in the last few years to stimulate technological advance in their own territory have largely been inspired by the growing menace to their own position. Particularly in Europe, political folklore at one time demanded every public address to open with the warning that Europe had got behind the East and that something had to be done about it. For these and other reasons, the growth of so-called innovating sectors in Europe and the USA has certainly speeded up. Technological progress, via automation, robotisation and computerisation, has caused a relatively severe fall in employment in traditional industries, and has essentially changed the nature of the articles produced. In the 1950s a calculator capable of not much more than the most elementary operations weighed some 10 kg, and in the 1960s an adult computer filled an entire hall. Since that time not only have dimensions and weights fallen dramatically, but prices have fallen similarly. Less weight, lower prices and much better quality are indeed typical of the evolution of all industry. Research by J. Vogelaar of the Netherlands Economic Institute has shown that between 1965 and 1981 GNP in the Federal Republic of Germany,

France and the Benelux countries increased by some 75 per cent, while the total weight transported within each country remained constant. The number of tonne-kilometers run, however, did rise, which indicated that a constant tonnage of goods was carried across ever longer distances. Similarly, international transport, also in tonnes, is still increasing with more goods than before crossing frontiers. On the other hand, the number of ton-km produced per European Currency Unit (ECU) of gross national product seems to have dropped since 1975.

This tendency will be consolidated in the future. Technological progress is knowledge-intensive and results in the accelerated evolution of the service sector, informatics taking the lead. Thus the industrial and agrarian production society with its intensive use of raw materials is turning into the more light-footed modern service society. Of course, industry and agriculture will still have a place in that new society, because it cannot function at all without them, but they will become much less important in terms of value added and employment.

Location factors for innovating activities

The arguments of these previous sections already touch on urban problems. Once society is increasingly oriented towards activities that are virtually independent of raw materials, we are apt to ask ourselves where such activities will locate and whether the larger towns have a role to play. The clue lies in the expression 'virtually independent of raw materials'. Indeed, if goods can be produced without raw materials and delivered without much cost to the final consumer, then traditional transport and the cost involved lose much of their significance. That applies to service transactions to a high degree, and it is practically 100 per cent true of communication via satellites. A telephone conversation between Glasgow and Tokyo via a satellite will cost hardly more than one from Glasgow to Edinburgh, for example. Once such communications are realised – and the time does not seem far off – modern service companies need not be much concerned about their location. Only firms relying strongly on personal contact with suppliers or consumers, for instance, suppliers of daily goods to final consumers, need still be established close to their contacts.

Thus modern techniques gradually bring about a situation in which sales prospects are largely independent of the place where the company is based. This upsets location theory, but it does not mean that the entrepreneur is now entirely free to settle wherever he fancies. The older spatial models, like Lowry's, assumed that an entrepreneur would choose a certain location in respect of the accessibility of markets and raw materials. Those working for the company would choose residence in the neighbourhood. On the one hand the company's transportation costs did not permit a location too far from the optimum, and on the other hand workers could not spare the time or the money to live far from the workplace. Under such rigid conditions certain activities and groups of population settled at clearly defined locations. It was the realistic thing to do at a time when the working population was barely mobile. Harbour towns are typical examples of such demographic concentrations, as are textile, coalmining, iron-and-steel towns, etc. Where the production was, the workers must settle also, whether or not the area was attractive. The workplace determined the living place, the quality of the latter was irrelevant.

As we have said, the description no longer fits our present society, least of all the new activities in it. They have indeed become 'footloose' in respect of the supply and dispatch of goods and services, that is independent of the characteristics of the location. But workers now clearly make high demands on the residential climate; in particular, the high-skilled workers on which hi-tech activities greatly rely have pronounced residential preferences.

The European framework

In Europe the residential preferences of highly-skilled manpower have already had visible results. A number of favourite residential areas in Europe are concentrated in the Alpine region, consisting of southern Bavaria, south Baden-Württemberg, Austria, Switzerland, Savoy, Dauphine, the Côte d'Azur, and the lake region in northern Italy. The area possesses beautiful scenery, a climate permitting two relatively long tourist seasons, a stable labour market, little unemployment, relatively little criminality and it is very clean.

That statement should not be interpreted to mean that in the future all Europeans will be moving to the Alps. Rather it means that economic developments in the Federal Republic of Germany will probably orient themselves more than before to the south. The same applies, *mutatis mutandis*, to the eastern part of France and the northern part of Italy. Within their national boundaries these regions will be more in favour than before. Similar processes will occur in other European countries: modern economic activities will concentrate in areas where the living is good.

The Alpine region is a vast area with at least seven international airports and as many sizeable towns. The area has also much to offer in the way of culture. It accommodates the Salzburger Festspiele

(Salzburg Music Festival) and La Scala in Milan as well as universities and scientific institutions of world fame. Indeed our statement about the Alpine area was clearly a macro one, emphasising the importance of the living environment in a general sense. The micro preferences still have to be looked at closely. In every country there are parts where living is pleasant, and these parts will play, within their national borders, the role the Alpine region plays in the European context.

Micro tendencies: the role of large towns

The developments in the larger towns of Europe have been the object of much research in the last few decades. The outcomes of the studies are highly similar: they all emphasise the process of suburbanisation of larger towns, with people leaving the central areas of agglomerations for the surrounding suburbs. This process has sometimes gone on until a whole agglomeration has suffered population losses, and the population has been dispersed and divided. The affluent and the higher educated have settled at a considerable distance from the centre (and thus, in most cases, from their workplaces), while the lower-skilled, lower-income classes have remained concentrated in the centre of the inner town. This process is still going on and has produced clear spatial separation between the inhabitants of different income and educational levels.

The consequences of this are twofold. In agglomerations consisting of different municipalities, the municipal councils of the suburbs, with their affluent populations, logically tend to be of a more conservative nature, while those of the central municipalities tend increasingly towards socialism. In many large towns this polarisation has doomed to failure all efforts to give the agglomeration its own central administration, as no one has been prepared to accept the risks and problems entailed in trying to co-ordinate these different ideological tendencies. This polarisation is also responsible for the central municipalities, almost absolute priority for social housing, and their neglect of the demand for houses of better quality. In the suburbs the reverse has happened. Thus the tendency towards segregation of qualitatively different population groups has been reinforced.

With most business companies established in the central part of the central town, large traffic flows – to the centre during morning peak hours, and back to the ring of the agglomeration at the end of the working day – have become unavoidable. As congestion has become worse companies in the centre have become less accessible, and businesses wanting to expand have found themselves pressed for space. In the end entrepreneurs have realised that, in the best interest of their companies and their staff, they had better move to the ring around the town, where their workers are already living. And so the decentralising tendency has begun to spread from the inhabitants to workplaces.

The tendency observed here is identical with the one discussed earlier, i.e. the quality of the living environment determines the economic development prospects not only in regions, but also within agglomerations.

Municipal governments or, more precisely, the governors of the central towns of agglomerations have not remained mere spectators. They have adopted a policy of re-urbanisation or revitalisation, as has been manifest from their efforts to render towns more pleasant to live in. This has been done by creating more public greenery, pedestrian precincts and traffic-sheltered zones, by building better houses in the inner city and, in brief, by showing more consideration for human beings in a modern town. How far this policy will be effective cannot yet be appraised. People seem less eager now to leave town than they have been for a long time, but we do not exactly know why. Perhaps one explanation is that the economic recession, now partly overcome, made buying a house somewhat risky. Past and present efforts made by municipal governments to make the town more liveable may have helped. If that is true, towns have at least done something to fight the lure of regions that offer not only more attractive scenery, but also a more hospitable environment.

In fact, if towns have little to offer in 'outstanding natural beauty', they make up for it in cultural values. Who knows, in the long run these values, in an adjusted and improved residential climate, might tip the scales for some people, including families with growing children, towards the town?

Synthesis

Looking back over the ground we have covered, we can see clearly that pondering on the future of towns in Europe, we have to reckon with several factors.

There is, first of all, the fact that we can hardly speak of the typical European town. There are ancient towns and young towns; cities enjoying the most important cultural heritage of Europe; and nineteenth-century industrial towns lacking everything that could make a town at all attractive. There are also towns set amid beautiful surroundings, with easy access to leisure-time and tourist areas. Towns on the coast or among gentle hills with a pleasant climate make more attractive places of residences than towns in vast old industrial areas with more rain and fog than sunshine. These factors are not new, but they are often forgotten and had better be reconsidered in the new light shed on them by latest developments. So long as the locational exigencies of trade and industry dictated the development of employment and thus of the population, climate and scenery were of negligible locational importance. Business came first. Now, however, helped by technical progress, companies are increasingly escaping from that type of dictatorship, and the interests of the employee are becoming the decisive factor in the choice of location and expansion.

There are of course some constraints. Any company will appreciate the proximity of an international airport and good connections with the country's network of motorways. But these secondary conditions do not clash with the interests of the staff. Indeed the demands high-grade workers make of the quality of the living environment include the presence of good schools and cultural services. Clearly the secondary requirements of companies and staff can only be fulfilled in or near urban areas. Nowhere else is there likely to be an international airport near at hand, nor can an adequate connection with the network of motorways be guaranteed elsewhere. Similarly, a high level of cultural and educative services tend mostly to be found in urban areas. Thus the interests of both entrepreneurs and staff can be seen to run on parallel lines.

The conclusion to be drawn is that the economic development of Europe is unthinkable without its towns. The services that a town has to offer are included in the requirements which staff members and their families demand from the living environment, and other elements of the residential climate are also influential; only in the overall surroundings of the towns can all these demands be satisfied. A place of residence too far from the town would jeopardise the cultural and educative component, while a residence too close to town cannot fulfil the other demands. Therefore, the so-called intermediary areas have the best prospects for a prosperous future. Several examples can be pointed out in Europe: in England, Cambridge is a good example, while others can be found in the Alpine region, already cited; in the Netherlands, Amstelveen is such a development pole, situated at equal distances from Amsterdam and Schiphol Airport.

High-technology developments like that of the Sunbelt in general, and Silicon Valley in the USA in particular, can also be expected at several new places in Europe. Although these developments are not likely to occur in the large towns themselves, in their own interest these towns should go on improving their living climate, maintaining their level of education and cultural services, maintaining the quality of their shopping services and making them more accessible. If in that way they cannot lure back many people to live there, at least they can attract an income flow from those living some way off. People's mobility, still increasing, makes such a development easily possible and desirable.

The process we have just described points to a large-scale dispersion of living and employment across a wide area around urban agglomerations. Those living in that area will, in some way, keep in touch with the original town, so that interaction albeit across longer distances than before will be continued.

Political aspects

When suburbanisation set in and many people working in the town went to live in the municipalities around it, there arose at once an administrative – or democratic – problem: those who lived in the suburban municipalities but still had great interests in the central town had no influence whatsoever on that town's administration. They did have influence on the government of their residential municipality, but that formed but a small part of the agglomeration to which they belonged. Thus there was an asymmetry between interests and influence in the central town. On the other hand, the inhabitants of the central town have interests in the suburbs, where they spend their leisure time, practice their sports and often go shopping in the supermarkets; in the future they will progressively work there as workplaces move to the ring around the central town. They, too, have interests in municipalities where they have no vote.

These problems will spread as the developments we have been speaking of continue. It is a logical consequence of greater personal mobility and of economic activities becoming more and more footloose. How much personal mobility has increased is revealed by some figures referring to the Netherlands: while in 1936 all personal moves were made within a range of 5–6 km, now the radius is 30 km. That means that humans, who fifty years ago moved within an area of 100 km^2, now need an area of some 3,000 km^2 for their activities, that is 30 times as much as before.

The extremely fast growth of physical interaction has coincided with a considerable increase in interaction by telephone. In comparison to the year 1936, the number of telephone calls has increased a hundredfold. Even the number of letters has increased by some 400 per cent in the same period. This increased interaction on all fronts reflects the increased intensity of all sorts of relationships which, in turn, implies a closer interweaving of mutual interests. Logically anybody participating in that interaction, and by so doing acquiring interests in contiguous or even more distant municipalities, more or less voluntarily waives part of his democratic rights with respect to municipal affairs. This disadvantage could, to some extent, be compensated for by introducing a larger scale of administration, for instance, by passing certain tasks of the municipalities of an agglomeration to higher bodies of administration. Regrettably but understandably, there is not much enthusiasm for such changes. Nevertheless, certain financial rearrangements are indispensable. If the distribution of services no longer matches that of the population, the financial structure of agglomerations must be adjusted.

Logical as all this may seem, we cannot hope for a fast and smooth progress of necessary administrative and financial adjustments to societal changes. They will have to be made some time, however. Until that moment the situation will tend towards consolidation. The socialist policies pursued by central municipalities will make those with different views even more inclined to leave central towns for the more conservative ring, while the suburban municipalities will be more and more conservatively inclined. While a subtle policy for the whole agglomeration would be preferable by far, the possibility cannot be excluded that polarisation will proceed until the central town's pauperisation has reached a point where even the most fervently socialist municipal board will undertake revitalisation, even if that implies gentrification.

Revitalisation

The question arises whether present agglomeration problems could not be solved with more success by other approaches than the very long-term solution of administrative reforms. The present practice is that all the actors involved, such as municipalities (sometimes quite a lot of them), all manner of business companies and financial institutions, follow their own independent course of action, a practice which by no means makes for satisfactory urban development. However, the individual actors are responsible only for the woe-and-weal of their own municipality or their own business. They may have made (without committing themselves!) the occasional gesture towards the common welfare, but cannot be said to have had the interests of the urban community as much at heart as their own. Municipal boards care most for their own inhabitants, without consideration for the interests of people living in other parts of the agglomeration. They have invariably tried to stimulate activity within their own territory and to attract new industries, even if these could have found better locations elsewhere in the agglomeration. Central towns, in particular, have a regrettable tendency to try to claim everything for their own, blind to any sensible wider view. Companies have shown the same lack of vision, letting the company's profit decide their strategy, irrespective of the town's interests.

Naturally that way of approaching problems of agglomeration has not led to optimum results. We have already pointed to the destructive forces that are threatening the agglomerations; we should note that they spring largely from the urban actors' lack of co-operation.

Nevertheless, changes seem imminent. More and more people have begun to understand that by operating jointly, or at least keeping their eyes open to the interests of the whole town, they will in the long run serve both the general welfare and their own interests better. The joint action of actors creates synergetic effects which benefit both the whole group and each of the partners within it to a high degree.

We suggested above that to fuse all municipalities together into one metropolitan municipality was a possible solution to urban problems. The spirit of the present proposal is the same but its form, and therefore its range and political feasibility, are different. The present proposal is to try for voluntary co-ordinated action by *all* actors (notably the political ones) by convincing them that such co-ordination is necessary to achieve a better, more attractive town, in which all actors obtain a better position than by isolated efforts.

While undeniably resting on an idealistic basis, this proposal is, at the same time, realistic. Several towns in the world have already demonstrated that the ideas presented here can, at least in part, be carried out in practice. Examples are the joint efforts of government and enterprise to revitalise the water front of Baltimore, the old industrial sites of Pittsburgh, the inner city of Boston, and Docklands in London. In the town of Rotterdam, too, the municipality and trade and industry have all been inspired to undertake and carry out various similar types of project.

Such developments prove that impressive results can be accomplished by co-ordination and co-operation of the central municipality and business enterprise. Why, then, would it be impossible to achieve co-operation among all municipalities in the agglomeration or, even better, between all these municipalities, business enterprise and financing institutions? True, this would imply a considerable extension of the so-called public–private partnership idea, which ordinarily involves only one single municipality, but the principle remains the same, namely a joint attack on the town's problems for the eventual benefit of all participants. The approach has been tried and proved fertile in several instances, and thus one hopes there is reason to expect that present political inflexibilities will gradually become a thing of the past. Once a town has been reanimated in this way, the stage of re-urbanisation has definitely commenced and a period of revitalisation lies before us, in which the town, Europe's cultural asset *par excellence*, can once more assume its rightful position.

References

Beesley, M.E. (1972), 'Economic alternatives in urban transport' in *The Quality of Life, IG Metall. Meeting Papers*, Oberhausen, West Germany.

van den Berg, L., Drewett, R., Klaassen, L.H., Rossi, A. and Vijverberg, C.H.T. (1982), *Urban Europe: A Study of Growth and Decline*, Oxford: Pergamon.

Busch, H. (1972), 'Technical alternatives in traffic' in *The Quality of Life, IG Metall. Meeting Papers*, Oberhausen, West Germany.

The Economist (1972), 'Shopping goes out of town', 15–21 April.

Hall, P. and Hay, D. (1980), *Growth Centers in the European Urban System*, Berkeley, Calif.: University of California Press.

Klaassen, L.H. (1972), 'The quality of traffic' in *The Quality of Life, IG Metall. Meeting Papers*, Oberhausen, West Germany.

Klaassen, L.H. and van der Meer, J. (1986), *The Changing Function of Public Transport in a Changing Agglomeration*, Netherlands Economic Institute, Rotterdam.

Klaassen, L.H. and Molle, W.T.M. (eds) (1983), *Industrial Mobility and Migration in the European Community*, Aldershot: Gower.

Klaassen, L.H., Molle, W.T.M. and Paelinck, J.H.P. (eds) (1981), *Dynamics of Urban Development*, Aldershot: Gower.

Klaassen, L.H. and Wagenaar, S. (1971), 'Measuring the psychological distance between the Flemish and the Walloons', paper presented at Meeting of Regional Science Association, Rome, August.

Klaassen, L.H. and Wagenaar, S. (1972), 'Towards an operational definition of psychological distance', *NEI Research Papers*, no. 3.

Lowry, I.S. (1964), *A Model of Metropolis*, no. RM4125, Land Corporation, Santa Monica, Calif., USA.

NRC-Handelsblad (1972), 'Manhattan rukt op in Parijs', Amsterdam/Rotterdam, 1 April.

Parr, J.B. (1979), 'Regional economic change and regional spatial structure: some interrelationships', *Environmental Planning A*, vol. 11, pp. 825–37.

van der Vlist, J.A. (1986), 'Politieke consequenties von suburbanisatie', discussion paper, Netherlands Economic Institute, Rotterdam.

4 Transportation

4.1 Urban change and transport*

Introduction

This section sets out to sketch the long-term influence of recent urban developments on the performance of public transport in the larger towns. The underlying assumption is that this performance is largely determined by the characteristics of ridership during peak hours, in other words, by the spatial structure of home-to-work travel. Naturally that structure depends on the location of homes and workplaces and on the pattern according to which the available jobs are distributed among people living at various residences. So the first important thing is to try to find out how such spatial patterns have developed in the recent past and will presumably develop in the not-so-near future.

From the changes of the past decades in the spatial structure of urban agglomerations has sprung the de-concentration of the functions of living and working which so strongly marks the phase of suburbanisation following upon the urbanisation phase of metropolitan growth. The phenomenon is common to urban change in many large and medium-sized urban regions in the Western world,

*See L.H. Klaassen and J. van der Meer, 'Urban change and public transport', *International Journal of Transport Economics*, Rome, 1987.

and is closely associated with national and regional economic development. The background is commented on in the first subsection, which focuses on the development of spatial-economic structures, and the following subsection highlights how the present developments affect public transport in urban areas, touching briefly on the effects of the growing popularity of part-time work.

Spatial population and business dynamics

The increasing prosperity which in the 1960s and early 1970s prevailed in a large part of Western Europe has greatly influenced the spatial structure of urban regions and thus the performance of the system of public transport. General car ownership enormously widened the possibilities of individual travel, and enabled many people to settle at some distance from their workplace, thus satisfying their desire for a more attractive house in pleasant surroundings. Large towns offered them little scope. Here the emphasis was still on large-scale efforts to beat the quantitative scarcity of housing, while at the same time increasing congestion necessitated a check on growth. Moreover, they were fast losing countenance as to living and housing conditions. Metropolitan ring areas, on the other hand, either responded to the demand for more attractive residential locations by pursuing an active municipal housing policy, or profited from the central government's growth-core or 'New Town' policy intended to accommodate the overspill population from the central towns.

Those circumstances, which are common to urbanisation processes in a large part of the Western world, led to extensive selective migration from the large towns towards 'greener' suburbs. Table 4.1 presents these migratory movements for a number of West European cities for which data are available. The first column gives the relative change of the population of the central city of the metropolitan area; the second column shows the same figure for the surrounding municipalities belonging to the metropolitan area; and the third column shows relative change of the population of the metropolitan area as a whole. Apparently the population decreases in all central cities. In some cases (British metropolitan areas), people are even leaving the metropolitan ring.

In general, the house moves had no direct influence on the workplace; at the first stage of suburbanisation, most work locations remained in the large central towns.

The entailing unbalanced distribution of home and work locations drastically affected the traffic pattern of the metropolitan areas during peak hours. The results were devastating, with huge, unbalanced

Table 4.1 Population changes in some West European metropolitan areas (percentage per annum)

	City	Rest	Metropolitan areas	Period
Antwerp	-0.8	+1.2	0.0	(1970-81)
Birmingham	-0.8	-0.3	-0.5	(1971-81)
Copenhagen	-1.5	+1.0	-0.1	(1970-85)
Hamburg	-0.8	+1.9	+0.1	(1970-81)
Liverpool	-1.6	-0.4	-0.9	(1971-80)
Marseilles	-0.1	+4.5	+0.5	(1971-81)
Milan	-0.6	+1.3	+0.2	(1971-82)
Paris	-1.1	+1.0	+0.4	(1968-82)
Rotterdam	-1.6	+2.2	-0.2	(1970-80)

Sources: Various.

commuter flows during morning and evening peaks, involving public as well as private transport.

The increasing interaction between the central cities and the suburban towns led more and more to so-called functional units, that is units whose complementary parts are increasingly dependent on one another. Municipal borders were more and more losing their function; very often they became hindrances to the efficient control of developments with respect to the labour market, the traffic system, etc. A change could also be observed in the spatial distribution of living densities, which decreased in the central towns while increasing in the suburbs; however, a wide discrepancy persisted. Research in various West European countries has proved that demographic suburbanisation tends to be followed in due time by the suburbanisation of business companies; this is illustrated in Table 4.2; the data

Table 4.2 Annual percentage change in the number of people employed in some West European metropolitan areas

	City	Rest	Metropolitan areas	Period
Copenhagen	-0.3	+3.2	+1.3	(1970-83)
Antwerp	-0.7	+0.4	-0.5	(1974-84)
Liverpool	-2.6	-3.1	-2.9	(1978-84)
Milan	-0.9	+1.9	+0.7	(1971-81)
Rotterdam	-1.1	+1.5	+0.6	(1975-84)
Hamburg	-0.8	+1.9	-0.3	(1961-83)
Rhine-Ruhr	-0.8	-0.2	-0.6	(1961-83)
Bremen	-0.7	+0.5	-0.2	(1961-83)
Hannover	-0.7	+1.1	-0.3	(1961-83)
Stuttgart	-0.5	+1.2	+0.6	(1961-83)

Sources: Various.

available do not refer to exactly the same series of cities as mentioned in Table 4.1, but the tendency is clear.

The figures in the table indicate a rather strong growth of the number of workplaces in the ring and a decline in the central cities, largely due to outward migration from the city. That development is the mirror image of urbanisation, the stage at which people tend to follow trade.

The underlying factors of business migration are of a varied nature. The most important is somewhat similar to the factor governing residential migration, namely the need for a quantitatively and qualitatively more suitable accommodation, in terms of expansion prospects, parking, a favourable situation with respect to traffic and last but not least status. Such conditions can hardly be fulfilled in the older town quarters and at superannuated locations.

A second factor is that company executives, having moved to places of residence more to their liking than the old cities, often know about alternative locations in areas surrounding the larger towns. Moreover, for certain categories of companies a large portion of the sales market has moved from the central town to the suburbs.

Finally, now that the urbanised area is functioning more and more as an integrated whole, the specific location advantages that used to be the prerogative of large towns are now available in a far larger area. That has greatly increased the relevant area of locational choice. The fact that companies in the principal growth sectors become more and more 'footloose' strengthens the de-concentrating tendency.

Urban dynamics and public transport

The previous sections have made it clear that demographic suburbanisation is increasingly followed by the suburbanisation of employment. At the urbanising stage, employment as well as population were concentrated in the central town. During the first part of the suburbanisation stage houses and workplaces came to be separated, workplaces staying in the city, while people began to move to housing in the ring around it. To public transport, the changing spatial structure spelled three handicaps of a business-economic nature.

The first is the outsize demand for the services of public transport during the few hours of the morning peak. The large capacity needed for that short period is inefficiently used during the rest of the day. The second is that all traffic in the morning peak moves in one direction, from the suburbs to the centre; the picture is mirrored in the evening peak. So too, in terms of direction, the capacity is used inefficiently.

The third, which results from the inefficient use of material of which the total capacity costs are very nearly inflexible, is the high capacity cost by traveller-kilometres. Indeed total capacity costs are made up of capital costs and labour costs; the former are higher for a rail system than for buses because of the additional infrastructural investments needed; the latter have been inflexible up till now because the number of staff also had to match peak-hour requirements.

At the second stage of suburbanisation, now in progress, companies are leaving the central town as well, to relocate in mostly the same suburban municipalities as the population did earlier. What are the implications for public transport?

To answer that question a somewhat closer study of the factors determining the financial results of public transport in urban areas is in order. We will assume public transport tariffs to be proportional with the distance travelled and constant by unit of distance; actually, the argument remains valid for a linear tariff with a fixed base. If the average distance travelled is denoted by $\bar{d}$, the number of trips by r and the total returns by R, then, at a tariff p:

$$R = pr\bar{d} \qquad (4.1)$$

A further assumption is that the capacity of the public transport network is adjusted to the demand for transport services. In practice, that means that the capacity is adjusted to correspond with the maximum demand occurring at a given hour of the day. If that demand is V_1^{MAX} in direction 1, the daily capacity of the corresponding part of the network equals:

$$C = 2TV_1^{MAX} \qquad (4.2)$$

in which V_1^{MAX} is the traffic at the busiest hour of the day and T the number of (relevant) hours a day. The factor 2 has been introduced because the capacity must also be available in the opposite direction.

If the maximum total traffic expected during the peak hour in both senses is V^{MAX}, the ratio between V^{MAX} and $2V_1^{MAX}$ can be taken as the first factor determining the returns from the transport system, $2V_1^{MAX}$ being the traffic which the network could deal with and V^{MAX} the actual maximum traffic under peak conditions. As the spatial distribution of demand becomes less favourable, V_1^{MAX} will become larger in relation to V^{MAX} and hence the ratio smaller:

$$\sigma = \frac{V_1^{MAX}}{2V_1^{MAX}} \qquad 0.5 \leqslant \tau \leqslant 1 \qquad (4.3)$$

where σ is the coefficient of spatial distribution.

An example may be illustrative for a given link, on which a quantity of traffic equal to 1,000 has to be dispatched; its capacity has to be 2,000. If the total maximum traffic in both directions occurring on this link is 1,200 (V^{MAX}), the coefficient of spatial distribution is:

$$\sigma = \frac{1{,}200}{2{,}000} = 0.6$$

Apparently the lowest value that σ can adopt is 0.5; it would occur when all workplaces are concentrated in the town centre and all houses in the suburbs, so that then all peak-hour traffic goes one way. The maximum value is 1.0, a figure reached when workplaces and housing would be spatially arranged to entail balanced commuting backwards and forwards, the two sides of the road being used at equal intensity during the peak hour.

Another factor with great impact on the returns from public transport is the way demand for transport is spread through time. Let us call $\bar{V}$ the average demand for traffic during relevant hours; the ratio between that variable and V^{MAX} can then be denoted as the coefficient of temporal distribution:

$$\tau = \frac{\bar{V}}{V^{MAX}} \quad 0 \leqslant \tau \leqslant 1 \tag{4.4}$$

Obviously the value of τ lies between 0 and 1. Value 1 is reached when the traffic is quite evenly distributed over the day, showing no peaks.

An efficiency coefficient is now simple to derive from the two partial coefficients; indeed:

$$T\bar{V} = \bar{r}d \tag{4.5}$$

i.e. average hourly traffic in terms of passenger-kilometres multiplied by the number of relevant hours equals the number of trips multiplied by average distance.

Furthermore, we may write:

$$C = 2TV_1^{MAX} = \frac{TV^{MAX}}{\sigma} = \frac{T\bar{V}}{\sigma\tau} \tag{4.6}$$

Substituting expression (4.5) for (4.6) we find:

$$C = \frac{r\bar{d}}{\sigma\tau} \tag{4.7}$$

or

$$\frac{r\bar{d}}{C} = \sigma\tau \tag{4.7a}$$

This very simple outcome means simply that the product of the spatial and temporal distribution coefficients yields the degree of utilisation of public transport. If both coefficients are equal to unity, the degree of utilisation is 100 per cent; so we may write:

$$\epsilon = \sigma\tau \qquad 0 \leqslant \epsilon \leqslant 1 \tag{4.8}$$

in which ϵ represents the efficiency of the system.

The foregoing does not yet give us sufficient information to formulate the cost function of public transport. Evidently the technical equipment consisting of infrastructure and vehicles entails fixed costs, whatever their degree of utilisation. Whether the same is true of manpower is questionable. On the safe assumption that staff costs are neither completely flexible nor completely rigid, we introduce a coefficient ϕ. Complete flexibility would mean that manpower can be fully adjusted to the daily fluctuations in the demand for traffic; in that case, ϕ is equal to unity. In the case of complete rigidity $\phi = 0$, all manpower is in permanent employ, the volume being tuned to the demand during peak hours.

We can now draw up the following cost function:

$$K = k_0 C + k_1 \left\{(1 - \phi) 2 V_1^{MAX} + \phi \bar{V}\right\} T \tag{4.9}$$

where: k_0 = capital costs by unit of capacity;
k_1 = labour costs by unit of traffic;
ϕ = flexibility coefficient.

Substituting expression (4.6) for (4.9), we find:

$$K = \left\{\frac{k_0}{\epsilon} + \frac{k_1}{\epsilon}(1 - \phi) + \phi k_1\right\} r\bar{d} \tag{4.10}$$

Substituting expression (4.1) for (4.10) and dividing by $r\bar{d}$, we find for the return by passenger kilometre:

$$\rho = \frac{W}{r\bar{d}} = \frac{R - K}{r\bar{d}} = \mathrm{p} - \frac{k_0}{\epsilon}(1 - \phi) - \phi k_1 \tag{4.11}$$

or

$$\rho = p - \frac{k_0}{\sigma\tau} - \frac{k_1}{\sigma\tau}(1 - \phi) - \phi k_1 \quad (4.12)$$

Note that if $\epsilon = \sigma\tau = 1$, flexibility no longer counts because it is not needed; and in that case:

$$\rho = p - k_0 - k_1 (1 - \phi) - \phi k_1 = p - k_0 - k_1$$

in which ϕ does not occur.

Parallel with spatial urban development another evolution is in progress in society, in general, and in the towns in particular, an evolution of great import to public transport: the tendency towards part-time jobs. There is reason to devote some words to that phenomenon before going into the more specific spatial urban developments. Part-time work is very popular among townswomen; more and more men, too, are preferring part-time to full-time work. As that tendency progresses its effects on public transport will be of two kinds. On the one hand, adjusting the staff to daily fluctuations in the demand for the services of public transport will be easier, so that coefficient ϕ will reach higher values. On the other hand, part-time work tops off the peaks because some people start not in the early morning, but later in the day. Peak-hour traffic in both senses will diminish, approaching the average, and the temporal distribution will improve. The two tendencies may well have a positive effect on the returns from public transport, reinforcing its position.

On the whole, part-time working, by spreading passenger transport over the day and thus ensuring a better utilisation in off-peak hours, besides diminishing the cost of labour, does much to overcome the first handicap. The question remains whether the second handicap, the one-way character of peak-hour traffic, will also be shortened. At any rate, it will become less of a trouble as both residences and employment are progressively located in the ring around the central town and most commuting will take place among suburban municipalities. Peak-hour travel to and from the centre will decline and be replaced, in part, with peak-hour travel in the ring. The interesting fact is that such peak-hour travel will be two-way as long as housing and employment suburbanise to dispersed secondary centres which, as we have seen, they indeed tend to do.

Apparently all factors make for better exploitation prospects for public transport in the future metropolitan area. Peak-hour traffic diminishes, two-way traffic relatively increases and the flexibility of the manpower reserve grows. However, two comments must be made on that rosy picture.

The first is that one major motive for the decentralisation of job opportunities is the lack of space in the centre. That motive does not apply to the rest of the metropolitan area, where establishments tend to be laid out far more spaciously right from the start, with a view to future expansion and certainly also with a view to creating parking space. Home-to-work traffic in the ring, including parking, will be smoother than before when it was oriented to the centre. Probably therefore the modal split will change in favour of the car.

The second comment refers to the response of public transport to the developments we have sketched. As far as buses are concerned there are few problems; needing relatively little specific infrastructure, they can flexibly adjust to the new situation. One or more ring lines can easily connect up with the traditional radial lines to the city centre which, though no longer all-important, will be far from superfluous. A major portion of home-to-work travel will go on as before, and the centre will continue to function as the principal shopping and amusement centre of the whole area.

Things are different for the metropolitan railway. A ring-shaped addition to the metro network for the sake of traffic in the ring will call for a very high investment of capital, and the question is whether its benefits would reasonably justify the costs. To move with caution on that score and to study the prospects of bus lines, first, seems a wise course of action. Another suggestion is to combine existing metro and train connections, extending the latter's contribution to public transport in the urban region for instance by opening more stations in suburban municipalities. The combined network might serve the same purpose as a metropolitan ring railway, if not in the most efficient way possible, at any rate without undue capital investments.

The interesting conclusion from the above is that in the future at least some factors will favour public transport. The question remains unanswered whether the urban developments warranting that conclusion must, on the whole, be considered desirable. A point of view repeatedly voiced is that the move of job opportunities is to be regretted because it implies loss of employment in the central municipality. To our mind, however, that point of view displays a regrettably narrow vision of the function of a central municipality, which is to provide the entire metropolitan area with high-grade services and goods. The central municipality fulfils a shopping function, a cultural function, an amusement function and a social function. Incompatible with those functions are activities which bring a large number of workers but relatively few visitors to the town. Such activities can much better be established elsewhere in the agglomeration, at places within easy reach of both workers and visitors. The town centre ought to be reserved for activities on a high level with many visitors for each worker and relatively little claim on space. The fewer activities of the former kind and the more of the latter, the more accessible the centre remains and the better it can go on fulfilling its central function.

Apparently, then, the spatial structure proposed here, of a high-grade service centre and secondary cores spread along the ring, calls for an infrastructure for public transport which (naturally) looks very much like that which already exists for car traffic in many European and American urban areas, namely a ring road, which apart from its important interregional function serves to guide local traffic towards the centre by branching roads and to cores at the outside of the ring.

Keeping all that in mind, one readily comes to the conclusion that profound study of the long-term function of public transport in the larger metropolitan areas is highly commendable and could even bring forth new insights into the way public transport should be structurally adjusted to the spatial dynamics of large metropolitan areas. The fact will then become apparent that public transport cannot and must not be considered exclusively from the point of view of the central municipality, for indeed its main function has been and will be to promote interaction among all components of a metropolitan area, whatever their municipal division.

4.2 Optimum use of transport networks*

Introduction

When discussing the optimum use of transport networks, one is inclined to focus on the question how *given* transport networks (for public as well as private transport) could be used in an optimum way. Almost naturally, one then thinks of such solutions as goods transportation during the night and passenger transport in the daytime, charter flights from airports during the very early and late hours of the day, and regular flights during normal hours, park-and-ride systems, etc. In these cases one considers the networks as given and tries to distribute the traffic that has to be accommodated in such a way over the existing network(s) that some sort of an optimum is reached.

Another more general approach could be, however, to start from

*See L.H. Klaassen, Report for the European Conference of Ministers of Transport (ECMT), Paris 1977; and J.B. Polak and J.B. van der Kamp (eds), *Changes in the Field of Transport Studies*, The Hague/Boston/London: Martinus Nijhoff, 1980.

a given spatial structure of a country, i.e. a given distribution of activities and population across space, and to design on the basis of the traffic supposed to result from that spatial structure a network or networks that serve this traffic in an optimum way.* Although the latter kind of approach has not dealt satisfactorily either with the existence of several sorts of network, or with the multiple use of one and the same network (like the use of roads by buses and private cars), it does provide us with a great deal of insight into the needs for extending particularly the road network in order to assure that the spatial structures foreseen as needed for the future will coincide with actual future structures.

It is, in particular, the last-mentioned point that is important, first and foremost in urban areas. If the networks designed influence the location of people and business activities, it may not be possible to solve the transportation problem in the sequential way indicated above, i.e. by designing, first, a spatial structure, and proposing then a network that meets the demand of traffic resulting from it. Rather the problem would call for a simultaneous solution, i.e. the simultaneous designing of the spatial structure and the networks in such a way that some sort of general optimum is achieved. It should be added immediately that such an optimum should not be defined as an optimum existing at a given moment of time, but as a design that guarantees an optimum situation for an essentially infinitely long future period.

It is particularly the nature of the sought optimum that should interest us. Obviously a general optimum could never be reached with a solution that minimises total traffic flows. Traffic flows reflect the desire of people to optimise their well-being in view of the location of their desired destinations and the quality of the network that enables them to reach these destinations. A network of lower standard could force them to limit their total effective demand for travelling, but thus their well-being would certainly not increase as a result. Travel time is one of the sacrifices that have to be made in order to reach a certain degree of well-being. Less travel time could as such be considered a benefit, but would have to be weighed against the disadvantage of reaching fewer destinations or reaching destinations less frequently.

A simple example may elucidate the point. Suppose a household is living and working in a city without a rapid transit system. The difficulties involved in travelling to and from the workplace have made the household decide to reside in the city itself, although they

*A good example of such an approach is the study by Dr P.A. Steenbrink, *Optimization of Transport Networks*, New York: Wiley, 1974.

would have preferred residence in the green outside the city. If a new public transport facility is introduced which enables the family to combine working in the city with living in more pleasant surroundings at some distance from the city, they might decide to do so moving from the city to a neighbouring community served by the new transport facility. The improvement of the transport facilities would have induced them to travel longer distances and thus increase their individual well-being. The costs of more travelling would, in this case, have been considered less important than the benefits of improved living conditions.

Whether or not the same holds for society as a whole is a matter that will be discussed later. For the moment, suffice it to state that an individual household's well-being depends on the attraction of the different destinations as well as on the travel costs or travel sacrifices. The household determines its location by maximising the difference between the two in such a way that marginal benefits caused by a shift in location equal marginal travel costs from such a shift. In order to analyse the problem more properly, it seems useful to consider the nature of the costs and benefits involved in some more detail.

Travel costs

Travel costs are defined as the costs that have to be made to bridge a certain distance. Costs, in this sense, are to be interpreted as sacrifices to be made. These sacrifices consist of money costs, time and risks involved. Other elements, such as resistance due to the 'strangeness' of the destination, and the psychological distance to be bridged, could also be mentioned here, but will be left out of our consideration. It follows that generalised transportation costs can be defined as the weighted sum of the three elements first mentioned, or:

$$D_{ij} = a_1 C_{ij} + a_2 T_{ij} + a_3 R_{ij} \qquad (4.13)$$

where D_{ij} = total generalised transportation costs between i and j;
C_{ij} = total money costs (or perceived money costs);
T_{ij} = total time costs;
R_{ij} = total risks (or perceived risks);
a = weights of different cost elements.

Obviously costs, time and risk can also be expressed per unit of physical distance (f_{ij}). Expression (4.13) then becomes:

$$D_{ij} = a_1 c_{ij} f_{ij} + a_2 t_{ij} f_{ij} + a_3 r_{ij} f_{ij} \qquad (4.14)$$

Since $t_{ij} = \frac{f_{ij}}{v_{ij}}$ in which v_{ij} is the average speed, we may write:

$$D_{ij} = (a_1 c_{ij} + a_2 \frac{f_{ij}}{v_{ij}} + a_3 r_{ij}) f_{ij} \qquad (4.15)$$

The expression between brackets represents the generalised transportation costs per unit of distance between *i* and *j*.

A few remarks concerning the coefficients in equation (4.15) seem in order. In many transportation studies it is tried to choose one specific dimension in which to express the generalised transportation costs; often the monetary unit is chosen. In that case, obviously $a_1 = 1$, a_2 reflecting the money value of one unit of time. According to economic theory, the marginal value of one unit of time equals the value of net earnings per unit of time minus the disutility of labour experienced during a marginal time unit; a_3 expresses the sum of money that could be looked upon as the trade-off of one unit of risk, this expressed as the probability of an unfortunate event taking place per unit of time.

An internationally more comparable unit would be the time unit. In this case $a_2 = 1$, a_1 expressing the number of time units per unit of money, and a_3 the trade-off between one unit of risk and the number of money units.

Whatever unit is chosen, D_{ij} expresses the total generalised transportation costs to be made if one individual decides to undertake the trip from *i* to *j*.

It should be mentioned here that all the coefficients in the equation are certainly not equal for all individuals. If the monetary unit is chosen as the basic unit, a_2 represents the translation of time costs into money costs; and the value of one unit of time having been defined as the earnings per time unit corrected for the disutility of labour per time unit, it seems reasonable to assume that this value is an increasing function of income. A similar reasoning holds for a_3: if the risk of an accident is defined as the sum of the human suffering, the money costs of the accident, and the earnings lost, a_3 becomes a function of income, too. On the other hand, a_3 might be a function of travel experience, decreasing with experience for air travel and increasing for car travel.

The foregoing leads us to the extremely important conclusion that generalised transportation costs are in fact a function of an individual's specific situation regarding his/her income (Institut d'Aménagement et d'Urbanisme de la Région Parisienne, 1966) and travel experience. It seems reasonable also that the socio-economic characteristics of the household that an individual belongs to affect the weights in the generalised costs function. Of course, even for individuals in the same situation as far as income and household characteristics are concerned, subjective evaluation of time costs and risks might differ considerably. It is assumed, however, that such random differences cancel out one another when groups of individuals are considered.

It is not a new but still valid assumption that the individual's (or household's) income level is one of the most important factors when it comes to explaining the distribution of traffic among the different transport modes. Neglecting for a moment that a traveller will consider not only overall travel time, but also the manner in which that time is spent (in waiting, changing, actual travelling, etc.), we may state that certain modes involve considerably less expenditure but also considerably more time than others. Comparing the generalised transportation costs of private car and public transport, we observe that, particularly for the smaller distances, the private car is preferred to public transport because of its low time costs and in spite of its high money costs, while for long distances public transport is often preferred (Klaassen, 1969) because it is cheap in relation to the travel time. The higher the income, the heavier the time costs will count, and the readier an individual will shift to the most time-saving transport mode. Or in terms of the above argument that the higher a person's income, the higher the value he/she attaches to time, and consequently the longer the distance for which they will be inclined to use a car, and the shorter the distance for which they will prefer to take an airplane. The train as the intermediate mode will, for as long as conventional speeds are maintained, lose at both ends as income rises.

Travel benefits: accessibility

In the former section we treated the concept of generalised transportation costs, defined as the sacrifices in money, time and risk the individual has to make in order to reach a certain destination. Now it is time to turn to the benefit side of travelling on which it depends how heavily the individual will count the travel costs.

Let us consider a specific case. An individual living in a region i considers visiting a recreation area of given quality and size in region j. In order to do so, the individual will have to bridge the physical distance f_{ij} and sacrifice generalised transportation costs to the amount D_{ij}. Furthermore, he/she will have to pay an entrance fee of

P_{ij}, so that total costs will amount to $D_{ij} + P_{ij}$. In this case, it is of course assumed that D_{ij} is expressed in monetary units. The attraction exerted by the recreation area is now determined by two factors: on the one hand the benefits derived from the visit, and on the other hand the costs of the trip, or, more exactly, the perception of the benefits and the perception of the costs of the trip.

Starting with the latter, it seems reasonable to assume that the perception of the costs is an increasing function of the costs themselves, so that:

$$p^c_{ij} = \psi_c (D_{ij} + P_{ij}) \tag{4.16}$$

where p^c_{ij} = perception of costs.

$$\frac{d\,\psi_c}{d(D_{ij} + P_{ij})} > 0 \qquad \frac{d^2\,\psi_c}{d(D_{ij} + P_{ij})^2} > 0$$

The last expression indicates that marginal costs are assumed to be increasing with 'distance' and entrance fee.

The benefits depend on the 'quality' and size of the recreation area x_j:

$$p^b = \psi_b (x_j) \tag{4.17}$$

where $x_j = q_j s_j$;
q_j = quality index of the recreation area;
s_j = size of the recreation area

and:

$$\frac{d\psi_b}{dx_j} > 0, \qquad \frac{d^2\psi_b}{dx_j^2} < 0$$

These expressions indicate that it is assumed that benefits are an increasing function of the size and quality of the recreation area, but that marginal benefits are a decreasing function of these two variables.

It seems logical to define the attractiveness of the recreation area as the ratio between perceived benefits and perceived costs; in other words, to define:

$$\Pi_{ij} = \frac{\psi_b (x_j)}{\psi_c (D_{ij} + P_{ij})} \tag{4.18}$$

A specific example of expression (4.18) could be $\psi_b\ (x_j) = x_j^\beta$ in which $0 < \beta < 1$ and $\psi_c\ (D_{ij} + P_{ij}) = \exp(-a[D_{ij} + P_{ij}]$, so that expression (4.18) can be written as:

$$\Pi_{ij} = x_j^\beta \exp(-a[D_{ij} + P_{ij}]) \tag{4.19}$$

Equation (4.19) has a number of important features which need further attention. The coefficient a represents the friction a consumer experiences in making the sacrifices $D_{ij} + P_{ij}$ for visiting the recreation area, or rather *a* recreation area. It is therefore *activity-specific*. The element $\exp(-a[D_{ij} + P_{ij}])$ may be said to represent the *accessibility* of the recreation area in j for an individual living in i.

If we consider not only the recreation area in j, but all recreation areas, we obtain a variable describing simultaneously the accessibility and the size and quality of all recreation areas seen from the region i. We then arrive at defining of the *recreation potential* for i.

Obviously:

$$\Pi_i = \sum_j \Pi_{ij} = \sum_j x_j^\beta \exp(-a[D_{ij} + P_{ij}]) \tag{4.20}$$

where Π_i is the recreation potential for i.

The next step is to assume that the number of trips originating from i to a recreation area anywhere is a function of this potential and of the income level of the individual (household). To that end, we write:

$$n_i = \gamma_0 \Pi_i^{\gamma_i} y^{\gamma_2} p_i \tag{4.21}$$

where n_i is the number of trips to recreation areas, y the average income and p_i the size of the population in i. From equation (4.21) it follows easily that it is reasonable to assume:

$$n_{ij} = \frac{\Pi_{ij}}{\Pi_i} n_i \tag{4.22}$$

This equation together with expression (4.21) determines the number of trips to each recreation area.

It should be mentioned here that the potential as defined is not uniquely determined. Usually there are different ways to make a trip from one place to another; consequently there are as many potentials as there are ways to make the trip. With two possibilities, e.g. by public and by private transport, there are two potentials. In that case, it can reasonably be assumed that the fraction of total trips made by public transport equals:

$$\psi_{ij}^{PV} = \frac{\Pi_i^{PV}}{\Pi_i^{PV} + \Pi_j^{PV}} \tag{4.23}$$

and the fraction performed by private transportation means:

$$\psi_{ij}^{PR} = \frac{\Pi_i^{PR}}{\Pi_i^{PV} + \Pi_i^{PR}} \tag{4.24}$$

If both potentials are equal, 50 per cent of the trips will be made by public and 50 per cent by private means of transportation. A similar reasoning as developed above for recreation can of course be made for shopping, job opportunities and environmental qualities. For each of these a potential can be defined from which, in the way indicated in the paragraphs above, trip creation can be derived.

A spatial welfare function

The theory so far presented can be extended by assuming that from a total set of potentials that could be derived, three main potentials can be determined:

(a) a potential describing the living conditions (Π^L);
(b) a potential describing working conditions (Π^W);
(c) a potential describing the availability of amenities (including recreation areas) (Π^A).

A social (spatial) welfare function could be defined then as:*

$$\omega_i = \omega_i\,(\Pi_i^L, \Pi_i^W, \Pi_i^A) \tag{4.25}$$

or, more specifically, as:

$$\omega_i = (\Pi_i^L)^{\delta_1}\,(\Pi_i^W)^{\delta_2}\,(\Pi_i^A)^{\delta_3} \tag{4.26}$$

It is important to note that the δs in this function will be mostly

*Cf. L. van den Berg, L.H. Klaassen and C.H.T. Vijverberg, 'Evaluation of governmental welfare policy by means of a social welfare function', FEER, Netherlands Economic Institute, Rotterdam, 1975/7.

household-specific. If there are children in the household, the availability of schools will play an important role. If the household consists of a pensioned husband and a housewife, job availabilities become unimportant and δ_2 will become zero, etc.

Since expression (4.26) describes the satisfaction that a given individual household derives from its location in i, the same function could be used to explain the movement of households from one region to another. This could be done in the following way. The absolute attraction the welfare of region j exerts on an individual living in i could be defined as:

$$a_{ij} = \omega_j \exp(-\epsilon f_{ij}) \tag{4.27}$$

Consequently the attraction of the welfare levels of all regions on a household in j could be defined as:

$$a_i = \sum_j \omega_j \exp(-\epsilon f_{ij}) \tag{4.28}$$

so that the relative attractiveness of j can be written as:

$$\frac{a_{ij}}{a_i} = \frac{\omega_j \exp(-\epsilon f_{ij})}{\sum_j \omega_j \exp(-\epsilon f_{ij})} \tag{4.29}$$

The factor f_{ij} is introduced into these equations in order to express that the 'strangeness' of a region, the lack of familiarity with conditions prevailing in that region, creates a resistance which assumedly will increase with physical distance f_{ij}; ϵ expresses the intensity with which this factor works.

Now assuming that migration between regions takes place according to the relative attractiveness of regions, we may write:

$$\frac{m_{ij}}{m_i} = \frac{a_{ij}}{a_i} \tag{4.30}$$

in which m_{ij} is the number of individuals or households migrating from i to j, and m_i represents all migrating individuals or households including those migrating from i to j. That means that:

$$m_i = p_i \tag{4.31}$$

Accordingly, we may write:

$$m_{ij} = \frac{\omega_j \exp(-\epsilon f_{ij})}{\sum_j \omega_j \exp(-\epsilon f_{ij}) p_i} \tag{4.32}$$

This expression, together with equation (4.26) allows us to estimate the size of the δ-coefficient.

Government policies

Introduction Let us assume for a moment that the theory presented above is a reasonable one. Parts of it have been tested at the Netherlands Economic Institute and elsewhere, and the results of the testing show that one may have a fair amount of confidence in the general framework of the theory.

Of course, one could question the type of functions chosen and even fortify one's arguments with some statistical evidence. That has been done in, for example, a study about commuting in the north ring of the Rimcity in the Netherlands, in which it has been shown that there is no evidence of an influence of distance on commuter behaviour for time distances less than 30 minutes (De Langen and Verster, 1976). A reasonable explanation for that phenomenon has not yet been found, but one of the reasons could well be that people derive certain benefits from travelling over a small distance, that many people actually like to drive some distance, particularly with their car, between work hours at their job and leisure hours at home. If this were true, it would change the shape of the job-potential function, at least for the short distance. A similar reasoning could hold for recreation, where part of the benefit might also be the enjoyment of the trip itself, again of course only as far as the shorter distances are concerned.

Future studies will have to show to what extent the individual functions will have to be corrected. For the following it suffices to assume that the general framework of the theory remains upright.

It now will be assumed that the general welfare level of a country can be defined as:

$$\omega = \sum_i \omega_i p_i \tag{4.33}$$

i.e. as the sum of the individual welfare levels of households in all regions. Now it is the task of the government for a given budget year to spend the budget in such a way that the increase in welfare of the country as a whole is maximum. In so doing, of course, the government could attach more importance to a certain increase in welfare of a poorer region than to the same increase in welfare of a richer region. Such a policy could easily be taken into account if the government would be able to specify the weights involved.

It is important that to the government there are several ways open for pursuing a welfare policy. In principle, the government can influence each element of the welfare function, and accordingly there are at least five different policies:

1. amenity policy;
2. industrial location policy;
3. housing policy;
4. infrastructure policy;
5. pricing policy.

Amenity policy Amenity policy is one that influences the quality, size and location of so-called social amenities, such as schools, theatres, recreation areas, health facilities, etc. If we consider the amenity policy in isolation from the other policies, government expenditures would have to be distributed in such a way that: (a) the marginal contribution of one additional amenity to social welfare in a given region equals that of any other additional amenity in the same region; and (b) the marginal contribution of one given amenity in one region equals that of the same amenity in any other region.

These first-order conditions are in fact similar to those in consumption theory, where a consumer spends his income in such a way that the marginal utility of a given money unit spent in one direction equals that of a money unit spent in any other direction. The difference is of course that in our case the spatial element, usually absent in consumer theory, is introduced.

In many countries amenity policy is not, or at least is not exclusively, a matter for central government. Many decisions in this field are taken on the lower level of the province or the municipality. In these cases, the central government pursues its amenity policy in an indirect way, through subsidies for specific purposes, or through subsidies that municipalities are entitled to if given conditions are fulfilled (as often happens for educational purposes).

Whatever the way in which the policy is carried out, it is evident that it influences the traffic flows in the country, to say it somewhat differently, the amenity cannot and will not be made available irrespective of the consequences for the traffic flows and thus for the use that is made of the infrastructure network.

Let us consider a special case. In the Dutch Rimcity, which actually is an almost full ring of cities around a green centre, providing recreation areas in the green heart is a matter of concern to the central government. Discussions have been focused on two options. The first is the construction of large recreation areas, centrally located and connected with the cities by appropriate infrastructure. The other is the creation of smaller areas closer to the cities. The difference in effects between the options is clear. In the case of larger recreation areas, the costs per hectare may be smaller, but the infrastructure costs as well as the traffic costs will be larger. For the individual there is of course a certain trade-off. If we assume (as before) that the benefits of visiting a recreation area to the individual or to the individual household are an increasing function of the size of the recreation area, they will be prepared to make a larger sacrifice in transportation costs to reach the area, and derive from their visit the same satisfaction as from going to a smaller area at lower transportation costs. From a societal point of view, however, the situation might be different. Although the total costs of constructing the larger recreation areas plus the infrastructure equal those of smaller areas, the space required for the former solution as well as the environmental damage due to the traffic generated, may exceed considerably those of the small-scale solution. It is perhaps not so much a question of serving well the individual living in the city, as whether or not society as a whole is served well. And if that is true, the environmental potentials of the regions that lie between the cities and the recreation areas will have to be taken into account as well,* potentials that will be influenced negatively in two ways: because roads take up space, and because the traffic using the roads spoil the environment.

There are of course intermediate solutions worth considering. New, large recreation areas could be situated close to main roads already cutting through the green heart, or being constructed anyway for other purposes. It should be kept in mind, however, that roads are no longer unlimitedly constructed for 'other purposes' either – and besides, would a situation near the main road be the most desirable for recreation areas? Whatever solution finally will be chosen in this and other cases, the important fact remains that amenity policy influences the use of the infrastructure network and can be designed either to create large traffic flows or to keep such flows within certain limits.

Industrial location policy A similar reasoning as has been presented for amenity policy can be given for industrial location policy. That is particularly true as far as the location of business activities within urban areas is concerned. A simple example can make this clear.

*Included in the potential for living conditions (Π^L).

Suppose we have two centres, one of them an employment centre and the other a residential centre. Suppose 20,000 people are living in centre I and are working in centre II (Figure 4.1). Every morning there will be a flow of 20,000 people moving from I to II, and every evening the same people will move back from II to I. As far as road traffic is concerned, each car will need two parking places, one in I and the other in II. Public transport will suffer from one-sided traffic both in the morning and in the evening.

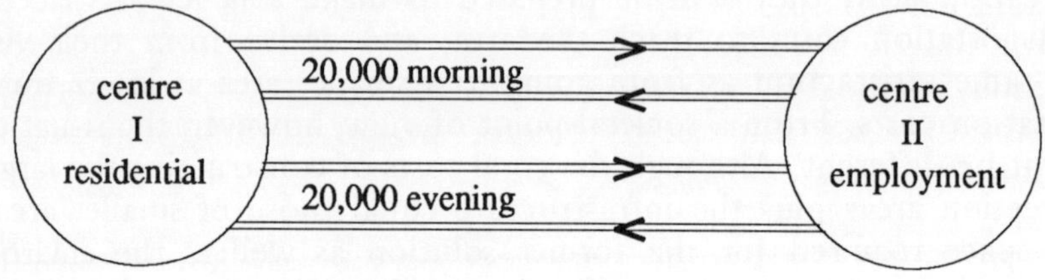

Figure 4.1 Unbalanced traffic structure

Now consider another case in which both centres are mixed employment/residential centres (Figure 4.2). Assume that each centre has a mixture of 10,000 workplaces and 10,000 active residents, 50 per cent of whom work in the other centre and the remaining 50 per cent in their living zone.

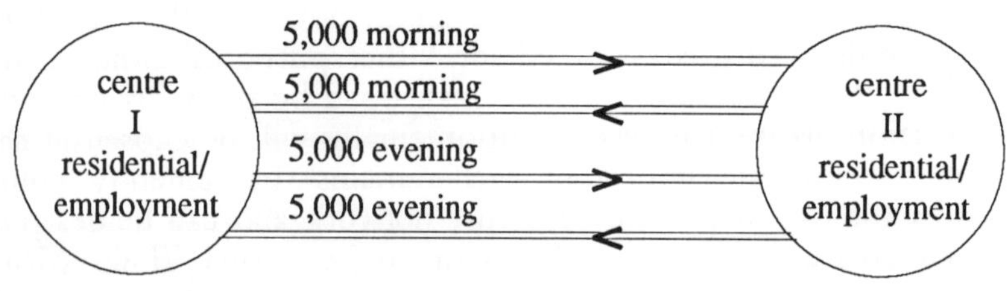

Figure 4.2 Balanced traffic structure

It appears, then, that the total traffic flow reduces to one-half of that in the first case, while the number of parking places required can also be reduced considerably (by 50 per cent at the most). The required capacity of the road infrastructure is reduced by 75 per cent.

So, by influencing the location of industry, the government is able to diminish the traffic flows, to reduce considerably the need for infrastructure and to cut the need for public transport at peak hours while achieving a much better general occupancy rate.

Of course, the example presents an extreme case. It does not do justice to the linkages between industries (inter-industrial relations) which do not permit their being distributed freely across space; it does not take sufficient account of the preferences many people have for living in purely residential areas, and so on. Still, it demonstrates that within certain limits industrial location policy might make for smaller traffic flows as well as for better use of the existing networks, both for private and for public transport.

We may conclude, then, that like amenity planning, physical planning of the kind referred to above affects the way transportation networks are used and cannot therefore be carried through in isolation from infrastructure policy.

Housing policy From the previous subsection it follows at once that the housing policy pursued by the (local) government will have considerable influence on the structure of traffic flows. In many cities the local government is promoting the development of residential areas in city centres, although the possibilities are often limited. Still, rehabilitation of the older houses, re-designating buildings for residential purposes, prohibiting the construction of further offices, etc., are becoming more and more common in West European cities. By policies to that effect a more reasonable balance between working and living is being obtained, and a balanced use of the infrastructure network achieved in much the same way as was contrived by industrial location policy.

Contrary to the trend towards balanced spread of working and living, and the balanced use of infrastructure, works the construction of systems for rapid public transportation connecting city centres with suburbs far out. Although the main purpose of such systems is to facilitate existing traffic between the suburbs and the centres, they tend to create new traffic in the same directions, as they make it considerably easier than before to reside in the suburb and work in the centre. As far as these systems are 'successful', they promote the increase in distance between work and residence by shifting the latter outwards, thus providing room for more employment in the centre.

It looks as if authorities who pursue such policies have their prestige more at heart than the ultimate effects of their grand projects on the spatial structure of their cities. Fortunately the disproportionate enthusiasm for rapid transit systems is on the wane, and it may safely be assumed that systems now under construction are among the last of their kind.

Infrastructure policy (1) We now come to infrastructure policy which, as has already been indicated in the preceding sections, may be regarded as a complement to amenity policy, industrial location policy and housing policy. The degree to which infrastructure policy is connected with, for instance, amenity policy may be demonstrated by the example of pedestrian zones.

In the section 'Travel benefits: accessibility' we indicated the attraction of a recreation area in j exerted on an individual living in i as:

$$\Pi_{ij} = x_j^{\beta} \exp(-aD_{ij}) \tag{4.34}$$

(the price level (entrance fee) is left out of the equation).

We now interpret x_j as the size and quality of a shopping centre and write again:

$$x_j = s_j q_j \tag{4.35}$$

where s_j indicates the size of the shopping centre and q_j as the 'quality' determined, among other things, by the assortment of goods offered by the centre. We may write then:

$$\Pi_{ij} = s_j^{\beta} q_j^{\beta} \exp(-aD_{ij}) \tag{4.36}$$

Now q_j may also be interpreted in a much wider sense than just as the goods assortment offered by the centre. We might include in the quality-index the atmosphere of the centre, its quietness, the cleanliness of the air, the street decorations and the traffic risks; many of these factors depend on the amount of traffic passing through the streets of the centre, the speed of the traffic and the number of cars parked there.

Turning the centre into a pedestrian zone contributes to its atmosphere and thus raises its quality. Simultaneously, however, D_{ij} will rise because of the decreased accessibility by car. Whether or not the transition of the centre into a pedestrian area will prove a success depends, then, on the trade-off between the two factors mentioned, the increase in q_j and the increase in D_{ij}. Parking facilities close to the centre will limit the increase in D_{ij}, and the set of improvements in the centre itself will, together with the absence of traffic, determine the increase in q_j. Careful planning of both might make the operation successful.

So far we have treated the creation of the pedestrian zone as the outcome of simultaneous infrastructure and amenity policy measures. Obviously one could also see it as the result of two different but well-coordinated infrastructure policies, one decreasing accessibility by car and the other increasing accessibility for pedestrians.

The interwovenness of infrastructure policy with other policies, including the pricing policy to be discussed later, will be our main consideration when dealing with our central theme, the optimum use of infrastructure networks. The foregoing may have shown that this interwovenness is not inherent to the policies mentioned, but simply stems from the fact that the search for optimum use of infrastructure networks is just one facet of the universal search for maximum welfare.

Solving the problem of maximising a country's social welfare, given the conditions prevailing in that country, would implicitly solve the problems of optimum size and quality of the network and of its optimum use. Because a proper pricing system is a condition for such optimums to be achieved, we will now dedicate some attention to pricing policy before returning to our main theme.

Pricing policy The above examples have made it clear that a consumer may easily make decisions which he/she would certainly have avoided if, from the first, he/she had been familiar with the costs of the external effects involved. The example of large-scale and small-scale recreation areas shows clearly that a governmental decision based on principles of optimum welfare might be strongly in favour of small, dispersed recreation areas, whereas a consumer might have no preference for either of the two solutions. However, as soon as he/she knows that the government is going to charge for the noise nuisance, air pollution and damage to the scenery caused by extra roads and extra traffic, then the consumer might well come to the same conclusion as the government, namely that smaller, dispersed recreation areas close to residential areas are to be preferred to larger, more central ones.

At first sight, then, the decision does not seem so very difficult. Just incorporate the external effects (positive as well as negative) in the prices to be charged to consumers, and the right decision will automatically be made.

Unfortunately the matter is not so simple. Many have seen the efforts made to translate noise nuisance and air pollution into money terms. The study of London's third airport is only one example out of many in which certain rules were proposed for treating these factors in such a way that they would neatly fit into a regular cost-benefit analysis. It remains to be seen, however, whether or not these efforts will in the end prove successful. The procedure described in the first section of this chapter does not leave much hope for a favourable outcome. The essential point presented there was that social welfare is not a cardinal but an ordinal variable. In equation (4.26) the constant was deliberately left out because it would be impossible to attach any fixed value to it; in other words, any value would do. It was assumed that the government would spend its budget in such a way that the increase in ω, whatever the unit in which ω is measured, would be maximum. This means that the government would apply the principle of cost-effectiveness rather than that of cost–benefit analysis. For the latter benefits must be measurable. Since evidently they are not, the next-best procedure is that of a cost-effectiveness analysis, the effect to be considered being the increase in social welfare resulting from spending the available means in an optimum way.

But if that is true, then it is also true that the only way to measure the damage to the scenery or noise nuisance is the indirect way of assessing how they affect people. People will react to infringements on their social welfare, and their reactions are an indication of the degree to which social welfare is diminished by environmental factors. However, it is hard to see how the indication thus derived could be translated into money terms.

The conclusion from the foregoing must be that although in principle it would be right to charge everyone for the direct costs as well as the external effects of policy measures, translation of the effects into money terms remains a doubtful procedure, fraught with more or less arbitrary decisions and estimates. The principle of charging a fee thus becomes somewhat shaky and the only thing that can be said is that we know, or at least think we know, what effects are positive and what effects are negative; and that charging some fee for negative effects is, in any case, better than charging nothing at all.

The former considerations apply to the pricing system that was already proposed at an earlier stage for traffic, namely the *road-pricing* system. This system was in fact limited to the external effects of one's participation in traffic on the other participants. Obviously road-pricing should be one of the elements of a general pricing system in which all external effects are to be incorporated – not only of activities in the sphere of traffic, but of all activities. The negative effects of a hypermarket in the green on the scenery in the surroundings should be charged for as well as its contribution to congestion, and so should the adverse effects of intensive recreation on the ecology of the recreation areas. To what extent charges should be made remains an open question.

It seems likely that the complete pricing system just proposed would end up in an extremely complicated and arbitrary set of rules according to which everybody is charged for something, everybody in fact paying everybody else, via the government, for the damages they inflict on general social welfare. Moreover, it can hardly be expected that every goal set by the government can best be achieved by pricing measures. If, for instance, the government aims at rehabilitating the centres of our cities, or protecting the scenery and nature, pricing measures may be of some help, but direct physical planning measures might prove much more efficient and immediately successful. It seems reasonable therefore that some measures are direct planning measures and others pricing measures. Road-pricing seems a good example of the sort of pricing measures that could be effected rather efficiently, while protection of the environment rather calls for direct planning measures.

Infrastructure policy (2) We may now turn back to infrastructure policy. From the preceding paragraphs we may derive that there are three important elements of infrastructure policy namely:

1 thc planning of traffic-creating elements;
2 the planning of the infrastructure itself;
3 the pricing system.

These three elements, and their interrelations, will determine the volume and nature of actual traffic flows. The scheme in Figure 4.3 indicates these interrelations and how accessibility, and hence the actual traffic flows, are ultimately influenced by the measures the government is able and willing to take.

Through the planning of traffic-creating elements and the application of a pricing system, the government is ablc, given the level of income, to influence the demand for infrastructure. Physical constraints (such as preservation of nature, and preservation of historical city centres) determine the willingness of the government to provide infrastructure. The infrastructure supplied determines, when confronted with the demand for infrastructure, the volume of traffic on the network and simultaneously the costs of using the infrastructure. The latter are decisive for the accessibility of jobs and amenities to the population. If the planning in this scheme takes place according to the rules laid down, it may be said that: (a) the infrastructure network is an optimum network; and (b) the use of this network is optimum.

The important questions that remain to be answered are how, in practice, the planning of traffic-creating elements must be effected, what pricing system is to be used and what physical constraints should be imposed in order to reach what might be called a societal optimum.

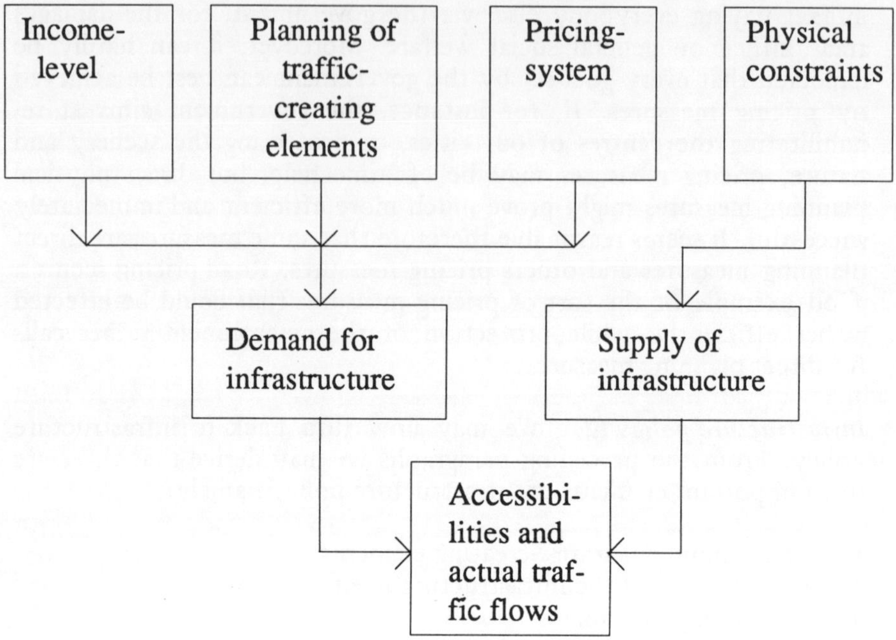

Figure 4.3 Determinants of accessibilities and actual traffic flows

Practical considerations

Introduction The analysis so far, although presented at a transportation symposium, has been general in nature. It has considered the behaviour of individuals in all their activities, in relation to their social economic situation as well as the characteristics of their environment in the broadest sense of the word. It would be easy to argue that such a general analysis, though perhaps interesting from a general societal viewpoint, is not operational enough for one thing, and for another that it is not of immediate relevance to transportation in the narrow sense. It seems worthwhile to attend to the points thus raised, particularly as, in my own eyes, transportation analysis has already suffered for too long from an all too narrow engineering approach, and one that is a far cry from the behaviouristic approach that is in fact required.*

When individuals go shopping, they do so in various ways, showing

*Cf. the conclusions of the ECMT Round Table, No. 32, 'Passenger transport demand in urban areas', *Methodology for Analysing and Forecasting*, Paris, 1976.

different behaviour for different goods; when they go to recreation areas, they may go to the beach, to the woods, etc., to whatever their region has to offer. Sometimes they go for sport, at other times for rest or for enjoyment of the scenery. People also have to go to school or to their jobs. They choose a place to live in an area where there are suitable homes and one which offers the greatest access to the kind of jobs and amenities they prefer. From their choice it follows what their transportation behaviour will be, account being taken of the available infrastructure and superstructure. As a matter of fact, if they have chosen their location well, they will have taken the infrastructure into consideration when making the location decision. A government that understands its task well will try to help individual citizens in their locational choice by improving local amenities and infrastructure, thus bringing about comparable welfare situations in all regions.

That, as simple as it may sound, is the theory presented in the first four chapters of this book. This theory is difficult to relate to transportation not so much because it would be too complicated to be properly tested, but rather because each element of the theory, though simple enough in its set-up, requires elaborate testing with data that are not generally available. Testing of the whole theory will be so time-consuming, and call for so much intensive research, that the temptation is great to fall back on much simpler solutions of the gravitation type. Such solutions demand not much more than a computer for finding the optimum network, where there is a given, 'reasonable' spatial distribution of activities and population to start from. Probably the pitfall hampering the development of transportation theory has always been the need for the proper integration of such a theory in a multidisciplinary approach to spatial consumers' behaviour.

An example may elucidate the point made here. If one wants to analyse the direction and extent of trips made for shopping, the analysis should be placed in the framework of a general study on shopping behaviour. Such a study requires at least:

(a) information per zone about shopping facilities in the study area, differentiated according to categories of goods supplied, size of the shops, assortment and prices;
(b) information per zone about residential households, their composition, income, social status, car ownership, age structure, etc.
(c) information (sample) on shopping behaviour, number of trips made and amount of money spent in each zone.

If all this information is available, the testing can be performed.

Testing is needed to measure distance friction per category of goods bought, for car-owning households and non car-owning households, to measure the attraction of the various shopping centres as a function of their size, assortment, parking facilities, etc. A team of the Netherlands Economic Institute (NEI) has over a period of about two years gone through this whole procedure and succeeded in estimating the most important coefficients (distance-friction coefficients) as well as in deriving from the material important conclusions relevant to shopping-centre policy in an area close to the city of Amsterdam.

What they could not do is to take into account sales to people living outside the study region, the amounts spent on trips originating from the workplace of the consumers, the extent to which multi-purpose trips play a role in shopping behaviour,* etc.; although some of these were provided for in the theoretical model underlying the analysis.† The total costs of a study of this kind can be estimated at a minimum of $200,000. It should be understood that in the NEI study referred to here only one region was studied, and only one activity (shopping) was considered. Application of its results to other regions without proper testing seems unjustifiable at the present stage in the study of consumers' shopping behaviour; application of, for example, the distance coefficients found to other activities, such as visiting cinemas or theatres or recreation areas, would be very hazardous indeed.

Reasoning thus, do we mean to discourage investigators from undertaking behavioural studies like the one performed by the NEI? Obviously the answer is in the negative. That the fruits to be picked from such studies in the narrow field of transportation alone are small is unimportant in view of the wealth of information they produce. What counts is that a full analysis of people's behaviour as regards shopping seems the only way to provide transportation experts with information on shopping trips that is based on actual shopping behaviour.

Analysing commuting behaviour appears even more complicated. An individual who lives at one place and works elsewhere may change his location to improve his living conditions while keeping his job. For that reason, commuting models have to allow for flexible commuting behaviour; in fact commuting behaviour is a function of the

*Cf. D.H. Hensher, 'The structure of journeys and nature of travel pattern', *Environment and Planning, A*, vol. 8, 1976, pp. 655–72, as well as the literature quoted there.
†Leo H. Klaassen, *A Shopping Model*, FEER, Netherlands Economic Institute, Rotterdam, 1974/13; in this report also the supply side of shopping facilities is treated.

living conditions in and around people's residence. Besides it is not so much the individual commuter as the household – in which there are usually more than one member working – that should be the unit to start from. A similar remark holds for other studies of the same kind. In recreation analysis it should be taken into account that the preference for a specific kind of recreation may well be a function of the composition of the household (which is apt to change as time goes on). The qualities of recreation areas form another variable that is difficult to assess; in fact they can only be measured indirectly as far as they exert an influence on behaviour. And that goes for all the variables required for the welfare function we are trying to establish.

When for all population groups in all regions potentials based on the outcome of all these studies have been calculated, the migration of various socio-economic groups of households from region to region will have to be analysed; the data required for such an analysis are in most cases not yet available. Only when the migration analysis has been completed will it be possible to estimate the group-specific weights of the different potentials in the welfare function.

And then, when all the obstacles are overcome and the welfare function completed, we shall still be faced with the question whether or not short-term individual preferences express adequately the societal long-term preference upon which government intervention should be founded.

This, then, is the dilemma that confronts us: should we continue to work with simple models by which potentials for all activities are calculated according to the same principles, deriving traffic flows and 'optimum' networks from them, or should we take the long road along which we shall find much more, and more detailed, information, but which will keep us going for many years to come? And years in which, after all, decisions will still have to be made: if for fear of doing wrong nobody makes any decision at all, we are heading straight for one gigantic traffic chaos. To this dilemma the next sections are devoted.

Towards better use of the transport networks

Introduction Hopefully, in the preceding sections we have succeeded in showing that the optimum use of transport networks can, in principle, only be accomplished along the road of optimising the spatial structure of social welfare. The use of the transport network resulting from such optimisation analysis is automatically the optimum use. It is the author's conviction that this road should be followed, however long and painful it may be. If in the following a different procedure is proposed, it is done for pragmatic reasons. The

The pragmatic approach is, rather than trying to find the optimum use of an as yet unknown network, to settle for a more effective use of the existing network. The matter can be further simplified by defining a bad use of the infrastructure network as a degree of utilisation far below its capacity.

Now that is a definition that seems to represent a shift from the approach adopted so far, by which underutilisation under circumstances could be considered the best possible use of the infrastructure network, rather than as a situation to be improved. However, in an attempt to reconcile the two approaches, we point out that at present the total volume of traffic is still growing, and that even if we accept that unlimited growth of what is called 'mobility' should be considered undesirable, adequate infrastructure must still be provided. As an alternative of constructing new infrastructure, we might consider using the existing infrastructure better; to a certain extent the same alternative would, as a matter of fact, be considered in the general solution. When a network is underutilised, the marginal costs of new traffic are low. So less investment will be needed for activities that create new traffic on underutilised parts than for activities that create new traffic on other parts of the system.

Therefore, other things being equal, the former activities would also rank higher than those that require additional infrastructure on the priority list according to the general approach. Underutilisation may take different forms, as follows:

1 General underutilisation;
2 Underutilisation during a given period of the day in one direction and during another period in the opposite direction;
3 Balanced utilisation with underutilisation during certain hours of the day;
4 Underutilisation during certain days of the week;
5 Underutilisation of one kind of infrastructure (public transport) and full or overutilisation of another kind of infrastructure (private transport).

We will now consider each sort of underutilisation in somewhat more detail. First, let us remark, however, that for the analysis of underutilisation as indicated, rather detailed information will be needed:

(a) traffic counts during all days of the week and the relevant hours of the day per direction per mode;
(b) information about the motives of people participating in traffic in the same subdivision as (a).

All these data are needed per link of the whole network with particular emphasis on the urban networks. These data will give us an insight into the degree of underutilisation, as required.

General underutilisation General underutilisation often occurs when too much confidence in the promotion of economic activities by providing a region with good infrastructure has resulted in networks that are only partly utilised, even during peak hours. For networks leading to employment centres, with the journey to work as a major motive for participation in traffic, the picture will be as indicated in Figure 4.4. The more balanced the distribution of employment and residential areas is, the more pronounced the evening peak in direction 1 and the morning peak in direction 2 will become. Figure 4.5 represents a full balance.

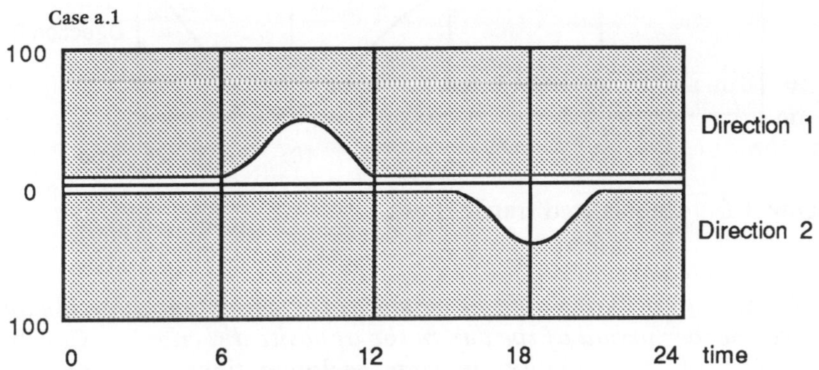

Figure 4.4 General underutilisation, unbalanced

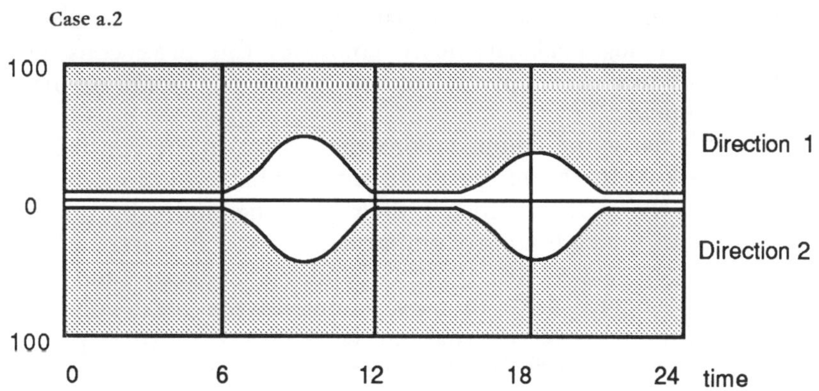

Figure 4.5 General underutilisation, balanced

In both cases the marginal infrastructure costs of a general increase in traffic are small, which means that on the one hand these costs can be practically left out of consideration in the physical planning of the regions where these cases occur (the more so as we get closer to case a.1), and on the other hand detailed studies about the motives of the travellers are less urgent than in other cases (Figure 4.6).

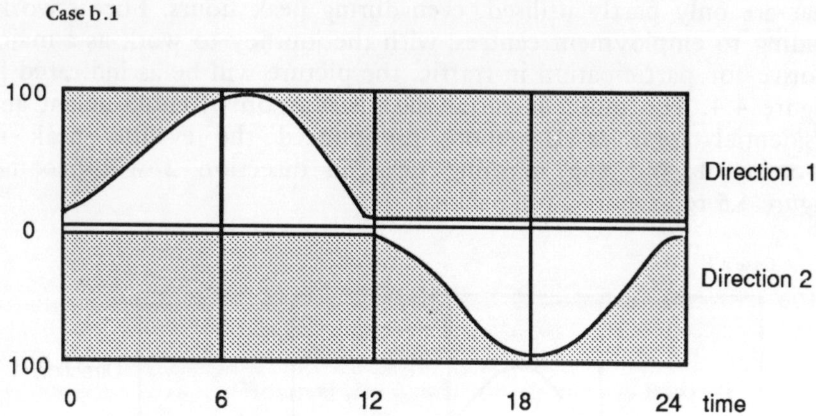

Figure 4.6 Unbalanced traffic flows

Underutilisation during a given period of the day in one direction and during another period of the day in the opposite direction Case b.1 is typical of the situation in large agglomerations with separated employment and residential areas. Usually the peak is broader because at certain times the maximum capacity is reached and trips are shifted towards later or earlier hours. In such cases, it is important to know the motives of participation in traffic, particularly during the evening peak. In many countries this peak consists of commuters as well as shoppers because the closing hours of offices and shops coincide.

It is particularly the labour unions that insist on the continuation of this situation. In the long run an intermediate solution could be found when the offices shorten their working hours by stopping earlier, while shopping hours are diminished by opening later.

Case b.2 represents the typical Sunday recreation and social visits pattern (Figure 4.7). In most countries the total volume of traffic on Sundays exceeds that on workdays with corresponding long peaks manifesting themselves later than on workdays. Measures to avoid at least some of this unbalanced use of the networks have been treated earlier and are returned to again in the next section.

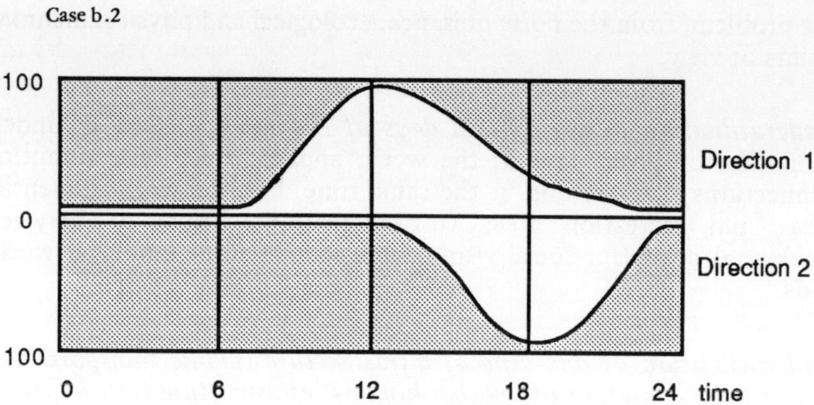

Figure 4.7 Sunday and social visits traffic pattern

Balanced utilisation with underutilisation during certain hours of the day With balanced utilisation, the peaks in both directions are equal in size. If during the peaks the road is used to capacity, underutilisation will be limited to certain hours of the day (Figure 4.8).

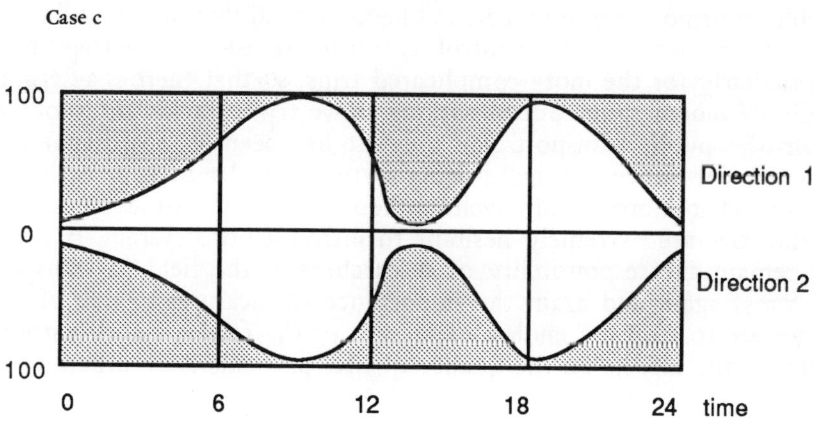

Figure 4.8 Balanced traffic flows

It may be said that, in this case, full use is made of the network. If there is no alternative for the connection for which this situation holds, its seems appropriate to enlarge the capacity of the network. Here extending the capacity of the existing links rather than constructing new links seems the most appropriate way of dealing with the problem, from the noise nuisance, ecological and physical planning points of view.

Underutilisation during certain days of the week Case d, underutilisation on given days of the week, applies to typical commuting connections that are not, at the same time, links between residential areas and recreation areas (for recreational trips) or between residential areas (for social visits); such roads will be empty at weekends.

Underutilisation of one kind of infrastructure (public transport) and full or over-utilisation of another kind of infrastructure (private transport) This final case is perhaps the most discussed of all, although in practice it may not occur as often as some people would suggest. The famous modal split question refers to it; often it is tried to influence the split by using the price mechanism, more specifically, by subsidising public transport. In the beginning of this section of the book, the concept of generalised transport costs was discussed, and it was shown that these consist not only of transport costs, but also of other cost elements that are not influenced by the rates charged. Apart from the question whether the cities of today could afford free public transport, we should always keep in mind that only to a limited extent are we able to control comfort, speed and waiting-times, particularly for the more complicated trips, so that there is a definite limit to modal split control as long as we try to tackle the problem from the public transport side only. It has been proposed time and again to introduce the road-pricing system in order to cope with it in a somewhat more elegant welfare-theoretical way, but it seems that authorities are extremely hesitant to introduce this system. It seems to remain the responsibility of researchers in the field of transport to stress again and again the importance of measures to that effect, if we are to stop the endless expansion of the road network without heed to the effects on the quality of life, particularly in urban areas.

A profile approach

The preceding subsection has dealt with the various traffic patterns emerging on specific links of the transportation network. Let us now imagine that an integrated regional study (including a transportation study) is going to be undertaken for a certain region. How would such a study be approached? The following steps could be conceived:

1 Investigating what potential growth possibilities the region has

that would contribute to higher future incomes and to a more stable economy.

2 Making assumptions as to how far such growth potentials could be realised.

3 Planning, on the basis of the assumptions in step 2, the social infrastructure needed.

4 Drawing up a spatial plan in which population and activities are distributed across the region in an optimum or rather an acceptable way.

This approach would have been the obvious one until very recently. In the early 1960s the main concern of the authorities in matters of regional development was to attract activities to a region that could contribute to growth and higher income as well as to the stability of the regional economy. The stability could be improved by diversifying the economy, avoiding the monostructures that have often shown themselves highly unstable foundations for a sound economy. However, of recent years other welfare elements have entered into the considerations about future development, and with them a different approach to the selection of activities to be attracted. Authorities have become concerned – and rightly so – with the structure of the labour market and the effect that future developments might have on the conditions prevailing there as well as with the quality of the environment and the effect new developments could have on that aspect of the quality of life. All such elements came to be taken into consideration in addition to the purely economic elements before permission was granted to start a new activity in a region.

This new approach was understandably most popular during the years in which economic growth and full employment prevailed and confidence was strong that the situation would continue like that. The philosophy behind it was in fact that the regional governments (as well as the municipal authorities) could take their pick out of all applications of industrial firms that wanted to start new activities in the region or extend their existing establishments. By imposing constraints in the above sense on those new activities the government could contribute to the decrease of discrepancies on the labour market, improve the environmental conditions and limit the volume of traffic, while pursuing at the same time the old goals of economic policy, namely growth and stability.

Conditions have considerably changed since then, particularly as a result of the oil crisis, and it seems that the change has also altered the opinion of the authorities. More than ever before, they are trying to promote along the old lines economic growth all over the country in order to reduce unemployment, with often little or no attention to the other elements of social welfare that a short while ago were considered of primary importance.

It does not seem unlikely that the world economy will recover from the influence of the fantastic increase in energy prices, and will gradually find, together with the OPEC countries, a new equilibrium with – probably modest – further economic growth. That will enable us to resume, perhaps on a more reasonable scale, the pursuit of a growth in welfare in which all five objectives play their role; that is,

1 reasonable economic growth;
2 stability;
3 acceptable environmental conditions;
4 acceptable discrepancies on the labour market;
5 acceptable traffic conditions.

If in the following considerations we go into somewhat more detail as far as the traffic conditions are concerned, we shall keep in mind that these represent only one objective out of five; thus we shall remain in complete concordance with the points stressed earlier that the optimum use of infrastructure can never be considered on its own, but rather should be defined within the framework of a more general social welfare framework. Sometimes heavy congestion will have to be accepted, sometimes heavy underutilisation, if the conditions prevailing in other fields require it; in the following we shall have to keep that constraint in mind.

Let us assume that the regional study has been performed to the point where the potential new activities have been defined and calculations performed regarding the nature and quantity of amenities that will be needed in the future. Further we will assume that a number of possible and acceptable scenarios for the region's future will at this stage be designed. Each scenario will define a certain spatial distribution of population and activities.

At this point, the behaviouristic approach should be introduced. From the distribution of employment, shopping centres, recreation areas and other amenities, and schools and population we should be able with the help of models that explain commuting behaviour, shopping behaviour, recreation behaviour, etc. to calculate the traffic flows created by each possible, acceptable spatial arrangement.

The additional traffic created, defined per direction, per hour and per day, will then have to be compared with the non-utilised infrastructure per direction, per hour and per day. If we denote the additional traffic by:

$$\psi_t = {}^{\delta}t^{\tau}_{ij} \tag{4.37}$$

to be called the *new-traffic profile* and where t is the number of passengers, δ the day of the week, τ the hours of the day and ij the direction in which the traffic takes place, and the non-utilised capacity by:

$$\psi_u = {}^{\delta}u^{\tau}_{ij} \tag{4.38}$$

to be called the *unused-capacity profile*, the plan should be chosen for which *for all* ${}^{\delta}t^{\tau}_{ij} > {}^{\delta}u^{\tau}_{ij}$:

$$\sum_{\delta} \sum_{\tau} \sum_{i} \sum_{j} [{}^{\delta}t^{\tau}_{ij} - {}^{\delta}u^{\tau}_{ij}] f_{ij} = \min$$

where f_{ij} represents the physical (or time) distance between i and j.

According to the principles laid down in the preceding section the plan envisaged, wherever possible and acceptable, should imply:

(a) extension of the general use of underutilised parts of the network;
(b) more balanced distribution of residential and employment areas;
(c) planning of recreation areas and residential areas in such a way that during the weekends those parts of the network are used for recreational and social visits purposes that during weekdays are used for commuting and shopping;
(d) improvement of public-transport networks on parts of the road network where congestion prevails;
(e) in all other cases, extension of the capacity of the existing network rather than the construction of new links.

A remark should be made concerning the situation in urban areas. The second recommendation says that the new activities should possibly be located in areas where they contribute to more balanced traffic flows (i.e. two peaks instead of one in each direction per day). This recommendation can obviously be carried out more easily the more rapid is the economy growth and, particularly, the more numerous are new activities. Recent developments in several West European countries (the UK, Federal Republic of German and Holland) have shown that employment in the larger urban agglomerations is decreasing rather than increasing. When that is the case, it is not quite so easy to achieve balanced traffic flows. In some cities employment in the service sector is still increasing. Where that happens, the first concern should be with preventing further concentration of existing service activities; what to do with new service activities is not a matter of urgent consideration. When it comes to decentralisation, efforts should be made to concentrate relocated as well as new activities in well-accessible, secondary centres, adequately linked with the main centre as well as with one another.

Considerations on the multi-modal use of infrastructure

The multi-modal use of infrastructure was more or less implicitly treated in the preceding sections; in this section we will treat this subject more explicitly. Let us start our considerations with a few examples of intervention in the multi-modal use. In recent years it has become more and more common to reserve extra lanes on highways as well as in city streets, for public transport and emergency transport (police, fire brigade and ambulances). Although opinions on the designation of lanes to specific purposes differ, it cannot be denied that there is in general a firm rationale behind it; as far as emergency transports are concerned, that is immediately obvious. The urgency of the trip and the importance of reaching the destination with the shortest possible delay demand priority in traffic, and the best way to obtain such priority is to reserve or construct a special lane for the purpose. However, also for public transport there is a rationale as soon as there is congestion on the road. That rationale is simply that the number of passengers in the bus is larger than that in a private car and consequently saving time is much more important for the bus than for the private car. A similar reasoning holds of course for tramways in cities, which used to share the roads with private traffic but are provided more and more with separate lanes. Here, too, the number of passengers is usually considerably larger than in a car, certainly during peak hours. This same fact also justifies the priority given to public transport at road and street crossings. The very number of passengers warrants the highest possible speed, even if it would increase the trip length of the private car users. Of course, the limit is reached when the measures in favour of public transport increase total travel time on the road by more than is saved on public transport, with the difference in comfort taken into account.

This first example shows that there is, at least on a limited scale, a tendency towards the creation of different lanes for different users of the road or, in other words, a tendency to reduce the multi-modal use of the road network in favour of the more urgent uses, as defined by legislative measures. Of course, one could argue that there are among the other users of the road also people who make extremely urgent trips, such as doctors going to patients or individuals going to important meetings, but there is no doubt that the partial measure taken means an improvement compared to the former situation. There is a definite move in the direction of separate sub-infrastructures for separate purposes, within the one basic infrastructure. We may denote this kind of measure as an *infrastructural split*.

Our second example refers to the measure taken in the Federal Republic of Germany to the effect that lorries are not allowed on the roads during weekends, except in special cases. It is considered that goods transport at weekends is less urgent than the social and recreational purposes which bring large quantities of private cars on to the roads. Once more, we have infrastructural split, but this time it is not a spatial but a temporal split: priority being given during certain times to certain uses of the road, while in the first example permanent priority was given to certain modes on certain lanes of the road. Another case of temporal split is found in pedestrian zones in cities, where loading and unloading of goods is permitted only during certain hours of the day, and pedestrians may claim absolute priority for the rest of the day, when the zones are inaccessible to any other kind of traffic.

Temporal infrastructural split differs from the spatial kind in effect: temporal infrastructural split does not affect modal split because goods and people are not competitive on that score; spatial infrastructural split does affect modal split, however, for the increased speed it allows to public transport may persuade people to use it, particularly for their journey-to-work.

Our fourth example concerns the use of railroad infrastructure by both slow and fast trains. Two tendencies can be discerned: (a) to use existing intercity railroads also for suburban traffic, and (b) to increase the speed of long-distance trains. To make railroads suitable for commuting, suburban stations can be created along existing lines. Here we are faced with a problem of weighted time saving similar to the one dealt with in our first example.

If suburban traffic is mixed with intercity traffic, the following things happen:

1. Regular trains have to stop more often at suburban stations; passengers from outside the agglomeration will lose time as a result.
2. People may switch from other means of transportation to the train because thus they gain time.
3. People who used to go by car but have switched to rail transport are released from the search for a parking place, but are either referred to additional transport to and from the train or

reduced to Shanks' pony (which, for that matter, might be a boost to their health!).

It seems rational to create suburban stations if the net gains of items 2 and 3 surpass the loss of 1.

So much for the first tendency. The situation becomes interesting if we introduce the second one into our considerations, which is the tendency to increase the speed of long-distance trains to over 200 km per hour. The Shinkansen line from Tokyo to Osaka is a real-life example of a connection by very fast trains. When, as in Japan, the capacity of the network is fully occupied, the tendency to create more and more suburban stations can apparently no longer be reconciled with the introduction of fast trains, unless separate infrastructure is created for the latter. Needless to say, separate infrastructure is anyhow preferable from a technical point of view as well as for reasons of safety.

This last example is, like the first we have given, one of spatial infrastructural split: separate lanes belonging to the same infrastructure are created for specific uses. Of course, the principle has been known and applied for a very long time in the Netherlands and Denmark with respect to bicycles (and pedestrians, for that matter). One wonders why it has been so sadly neglected by designers of traffic infrastructure in developing countries!

In most cases mentioned, the sort of infrastructure provided has a definite influence on modal split, in some cases through the decrease in risk (cycle paths), in other cases through the gain in time (separate bus lanes). The aspect of the infrastructural split links the problems treated in this section with that of the modal split, which even today is too often seen as a matter of money price competition rather than as a competition between levels of generalised transportation costs. It is to a considerable extent the quality of the infrastructure that determines the speed of the vehicles and the risk levels for the passengers using the infrastructure, factors that, as essential parts of the generalised transportation costs, are important for the modal choice.

Parallel to the tendency to create specific (sub)infrastructures for specific sorts of traffic, there is a tendency towards what is usually called integration of the existing transport infrastructure, both for private and for public transport. Manifestations of this tendency are park-and-ride systems (park-and-fly systems), and the construction of integrated rail systems that simultaneously caters for the intra-urban and inter-urban needs by using the same infrastructure for both regular trains and (fast) streetcars.

The objective of the measures taken in this field is to facilitate the transition from one mode of transport to another at the points where such a transition seems most desirable, either from a capacity point of view or for other reasons (such as the limited parking facilities available in urban areas). They tend to increase the flexibility of the system and to promote, by removing obstacles at interchange points, the optimum use of the system as a whole because they enable travellers to compose their total journey of such sub-trips as serve the purpose of the total trip best.

The two tendencies, namely the creation of specific infrastructural elements for specific trip purposes and the promotion of easy possibilities of changing from one mode to another, complement each other and together might contribute considerably to the optimum use of the system as a whole.

In the former section we reached the conclusion that better use could be made of the transport network if certain physical planning and pricing policies were pursued. Here we might conclude that these policies could be facilitated by measures that differentiate the network and measures that enable those who use the total network to do so in a flexible way, dependent on purpose, length, direction and time of the trip. Such improvements of the network itself, though perhaps of minor importance compared to the network as a whole, could contribute considerably to the efficiency of its use.

Final remarks

In the foregoing a number of theoretical considerations were presented which were partly of a highly theoretical nature, and partly of a somewhat more practical character. For an elegant presentation, the more practical conclusions ought to have been derived from the theory presented first. However, in this section it has not been possible fully to meet that requirement because testing the theory would have called for so much original research that only very partial results could have been presented now. For that reason, a simpler approach to the practical matters has been chosen, linked to the theory in many respects, but certainly not making full use of its potentialities.

The dilemma in which transportation theory finds itself at this moment is certainly not typical of transportation problems. More than ever, it is realised that all the major problems the world is faced with today are no more than facets of the much more general problem of how to find a societal optimum. In labour market studies, environmental studies, economic studies and physical planning studies the same problem arises. Improvement of the conditions on the labour market might create new traffic, and require the expansion of industrial production that harms the environment. Measures that promote the quality of the environment fast and efficiently could cause serious repercussions on the labour market and gravely infringe the individual's freedom to travel. To maximise economic growth has become as doubtful an objective as to minimise traffic flows and maximise the quality of our environment. All these objectives should get their proper weight in the social welfare function in order to enable society to find a solution that is acceptable for most people as the best solution that can be reached, given the prevailing conditions and financial and other constraints.

The procedure we have followed here finds its justification in the position in which most researchers in all the fields indicated find themselves. On the one hand they are inclined to concentrate on the general societal problem, and on the other hand they are faced with the necessity to propose solutions for practical problems – solutions that have to be realised at short notice. Society cannot wait until the long-term optimum solution has been found, and many politicians are even far from convinced that it is right to go on searching for it.

It is indeed my conviction that the two lines should be followed simultaneously. One line is the study of integrated models that, if made operational, could provide integrated solutions on many specific problems. The other line is to search for partial solutions, taking into account all external effects of any measure proposed, so that the solutions suggested are likely to fit into the framework of the general model.

Even a partial approach to each of the specific fields referred to above – including that of transportation – will require the formation of a multidisciplinary team. Transport experts may find consolation in the fact that multidisciplinarity is nowadays commonly required in all fields, not just their own. Compared to the general framework of societal models, every model, however complicated or sophisticated, and be it a transportation model or an economic model or an environmental model or a labour market model, is a partial model, and not more than that. Practical solutions, however, require more than the solution that a partial model is able to give. That is why we should try to walk along both avenues simultaneously, however difficult it may seem from a transportation point of view.

4.3 Allocating subsidies to public transport*

Some general thoughts on public transport and social well-being

The concept of social well-being To get an idea of the obstacles on the road to a plausible definition of *social* well-being, let us start from the notion of *individual* well-being. The most general definition one could give of individual well-being is, 'the degree to which the individual's needs are satisfied'. Somewhat mathematically formalised, individual well-being would thus be the individual's actual satisfaction of needs divided by his/her desired satisfaction of needs. Now an individual's desired satisfaction of needs is hardly likely to be independent of the actual satisfaction of other individuals in comparable positions. Indeed the higher their level of satisfaction, the higher our individual will set his/her aspirations, and the less satisfied he/she will feel; on the other hand, if the needs of the comparable group are less satisfied, our man/woman will feel more so.

Now that is no news, of course. We know that a person's absolute money income or absolute consumption is only partly decisive for his/her well-being. The well-being of a person living in a country with a high per capita income is not by definition higher than that of an individual living in a low-income country, at any rate so long as the lower income keeps above a certain threshold.

Accepting, then, that individual well-being is a relative notion, namely the ratio between an actual and a desired situation, and stating further that the desired situation is derived from the actual situation of those with whom the individual compares himself/herself, we conclude that the concept of social well-being is as complicated as it is because the well-being of every individual depends on the well-being of all other individuals. The relations are so involved that we cannot even be sure beforehand that general social well-being will improve when the needs of an individual or a group of individuals are better satisfied while the satisfaction of other individuals or groups remains the same.

In the same line of thought, an improvement in the conditions of living of an entire population need not necessarily enhance their social well-being. The hypothesis, for example, that aspirations keep in step with economic growth can by no means be discarded.

An interesting question now arises: with what group will an individual tend to compare his/her own situation? Probably both with

*See L.H. Klaassen, H. Vogelaar and Sj. Wagenaar, *Transport Reviews*, London/Philadelphia: Taylor and Francis, 1981.

those more prosperous and with those less prosperous than himself/herself. From the first comparison a relatively low appreciation of his/her own well-being could result, but from the second a relatively high one. As the individual climbs the prosperity ladder he/she will look upon his/her own position with more satisfaction; the inverse applies to a relatively low position. Probably, then, the distribution of social well-being among individuals is more askew than that of prosperity among the same individuals. The difference in skewness is so hard to measure, however, that a somewhat adapted definition of social well-being, or a replacing notion, seems worth looking for. We shall try to do so with an eye on the traffic problems which are the subject of this paper.

Social well-being and the need to travel Speaking about social well-being and transport, we should give attention to the average individual's mobility as well as his/her need to travel. Various documents dealing with transportation, both recent and older ones, often suggest the existence of a more or less exogenously determined and quantifiable need of individuals to travel. Should that need be known, then it would also be possible to determine to what extent that need is satisfied, for instance, by the public transport system. Obviously, however, we are coming up against the very question we mentioned previously, namely whether the individual's need to travel is a quantity that can be measured in independence of prevailing circumstances. If not, we have to find out what the intensity of the need for travelling does depend on and, more particularly, to what extent it is determined by the actual travelling, or ability to do so, of others. A locality which has a bus connection with the nearest town every three hours will be thought very poorly provided for by many West Europeans; however, people in much of Africa, used to having to walk such distances in their own countries, will look upon the bus connection as unparalleled luxury. Man has no absolute need to travel. His needs are relative, largely determined, like almost all needs in this world, by his social surroundings.

So we should not pretend that there is something like an objective minimum standard for the frequency of public transport. Minimum standards are fixed in surroundings where an *average* standard prevails, an average that is decisive for the level of the minimum standard. If the average standard can be raised as more financial means become available, there will be a tendency to raise the minimum standards as well. That is the common procedure in our society.

Optimum public transport One thing has clearly emerged from the foregoing: the notion of social well-being, whether used in general or in relation to the specific contribution of public transport, is difficult to operate because of its relative character. It represents the ratio between something quantifiable (the actual satisfaction of needs) and something not quantifiable (the desired satisfaction of needs); thus the notion is essentially inoperational.

So to make a meaningful statement about, for instance, an acceptable level of provision of public transport, we shall have to try to find another notion, lacking the relative character of social well-being, operational and also policy-relevant. While using this substitutive notion, we must keep in mind that we have purposely abstracted from the relative character of the concept of social well-being. We shall henceforth treat 'social well-being' as if it were an absolute notion; so a more frequent public transport in country A than in country B will be taken to mean that people in country A are more content with public transport than those in country B, and that therefore public transport contributes more to 'social well-being' in country A than in country B.

Now the question arises, when can the contribution of public transport to social well-being, thus defined, be said to be optimum? The authority which decides the level of provision and the tariff of public transport is supposed to do so by a certain behavioural rule. The behaviour consists in using the available instruments, so that an optimum defined by the behavioural rule is reached. Several behavioural rules are possible, in principle, but we shall assume here that the government aims at making the difference between social benefits and social costs of public transport as wide as possible, which implies substituting the narrower and absolute notion of net social benefits for the notion of social well-being. On the assumption that the government has two instruments available to reach the optimum, namely the price (by passenger-kilometre, for instance) and the level of provision (defined as the reciprocal of the weighted time sacrifice one traveller has to make to travel 1 km), that 'social' optimum is achieved if two conditions are met, namely that: (a) the price is equal to the marginal cost by passenger; and (b) provision has reached a level where its marginal improvement results in passengers saving an amount (of time and energy) equal to the marginal social costs of that improvement.

Indeed, for any one familiar with cost and demand functions, determining simultaneously the optimum tariff and the optimum level of provision is not a very complicated task. But the last word has not yet been spoken: we have not yet given any attention to the financial consequences of optimisation.

Financial constraints Let us begin by stating frankly that governments hardly every make serious efforts to find out about the optimum price of public transport, and rarely try to determine an optimum level of provision. As a consequence, not only are the results likely to be socially sub-optimum, but the financial deficits are probably also far greater than they would have been in a socially optimum situation. On the other hand, there is no reason to maintain, a priori, that in a socially optimum situation there would have been no financial deficits; that would hardly be credible in view of the unfavourable market situation and cost conditions in which public transport has to operate.

Here we are touching upon an extremely important question: is there a discrepancy between the funds available to the government for distribution among various uses, and the total of funds they would need to achieve for all provisions a 'social' optimum.

The moment we ask that question we know the answer. There is no reason at all to suppose that the funds required to achieve a situation considered optimum by the prevailing rule of behaviour will come forth, as it were, automatically. So the chance of a budget constraint becoming operative cannot be ignored.

Now it is interesting to examine the nature of such a budget constraint. It applies to individuals as well as to the government, and springs in both cases from the finiteness of the total available budget. An individual will distribute his/her budget in the well-known manner among the goods and services he/she buys, so that the marginal utility of a unit of money spent in whatever direction is the same. That seems good advice to the government as well. Unfortunately things are not so simple there as in the theory of consumer behaviour. Who will have the temerity of weighing the marginal utility of greater defence efforts against that of the improved care of senior citizens, health-care research, better training of agricultural engineers or the improvement of public transport? Such weigh-offs are not based on rational quantitative analyses, but come about through a large number of political, marginal small-scope decisions, made during a long series of years, and resulting finally in the actual situation of the moment. In the Netherlands the central government spends about 1 per cent of national income both on development aid and on making good the deficits of public transport. But who will say whether or not that is socially justified? Is one expenditure too high, or the other, or both? Or are both of them too low?

But if we cannot answer those questions, neither can we tell whether a budget constraint imposed on public transport is too high or too low. It is the outcome of a dynamic political process mostly of the past, influenced by the present financial situation, but not as such based on present and relevant social considerations. Admittedly, we have indicated in the foregoing what such a social consideration could look like and how one could compute exactly how much money should be put at the disposal of public transport to make it function in a societally optimum manner. The same could be done for some other government tasks. But not for all of them, and certainly not for all important ones. And that is what renders partial budget constraints on public transport rather 'soft', though they do make it impossible to realise the social optimum. But if the social optimum cannot be realised for lack of financial means, there is not much sense in talking about a social optimum. For the original behavioural rule of the government with respect to public transport cannot be maintained, and can even be dropped in favour of an entirely different rule under the restrictions of the budget. As the budget shrinks one becomes further removed from realising the social optimum, and hence from the behavioural rule which aims at realising it. To illustrate this, let us consider a situation in which the government limits the budget to the very lowest limit. In those conditions the behavioural rule can no longer be that of the social optimum. Indeed to minimise all possible deficits, a totally different behavioural code must be applied, namely that of minimising losses as would a monopolist. Bending over backwards, the government may go on pretending to keep the behavioural rule of aiming for a social optimum under a budget constraint, but actually the latter has become so strict as to force the government to monopolist behaviour with respect to public transport. Admittedly, if the margin between the amounts needed for a social optimum and those required to keep losses at a minimum is narrow, politicians do not have much leeway in which to manipulate the budget restriction.

Conclusions: realistic public transport We can draw the following conclusions from the previous sections of this chapter:

1 By its relativity, the concept of social well-being lends itself hardly or not at all to analysis, which renders it an unfit policy objective.
2 As a substitute for the concept of social well-being, that of net social benefits could serve; this is an absolute notion with theoretical drawbacks, but with the advantage of being quantifiable.
3 The behavioural rule for government policy, namely to try for the highest possible contribution of certain provisions to social well-being, can then be given substance by translating that objective into that of maximising the difference between social benefits and social costs.

4 The government may be hampered in implementing its policy to that effect if deficits are involved which the same government does not want to make good.
5 To maintain the system of public transport the government's subsidy need not be higher than corresponds with the social optimum, but cannot be less than the deficit manifesting itself when the system is run as a monopoly by aiming for maximum profit (or minimum loss).
6 As the available funds shrink, the government will stray further away from a policy aiming at an optimum contribution of public transport to net social benefits, and tend to behave more and more as a monopolist. That stage seems imminent now, and the government will be inclined to judge the financial situation with respect to public transport more and more keenly. In practice, that will be manifest from the critical analysis of tariffs demanded and levels of provision offered.
7 The possibility must not be ruled out that reconsideration of the last two points will not only lead to lesser financial deficits of public transport, but also to its contributing more to net social benefits than at the present time.

A theoretical model

Introduction The preceding considerations enable us to build up a model consisting of a few equations based on the 'operational' definitions of social well-being. It will be shown later that the model could serve as an instrument for public transport policy if some mathematical specifications of the equations used are introduced.

The demand for public transport Literature on the subject of the demand for public transport is abundant. Our purpose here is not to describe in detail the results of studies made in the Netherlands or elsewhere, but to concentrate on the theoretical problems inherent in defining the 'appropriate' level of public transport to be provided in urban areas by local or central authorities, the role that demand and cost functions play in that definition and the degree of subsidisation associated with an 'appropriate' level.

We assume a simple demand function:

$$P = P(c, exo) \qquad (4.39)$$

where P = demand for public transport services;

c = the level of cost for the user of public transport;
exo = the set of variables that could be considered exogenous; these are the geographic and socio-economic structure of the urban area, income and/or car ownership, population size, etc.

We will consider each variable in some detail. P represents the demand for public transport services and can be expressed in passenger-kilometres, number of passengers or number of trips. Each of these possible variables has its drawbacks. If we measure in passenger-kilometres, we treat longer trips with fewer passengers the same as shorter trips with more passengers. Taking the number of passengers means leaving out the average trip length, and taking the number of trips gives difficulties of measurement, as we do not know the separate numbers of linked and unlinked trips. In the course of a study carried out in the Netherlands by the Institute of Public Administration in Washington, together with the Netherlands Economic Insitute in Rotterdam on bchalf of the Dutch Ministry of Transportation, the number of passenger-kilometres was found to be probably the most appropriate measure, reflecting adequately the use made of public transport.

The second variable is c. It should be measured as generalised costs or generalised time. If measuring it as generalised costs, we should express the different time elements of a trip in monetary units. That means attaching different values to the time needed to walk to the nearest stop, travel time, perhaps time to change vehicle, again travel time and walking time to the final destination. To these should be added the fare, usually a function of the length of the trip. Obviously some more or less arbitrary decisions will have to be made to find a value for the average generalised costs per passenger-kilometre. In practice, these decisions are not too difficult, but for a proper calculation one needs to know, in principle, details of frequency and speed of public transport. Generalised time is in fact known when these calculations have been made and the fare has been expressed in time. The concept of generalised time is important, however, when later on we consider the relation between level of service and costs.

The variable in *exo* that is most difficult to measure is the efficiency of the structure of the urban area; we may proceed as follows. Assume that there exist an infrastructure for public transport and a given number of carriages and staff. Assume, further, that there is only one kind of public transport in each city with its own infrastructure; other kinds of public transport can be introduced without specific problems. The capacity of this public transport is expressed as the maximum number of passenger-kilometres that could be produced during the relevant hours of the day; it will be denoted by C.

Considering the network as the sum of unit-distance parts of links and assuming that each part is occupied to capacity in one direction during peak hours in expression (4.39), we may write:

$$C^i = 2TV_1^{max p}\ p_1^{max p} \tag{4.40}$$

where subscript 1 = the direction;
T = number of relevant hours per day;
$V_1^{max p}$ = maximum number of carriages used during peak hours (which is equal to the maximum number of vehicles that can be used during peak hours);
$p_1^{max p}$ = maximum number of passengers per carriage during peak hours (equalling maximum possible number of passengers);
C^i = the capacity of the ith part of the network in *two* directions.

If we write $\overline{T}\overline{V}\overline{p}$ for the total number of passengers transported over the ith part of the network during the whole day (i.e. the T relevant hours of the day), $\overline{V}$ representing the average number of carriages and $\overline{p}$ the average number of passengers per carriage during the T hours, the following expression holds:

$$\epsilon = \frac{\overline{T}\overline{V}\overline{p}}{2TV_1^{max p}\ p_1^{max p}} = \frac{\overline{V}\overline{p}}{2V_1^{max p}\ p_1^{max p}} \tag{4.41}$$

representing the efficiency of the use of the system on the ith part of the network, or in other words, the degree to which the available capacity is utilised during the T relevant hours of the day. Equation (4.40) can be written as:

$$\epsilon = \frac{\overline{V}\overline{p}}{V^{max p}\ p^{max p}} \cdot \frac{V^{max p}\ p^{max p}}{2V_1^{max p}\ p_1^{max p}} = \tau\sigma \tag{4.42}$$

where $V^{max p}\ p^{max p}$ stands for the total number of passengers transported over one part of the network in both directions during the peak.

The first term thus indicates the ratio between the average number of passengers in both directions and the maximum number observed during the peak. This ratio represents the *temporal efficiency* of the system. If $\overline{Vp} = V^{maxp}\ p^{maxp}$, traffic flows are distributed equally among the hours (T) of the day; temporal efficiency has then reached its maximum ($\tau = 1$).

The second term is the ratio between the actual number of passengers observed during the peak and the maximum number possible (which is equal to twice the peak number in the busiest direction). This ratio is denoted by σ and represents the *spatial efficiency*. If $\sigma = 1$, the part of the network considered is fully occupied in both directions during the peak.

Evidently ϵ can be equal to unity only if both $\tau = 1$ and $\sigma = 1$. In that case, traffic is distributed equally among the T hours of the day as well as between directions. For the system as a whole we may write (summing over all unit-distance parts):

$$\epsilon_{tot} = \frac{\Sigma\ \overline{Vp}}{\Sigma\ V^{maxp}\ p^{maxp}} \cdot \frac{\Sigma\ V^{maxp}\ p^{maxp}}{2\Sigma\ V_1^{maxp}\ p_1^{maxp}} = \tau_{tot} \cdot \sigma_{tot} \qquad (4.43)$$

The three efficiency symbols relate to total (public) transport. It should be noted that if all parts of the network have the same unit length, the sum of the number of passengers per part equals the total number of passenger-kilometres. Obviously ϵ_{tot} equals the number of passenger-kilometres divided by the number of place-kilometres produced by the system.

This variable is usually not difficult to compute. Primarily, as a result of the rigid spatial separation of workplaces and residences, the values reached for ϵ_{tot} will in general be low, a major cause of the bad financial results of most public transport systems. What follows in the next section should be placed in this general spatial context.

The supply of public transport The most important parts of the supply function of public transport are the relations among the costs, the level of service and the number of passengers carried. In this section we will first consider what is to be understood by level of service, and next dwell on the concept of costs which in all practical studies appears of considerable relevance. We write for the cost function:

$$K = K(\tau, P, exo) \qquad (4.44)$$

where K is the total economic costs, τ the reciprocal of the level of service and *exo* the set of exogenous variables among which the efficiency measure of the urban structure.

We will start with τ and consider its relation to c. We may write (in a simplified form):

$$c = t + v\tau \qquad (4.45)$$

where t is the fare to be paid and v is the value of time attached to one unit of time spent in travelling with public transport (in fact both v and τ are vectors).

Apparently, τ should represent (weighted) time per passenger-kilometre when using public transport, including time for walking to the stop, changing at transfer points, travelling and going to the final destination. An increase in the level of service is reflected in a decrease in one or more of these time elements; extensions of the network decrease time used for access to and egress from public transport, more direct lines as well as higher speed decrease transport time, etc. This indicates that $1{:}\tau$ is an acceptable measure for the quality of public transport (level of service) in an urban area. In principle, the weighting involved in calculating τ should take into account the level of comfort during travel, like the probability of getting a seat, the cleanliness of the vehicle and safety. We will not go further into this matter here, although it is quite possible to take those factors into account in the weighting of travel time.

Accepting τ as a good measure for the (reciprocal of) the level of service, we should now consider the costs of public transport. One of the fundamental difficulties in practical research concerned with determining cost levels is that calculations by municipalities, as well as other transport operators, are often made on the basis of financial costs rather than economic costs. A proper system of allocating funds in order to reach in each city a level of service that can be considered appropriate should, however, be based on economic costs.

If existing cost figures are expressed as financial costs, they have the following features (see Klaassen and Otten, 1980):

1. The depreciation of durable assets is calculated on the basis of historic cost prices.
2. The interest entered into the books of the transit operators reflects interest rates prevailing at the time loans were contracted.
3. Capital costs which have been covered by past grants no longer show up in the operating deficits (or cost) of the transit undertakings. This tends to lead to an underestimation of total cost involved in the provision of public transport services.
4. Interest and depreciation costs for bus and tram differ among public transport operators. The differences must be ascribed, in

part, to differences in the value of rolling stock (differences in historic cost price), differences in depreciation rate (different estimation of economic or technical life time) and differences in interest rates.

From what has been said, above, one can infer that to arrive at comparable and economically sound cost figures to be used for the correct allocation of government subsidies to urban transport operators, the following conditions need to be fulfilled. First, the annual cost (interest and depreciation) of infrastructure that benefited from a grant-in-aid in the past should be included in the yearly cost of public transport in a city. The cost of acquiring land, being an item that need not be replaced, should not be written off and should only be charged for the interest.

Depreciation should take place on the basis of the replacement value of assets rather than historic cost. In a situation of rising prices the concept of replacement value offers better opportunities for smooth adaptation. The rate of interest calculated by public transport operators should not be based on the rate actually paid, but on a rate that reflects the opportunity cost of capital.

The ways in which various public transport operators calculate their operating costs should be harmonised whenever possible. That applies, for instance, to the estimated life-time of buses, trams and other types of asset. In that way, differences in cost springing only from varying accounting methods are eliminated. The remaining cost differences have to do with, for example, different composition of rolling-stock, different structure of the city area served by the transit operators, different wage structure of the staff and differences in management. Only after correction of the existing cost figures according to the above mentioned principles will it be possible to estimate a cost function for public transport.

Appropriate levels of public transport In the *general model* we start from the following simple model:

$$P = P(c, exo) \tag{4.46}$$

This equation expresses that the total number of passenger-kilometres travelled by public transport depends on the generalised costs per passenger-kilometre in public transport and some exogenous variables, including the generalised costs per passenger-kilometre travelled by private transport. Among the latter is obviously a reflection of the physical and spatial-economic structure of the city.

The second equation expresses the influence of the weighted time needed for one passenger-kilometre (τ) (the reciprocal of the level of service) and the number of passenger-kilometres on the total economic cost of public transport:

$$K = K(\tau, P, exo) \tag{4.47}$$

As a third equation we add:

$$c = t + v\tau \tag{4.48}$$

where t is rate by passenger-kilometre in public transport and v the value of one unit of time for passengers travelled by public transport. Finally:

$$t = exo, \qquad \tau = exo \text{ (instrument variables)} \tag{4.49}$$

The structure of the simple model is given in Figure 4.9.

An 'appropriate' level of service and an 'appropriate' fare for public transport being the most important goals for the central or local government, transport operators should consider benefits and costs associated with such levels. Two approaches are open to them. First, they could adopt a policy of maximising profits (or minimising costs); and secondly, they could follow a benefit–cost approach. In what follows we shall see how the two differ with respect to users and operators of the transport system.

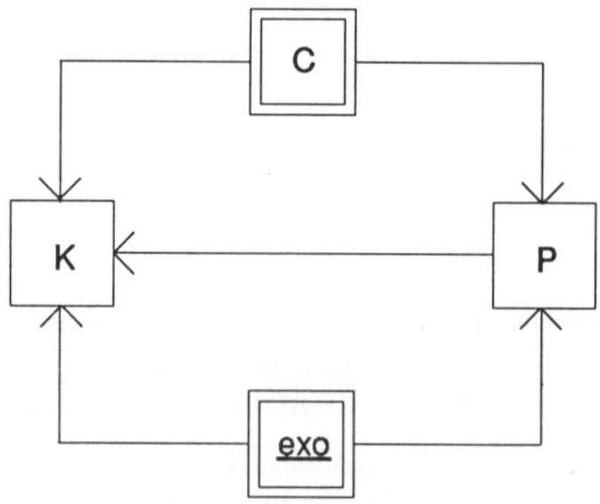

Figure 4.9 A simple economic transportation model

In the *maximum-profit approach* the income of the operator Y is, by definition, equal to:

$$Y = Pt - K \tag{4.50}$$

This income reaches an extremum for $dY = 0$; given that:

$$dPt = (P + t\frac{\partial P}{\partial t})dt + t\frac{\partial P}{\partial \tau}d\tau \tag{4.51}$$

and:

$$dK = \frac{\partial K}{\partial P} \cdot \frac{\partial P}{\partial t}dt + \frac{\partial K}{\partial P} \cdot \frac{\partial P}{\partial \tau}d\tau + \frac{\partial K}{\partial \tau}d\tau \tag{4.52}$$

$$dY = 0$$

if:

$$(1 + \frac{1}{\epsilon_t})t = \frac{\partial K}{\partial P} \tag{4.53}$$

and:

$$(t - \frac{\partial K}{\partial P})\frac{\partial P}{\partial \tau} = \frac{\partial K}{\partial \tau} \tag{4.54}$$

where ϵ_t is the rate elasticity, and which can be rewritten as:

$$(1 + \frac{1}{\epsilon_t})t = \frac{\partial K}{\partial P} \tag{4.55}$$

$$-\upsilon P = \frac{\partial K}{\partial \tau} \tag{4.56}$$

The first condition states that the marginal income from an additional passenger-kilometre should be equal to its marginal costs. Obviously this condition can be reached only if $\epsilon_t < -1$ which, in general, means very high rates.

The second condition says that the marginal improvements of the level of service should equal the marginal benefits to the user in the form of a reduction of generalised time costs.

In the *benefit-cost approach* the first elements to be taken into consideration as far as benefits are concerned is the sum of total expenditure (Pc) and the consumer's surplus. The latter can be expressed as:

$$C = \int_c^\infty P(c)dc \tag{4.57}$$

Total societal gross benefits thus equal:

$$B^G = Pc + \int_c^\infty P(c)dc \tag{4.58}$$

Pc contains an element $Pv\tau$ which is to be considered the value of the productive forces (time and human energy) sacrificed by the user in the transportation process. Indeed the net benefits to the user should be written as:

$$B^N = Pt + \int_c^\infty P(c)dc \tag{4.59}$$

The difference between benefits and costs Z reaches an extremum for:

$$dZ = dB^N - dK = 0 \tag{4.60}$$

or if:

$$t\frac{\partial P}{\partial t}dt + t\frac{\partial P}{\partial \tau}d\tau - vPd\tau = \frac{\partial K}{\partial P}\cdot\frac{\partial P}{\partial t}dt + \frac{\partial K}{\partial \tau}\cdot\frac{\partial P}{\partial \tau}dt + \frac{\partial K}{\partial \tau}d\tau$$

This condition is fulfilled if:

$$t = \frac{\partial K}{\partial P} \tag{4.61}$$

and:

$$-vP = \frac{\partial K}{\partial \tau} \tag{4.62}$$

We may summarise the results reached so far as shown in Table 4.3.

Table 4.3

	Rate	Level of service
BC approach	$t = \frac{\partial K}{\partial P}$	$-vP = \frac{\partial K}{\partial \tau}$
MP approach	$(1 + \frac{1}{\epsilon_t})t = \frac{\partial K}{\partial P}$	$-vP = \frac{\partial K}{\partial \tau}$

The way in which the optimum level of service is determined seems identical in the two approaches. The differences in outcome of the two approaches are now apparent. They are compared in Figures 4.10 and 4.11. From the graph in Figure 4.11, in the BC approach, the rates are clearly lower and consequently the demand (P) higher than in the MP approach. In the graph τ is replaced with l as a variable positively related to the level of service. The graph clearly shows that, since $P_{BC} > P_{MP}$, also $vP_{BC} > vP_{MP}$ and, the assumption being that $\partial^2 K \, \partial l^2 > 0, l_{BC} > l_{MP}$.

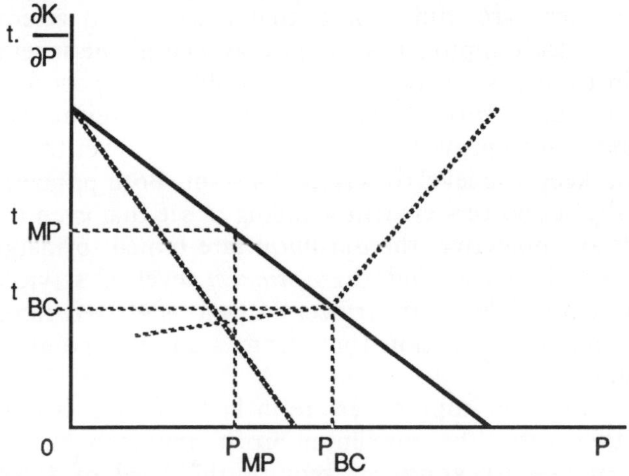

Figure 4.10 **Comparison of rate-setting in benefit–costs and maximum-profit approaches**

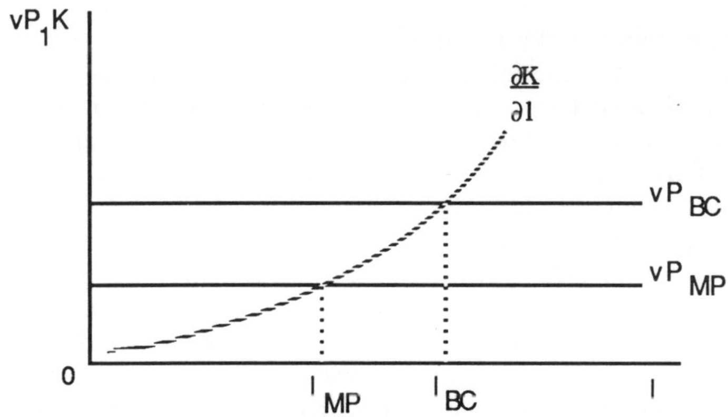

Figure 4.11 **Comparison of levels of service in thc BC and the MP approach**

To summarise, in the benefit–costs approach the level of service is higher, the rates are lower and consequently the number of passenger-kilometres (demand) is higher than in the maximum-profit approach.

Some further considerations So far, we have compared, with the help of an example, the welfare approach and the conventional maximum-profit approach applied to public transport. As could be expected, the outcomes of the first approach favoured the passengers, and that of the second, the operator.

However, there are some points that need special attention. The first is that in both approaches the fare as well as the level of service is used as instruments. In the practice of public transport management that is not the usual procedure. The policy will be either to keep the fare constant and improve the service level, or to lower the fares (even to zero) and keep the level of service constant. Both policies are often proposed, the supporters evidently failing to see that even if a societal optimum is the objective, the *optimum* fare (equal to marginal costs per passenger-kilometre) and the *optimum* level of service must be sought. An a priori level of service, as well as a fixed fare, are very likely to result in a situation that, from a societal point of view, is sub-optimum.

Note that the two approaches are in fact identical if the rates are given. In that case, the maximum-profit approach as well as the marginal benefit–cost approach require the level of service to be determined in such a way that the costs of marginal improvement are just equal to the benefits for the user (savings in generalised time). The two approaches differ not in the way the level of service is determined, but in the way the rates are fixed. Once again, in practice, there seems to be hardly any searching for a maximum profit or societal optimum, and none at all for an optimum rate.

Admittedly, the model used was a very simple one. Reality is much more complicated than can be expressed in a model. Often one hears that public transport fares should be low to induce a number of car users to shift to public transport, thus contributing to lower levels of pollution and energy use. The argument is only partly valid. Suppose many people were to shift to public transport, for instance, as a result of a reduction in fares (which could imply the need for an increase in capacity during peak hours). The improved level of service on the roads might well attract additional car travellers, a disappointing effect. Moreover, particularly in countries like the Netherlands and Denmark, people might well turn from their friendly bicycles to public transport, causing an adverse effect on the environment. And as far as energy use is concerned, one wonders if nowadays the real value of energy is not already sufficiently expressed in the price actually paid.

There are other arguments. One of them is that a good level of service and low rates are needed for the people who have no alternative. These 'captive passengers', i.e. children, senior citizens, people without a driver's licence and handicapped persons, should be provided with good public transport. However, that is a problem that could be solved efficiently by guaranteeing a minimum level of service in all zones of the urban area; it does not call for a very high level of service at very low rates everywhere.

There is one more point that needs attention. In the model the value of time was introduced as a constant, but in reality it is a function of income. People with high incomes attach a high value to marginal time and a relatively low value to marginal expenditures; an improvement of the level of service at constant rates therefore is more profitable to them than to people with lower incomes. A decrease of rates at a constant level of service is more attractive to the people with lower incomes than to the well-to-do, the former attaching a high value to marginal expenditures and a relatively low value to time. In public transport studies the fashion has become to work with an average value of time regardless of income, although this obviously is not justified by economic theory.

The exogenous variables In the introduction to this section considering the role of public transport in urban areas we pointed out that in urban areas with an 'inefficient' distribution of people and employment, the costs of public transport tend to be much higher than in urban areas where workplaces and places of residence are spread in a more 'efficient' pattern. The benefit–cost analysis has shown that the 'appropriate' levels of services and fares are related to marginal costs (see equations (4.56) and (4.57)), 'efficient' cities showing lower fares and/or higher levels of service than 'inefficient' ones. It follows that with fixed fares (as they are in the Netherlands) the optimisation procedure of the benefit–cost approach will inevitably result in levels of service that are distinctly lower in 'inefficient' than in 'efficient' cities. Moreover, such geographical factors as river-crossings may reduce the relative level of service in an area. Our analyses have made it clear that introduction of equal levels of service in all urban areas, in disregard of their shape and position of their cost functions, would be uneconomic and contrary to the interests of society.

There are other factors than fares and service level that affect modal split in Dutch urban areas. In a hilly town like Arnhem the bicycle is a less likely choice than in the flat cities of the western part of the country. So, in Arnhem, public transport will be more in demand. In the estimation of demand functions and cost functions, particularly if done on a cross-sectional basis, all these factors should be explicitly taken into account and quantified as far as possible.

A final remark The considerations so far have indicated that the marginal benefit–cost approach necessarily results in less favourable financial returns than the maximum-profit approach. This does not imply that there is a financial deficit if the marginal benefit–cost approach is followed. It only means that the financial results are less favourable. The actual financial result depends on the situation and shape of the demand function and the cost function. We know, however, that nowhere in the world, whatever the circumstances under which a public transport company works, are financial results favourable. This suggests that the costs functions and demand functions, probably mainly due to high levels of car ownership and unbalanced city structures, are so unfavourable that even in the maximum-profit approach hardly any positive results can be expected.

The optimum rates and optimum level of service resulting from the marginal benefit–cost approach correspond to an even more unfavourable financial position. However, if we accept the principle of the societal optimum, we should also accept the outcome even if this results in a considerable degree of subsidisation. Those subsidies would under these circumstances fulfil their proper role; they are, in this sense, *optimal* subsidies.

But we should also realise that the actual approach to public transport is far from being either a benefit–cost or a maximum-profit approach. Therefore, we may doubt whether the *present* subsidies fulfil their proper role.

An empirical approach

A study of allocation systems After the preceding theoretical considerations, it seems appropriate to demonstrate to what extent these considerations can be translated into an approach that enables us to tackle real-world problems. Following a short description of the problems of urban public transport in the Netherlands, it will be shown how the marginal-benefit approach could be applied to these problems. This does not mean that a final solution to the problem which is mainly a financial one is presented, but rather more to show that the approach is operational as far as the optimisation of the level of service at given fares is concerned. An extension of the approach to the simultaneous optimisation of the level of service and the fares is just one step further, and one that can be made without major difficulties.

As in many other countries in the world, public transport in the Netherlands has lately been suffering severe losses. Particularly in the 1970s the subsidies granted to urban public transport increased rapidly, at an average rate of some 15 per cent a year. At present they take up 1 per cent of the Netherlands gross national product. According to TRRL (1980), in percentages of operating costs, the Dutch subsidies to public transport are among the highest in the developed world.

According to an agreement in operation since 1975, the central government has reimbursed in full and automatically all losses on urban public transport incurred by municipalities. The government hoped to gain control of local budgets by demanding that local authorities should submit all changes in operations involving costs for approval. However, such a procedure proved to interfere too much with the details of local responsibility.

The Ministry of Public Works and the local authorities are now studying various allocation systems by which to quantify the appropriate level of service for each municipality and on that basis to calculate what deficits can be compensated, the responsibility for routeing and frequencies being left to local operators. A basic study considering these matters in detail was commissioned from the Netherlands Economic Institute and the Institute of Public Administration in Washington, DC.

By the terms of reference of the study, the allocation system has to satisfy the following policy objectives:

1. to establish a system of agreed standards to allow the equitable allocation of resources among Dutch cities such that the level of service provided in each city be perceived as appropriate to its needs and conditions;
2. to maximise the contribution of urban public transport to social well-being;
3. the method of relating levels of services and subsidies should be such as to allow sensitive responses to external policy objectives;
4. the system of standards should be capable of establishing the 'appropriate' level of service without reference to a budget constraint but also of adapting it to budget limitations.

In the first stage of the study the objectives were discussed and such methodological issues as the definition of level-of-service indicators and criteria for evaluation dealt with. Summaries were presented in 1981 at the PTRC's Summer Annual Meeting (Garden, Hockert and

Rühl, 1981) and to the Transportation Research Board (Fitch *et al.* 1981). The preceding sections of this chapter have provided a theoretical background for the problem in hand. In the second stage of the study a number of allocation systems were developed and tested on empirical data.

The present section deals with the methodology of the so-called Incremental Benefit–Cost Method, a discrete version of the marginal benefit–cost approach, which has been elaborated by the Netherlands Economic Institute. The basic principles of the method are next discussed and the quantitative model is presented. Finally, the procedure for allocating subsidies is outlined.

Principles of the incremental benefit–cost approach

Theory and practice: The fundamental question to be solved is how, in practice, the benefit–cost ratio of public urban transport can be determined. There are few conceptual problems on the cost side: the cost functions of urban public transport can be formulated unambiguously and, in principle, most of the data required can be taken from the accounts of the companies involved. True, as stated earlier, the financial accounting figures will have to be transformed into economic-cost data. Rather than the historical cost of rolling-stock, for instance, the replacement value should be used.

On the benefit side things are more complex. There are all sorts of benefits of public transport, and no 'account' is kept of them. Benefits to public transport ridership can be measured in terms of weighted travel time and travel cost, influenced by regularity and comfort. Some benefits spring from changes in modal split: a decline in car traffic will improve the urban environment (pollution, noise and safety). Others fit in with the societal and spatial objectives of municipalities such as making urban amenities accessible to all groups of the population and using public transport as a structuring element in spatial planning. The development of a formula for quantifying the benefits of public transport forms the hard core of the proposed allocation system.

'Integral' vs 'incremental' approach: To obtain a complete comparative survey of all relevant aspects of the demand for and supply of public transport in the municipalities involved the allocation system would have to calculate the total social benefits of urban public transport. That is practically impossible, however. In cost–benefit analysis two situations are compared, one with and one without the provision in question, the differences in costs and benefits determining the viability of the project. A large town without public transport may be theoretically possible, but calculating all the consequences for

other modes of transport and all social and spatial effects for a situation in which there is no public transport available is hardly a realistic exercise. Moreover, the absolute level of public transport provisions, and the benefits and costs involved, depend on a large number of specific characteristics of the municipalities. Think, for instance, of the *structure* of a town, which is largely determined by its history; and traffic and transport *policy*, as well as social and spatial policy, may also vary from one town to another.

There is no way to combine all these factors in one system. Such an allocation system would be unsuitable for practical and quantitative application. The system should allow, however, for the introduction of municipality-specific aspects by means of parameters.

For the reasons mentioned, the allocation system presented here starts from the level of service in the actual situation. This level is the outcome of a long period of development, in which each municipality has endeavoured to adjust the size, structure and service of its public transport as well as possible to its specific spatial and socio-economic features and political circumstances. There is no reason to assume that the actual level of service should be much further removed from what would be desirable from the social point of view in one municipality than in another; on the other hand, appreciation may be different.

Once the actual level of service is accepted, the question is whether *changes* in respect of the present situation move in the right direction. In other words, the allocation system to be applied becomes an incremental one. The benefit–cost ratio then refers to *changes* in the level of provision. By applying the benefit–cost principle in an incremental way, the system will eventually tend towards an equilibrium with optimum benefit–cost ratios, in which socio-economically desirable conditions have come about in the country as a whole and in the individual towns.

The incremental approach is preferable not only because, in contrast to the integral approach, it does envisage the quantification of social benefits, but also because it responds more readily to (fast-) changing (external) situations. Moreover, if the actual situation is chosen as a starting-point, hard to compute aspects of spatial policy with respect to transport and traffic, and social and spatial objectives, are implicitly taken into account.

Categories of benefits: The benefits of changes in the level of service can be split into two main groups, namely internal benefits, accruing to the users of traffic and transport systems, and external benefits or the benefits to the urban environment and the spatial structure. In the examples, below, the effects of an improvement in the level of service are illustrated, but the reasoning holds, *mutatis mutandis*, also for a deterioration.

Benefits to the users of traffic and transport systems: These include not only the benefits to public transport ridership, but also the benefits, if any, to users of other transport modes, should the change in the level of service entail a shift in modal split. The smoother dispatch of car traffic as a result of improved public transport comes to mind.

External benefits: A distinction could be made between direct and indirect external benefits. If an improvement in the level of service entails fewer car trips, direct external benefits may be enjoyed because noise, vibrations, toxic emissions, foul odour, etc. diminish. One should consider, however, that improved public transport also attracts those who so far have used their bicycles; the net result therefore is not, a priori, certain. Indirect external benefits refer to the function of public transport as a structuring element in spatial planning, especially for maintaining the economic and social significance of town centres.

The benefits falling to the users of traffic and transport systems can be quantified with reasonable accuracy; theories and methods developed in countless cost-benefit analyses of traffic and transport projects ensure that. Measuring external benefits is more difficult. Admittedly, this category of benefits has been given ample attention lately, but whether in the present stage of knowledge there is a fast and simple way to calculate them for all municipalities concerned is doubtful. That is true, in particular, of indirect spatial effects of changes in the level of service, which in the nature of things can only become visible in the long run.

One should keep in mind that the external benefits cannot (yet) be assessed by observing and appreciating consumers' behaviour through the workings of the market mechanism, but can only be inferred from judgements by the authorities. In terms of cost-benefit analysis, the exclusion of external effects implies that the benefit-cost ratio will be underestimated. It is for central government to decide, in consultation with the local authorities, what benefit-cost ratio warrants additional subsidisation, or to put it otherwise, what benefit-cost ratio the added service should at least satisfy. This marginal benefit-cost ratio is sometimes called 'pass mark' or 'threshold value', following the system developed in British practice. When the threshold value is known, cost-benefit analysis can help to determine, for each municipality, the appropriate level of service, which is in fact the level for which the marginal benefit-cost ratio is equal to this threshold value. Should the government be unable to determine a threshold, the cost-benefit ratio can only serve as a *distribution key* for a given total budget.

The benefit–cost model

Principles: The proposed model is concerned with the distribution of a given total budget; the distribution key is the benefit–cost ratio of changes in the level of service. In measuring the benefits of changes in the level of service, the external benefits will be abstracted from in this paper, only those benefits to users being taken into account.

As will be explained below, users' benefits can be appreciated in money terms on the generalised cost principle. The generalised costs of transportation contain both the money costs and the travel time, the latter expressed in money. Because the public transport rates have been harmonised in the Netherlands (van Dam, 1981), money costs play no part in the allocation, so that the generalised time concept can be used as a measure of users' benefits.

Indication of the level of service: Changes in the level of service can be 'translated' into changes of generalised travel time, namely:

(a) changes in speed affect in-vehicle time;
(b) changes in frequency affect waiting-times at the stops;
(c) changes in the routes affect walking-times to and from stops;
(d) changes in stop density affect walking-times to and from stops as well as riding speed.

Using the 'official' values for travel time savings, one can estimate users' benefits. These benefits can be assigned to various categories of users:

(a) travellers who already used public transport before the improvement;
(b) travellers who change from another travel mode to public transport;
(c) 'new' travellers who because of the improvement are making trips they had not undertaken before;
(d) users of other modes the quality of which has improved by a decline in demand due to the shift towards public transport.

With respect to the last-mentioned category, a distinction should be made between the car and other alternative modes of transportation. One can imagine that better public transport means less congestion and thus benefits to the 'remaining' car users. Preliminary calculations carried out for a medium-size Dutch town have indicated that the benefits accruing to car traffic come to no more than a tiny percentage of the total benefits (which is why they have been neglected in the present model). The benefits of an improved level of service to public transport users can be accounted to existing ridership and to new ridership generated by the improvement.

The incremental benefits and costs: If the demand function in the neighbourhood of the actual level of service is supposed to be linear, the incremental benefits can be written as:

$$\frac{\Delta B}{\Delta T} = (P + 1/2\Delta P)VOT \tag{4.63}$$

where P = existing travel demand in number of trips (it was earlier suggested that number of passenger-kilometres would be a better measure but figures on this score are unfortunately not available);
ΔP = generated travel demand;
ΔT = changes in (not generalised) travel time;
VOT = the value of time.

Equation (4.63) can be rewritten as:

$$\frac{\Delta B}{\Delta F} = \frac{\Delta B}{\Delta T} \cdot \frac{\Delta T}{\Delta F} = \frac{\Delta T}{\Delta F}(P + 1/2\Delta P)VOT \tag{4.64}$$

Now savings in travel (waiting) time ΔT will decrease with an increase of frequency. A functional relationship between the rate of frequency change and the change of waiting-times has been tested on Dutch data:

$$\Delta T = C_1 \ln\left(1 + \frac{\Delta F}{F}\right) \tag{4.65}$$

Substitution of (4.65) into (4.64) results in:

$$\frac{\Delta B}{\Delta F} = \frac{C_1 \ln\left(1 + \frac{\Delta F}{F}\right)}{\Delta F} \cdot (P + 1/2\Delta P)VOT \tag{4.66}$$

If the relative change in frequency is $\Delta F/F$, the change in ridership due to a change in frequency is:

$$\Delta P = \epsilon \frac{\Delta F}{F} \cdot P \tag{4.67}$$

Next, the model should describe the quantitative relationship between a change in (average) frequency and the corresponding change in travel demand. Because it is simple and easy to apply, the elasticity concept has been chosen to express this relationship. Empirical evidence is scarce in the Netherlands, but the TRRL (Transport and Road Research Laboratory) Report, *The Demand for Public Transport* (1980), provides a framework for estimating city-specific frequency-elasticity values, by city size, peak-hour intensity and mode of transport. Moreover, the frequency elasticity depends on the actual level of frequency; the following equation has been estimated:

$$\epsilon = C_2 - C_3 \ln F \tag{4.68}$$

Combining equations (4.68) and (4.67) we find:

$$\Delta P = P\frac{\Delta F}{F}(C_2 - C_3 \ln F) \tag{4.69}$$

Substitution in equation (4.66) results in:

$$\frac{\Delta B}{\Delta F} = \frac{C_1 \ln (1 + \frac{\Delta F}{F})}{(\Delta F/F)} \cdot \frac{\left\{P + \frac{1}{2}P\frac{\Delta F}{F}(C_2 - C_3 \ln F)\right\} VOT}{F} \tag{4.70}$$

It follows that:

$$\frac{dB}{dF} = \lim_{\Delta F \to 0} \frac{\Delta B}{\Delta F} = \frac{C_1 P \cdot VOT}{F} \tag{4.71}$$

As far as the (economic) costs are concerned, frequency changes are proportional to the number of vehicle-kilometres (VKM); the costs of changes in frequency are then determined by city-specific unit-cost values per vehicle-kilometre. We thus may write:

$$\Delta K = \frac{\Delta F}{F}k \cdot VKM \tag{4.72}$$

or:

$$\frac{dK}{dF} = \lim_{\Delta F \to 0} \frac{\Delta K}{\Delta F} = \frac{k \cdot VKM}{F} \tag{4.73}$$

The marginal benefit–cost ratio thus can be written as:

$$MBCR = \frac{dB}{dF}\bigg/\frac{dK}{dP} = \frac{C_1 P \cdot VOT}{k \cdot VKM} = C_4 \frac{P}{K} \text{(compare equations (4.62) and (4.56))} \qquad (4.74)$$

where P is the number of trips, K is the total variable operating cost, and C_4 is a city-specific constant.

Towards a practical allocation system

Constraints: The marginal benefit–cost ratio is not the only criterion used in the allocation of public transport subsidies to municipalities. A number of constraints are imposed to ensure an equitable distribution of the subsidy budget.

Minimum level of service is fixed by the national government. Discrimination by size of municipality may be desirable. The costs of maintaining the minimum level of service must always be reimbursed and should therefore be either left out of the distribution scheme or implicitly incorporated in it.

The fixed costs are always guaranteed; they are essentially, at least in the short term, dependent on the volume of traffic, at any rate for modest changes in the level of service.

The maximum permissible discontinuity is in respect of previous years. On various socio-political and organisational considerations, it may be preferable not to change subsidies to certain communities – in either sense – too drastically. Limits can be set, for instance, to the effect that the subsidy (to take care of variable costs) has to be at least x per cent of that of the previous year, or that the level of service, expressed in average frequency, must not drop by more than y per cent in respect of the frequency of the preceding year. By the same token, an upper limit can be imposed to the percentage increase of municipal subsidies or levels of service.

In sum, the allocation system proposed in this section aims at maximising the net social benefits by the application of the marginal benefit–cost principle, within the marginal conditions set before.

The functioning of the system: Part of the national subsidy budget is reallocated, municipalities with a low marginal benefit–cost ratio (and hence a higher level of service) having to make some sacrifice in favour of municipalities with a high marginal benefit–cost ratio (and hence a low level of service). The budget to be allocated by the MBCR (Marginal Benefit–Cost Ratio) method is determined by first reducing all municipalities by the maximum permissible percentage. The level of service resulting from the maximum permissible reduction is expressed in average frequency. The corresponding demand and supply situation is then determined, among other things, with the help of demand elasticities related to the frequency level.

The new transport volume and the economic supply costs together determine the 'initial values' of the MBCRs which, in turn, serve to decide on the priority ranking by which the portion of the subsidies to be reallocated will be paid out. The essence of the allocation system is that it aims at harmonising the social benefits to the users and the quality of public transport in the municipalities concerned by adjusting the level of services. The step-by-step process consists in making the highest MBCR equal to the highest but one by increasing the supply in vehicle-kilometres (account being taken of the increase in demand). On the basis of the financial costs applying to the municipality in question, the budget required for the increase is determined and allocated. The data pertaining to the new situation are next computed (average frequencies, elasticities, etc.).

Subsequently the quality in the two municipalities now possessing the highest MBCR is raised to the level of the municipality ranking highest but two. This process is repeated until either the budget is exhausted or all municipalities have the same MBCR, provided that the maximum permissible discontinuity – upper limit – is not reached. In the latter case, the quality in all municipalities can be improved further; in the former case, there will remain differences among municipalities which, however, can be reduced in subsequent years.

The procedure for one step is the following: write for the start value of the marginal benefit–cost ratio:

$$MBCR_1 = \frac{C_1 P_1 VOT}{k \cdot VKM_1} \tag{4.75}$$

and for the value to be reached:

$$MBCR_2 = \frac{C_1 P_2 VOT}{k \cdot VKM_2} \tag{4.76}$$

Since both ratios are known, their ratio is also known. The problem is then to find the change in frequence necessary to reach the desired ratio:

$$\rho = \frac{MBCR_1}{MBCR_2} \tag{4.77}$$

We write:

$$\rho = \frac{P_2}{VKM_2} \cdot \frac{VKM_1}{P_1} = \frac{1 + (\Delta P)/P}{1 + (\Delta VKM)/VKM} \tag{4.78}$$

Since:

$$F = C_2 \frac{VKM}{RL}, \; \Delta F = C_2 \frac{\Delta VKM}{RL}$$

and thus:

$$\frac{\Delta F}{F} = \frac{\Delta VKM}{VKM} \tag{4.79}$$

Further, we may write:

$$\Delta P = \epsilon \frac{\Delta F}{F} \cdot P \tag{4.80}$$

Substituting equations (4.79) and (4.80) into (4.78), we find:

$$\rho = \frac{1 + \epsilon(\Delta F)/F}{1 + (\Delta F)/F} \tag{4.81}$$

or:

$$\frac{\Delta F}{F} = \frac{1 - \rho}{\rho - \epsilon} \tag{4.82}$$

By substitution of $\epsilon = C_3 - C_1 \ln F$ (cf. equation (4.68) into (4.82), it becomes:

$$\boxed{\frac{\Delta F}{F} = \frac{1 - \rho}{\rho - C_3 + C_4 \ln F}} \tag{4.83}$$

In this function ρ, F, C_3 and C_4 are known, so that ΔF can be computed. The procedure is illustrated in Figure 4.12.

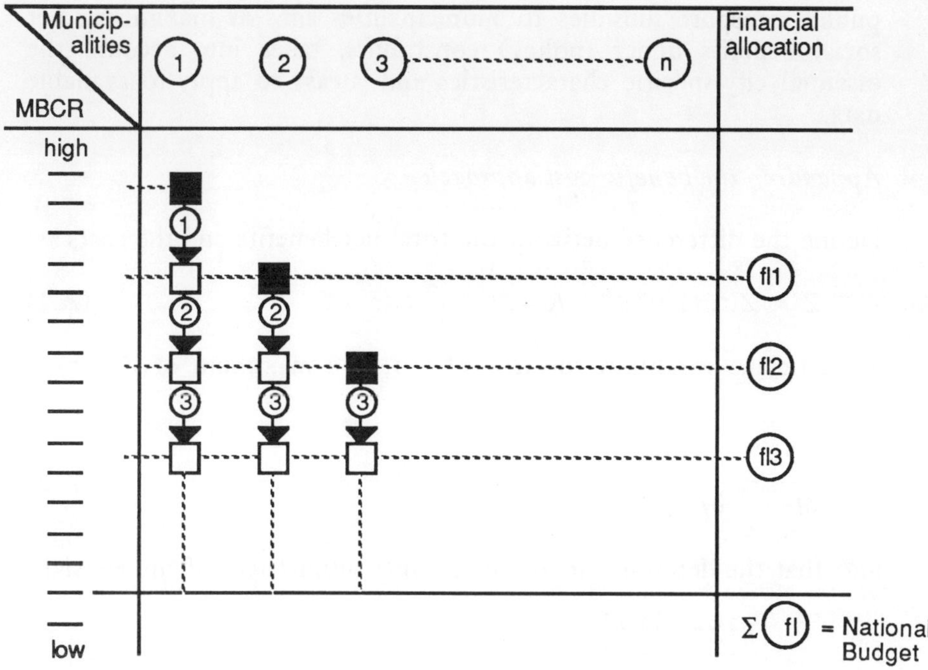

▪ Initial (start) value of MBCR.
○ Step-by-step recalculation of MBCR.
□ Value of MBCR after allocation.
fl Financial allocation to municipalities.

Figure 4.12 The allocation procedure

Calculations: The allocation system, including (policy) constraints and the marginal benefit–cost model, has been applied to the available data of the 50 Dutch municipalities. The calculations do not require more than the following (city-specific) variables:

(a) number of passengers;
(b) route length;
(c) number of vehicle-kilometres;
(d) unit cost;
(e) set of constants.

The calculation scheme, which is simple, has been programmed on a pocket calculator; alternative assumptions can be evaluated in an easy way.

The conclusion is that the system proposed for allocating urban public transport subsidies to municipalities aims at maximising net social benefits under (policy) constraints, takes into account the essential city-specific characteristics and is easy to apply to available data.

Appendix: the benefit–cost approach

Define the difference between the total net benefits and the costs as:

$$Z = Z(t, \tau) = B^N - K = Pt + \int_c^\infty Pdc - K \qquad \text{(A.1)}$$

A sufficient condition for (t^*, τ^*) to be a maximum of $Z(t, \tau)$ is that:†

$$\frac{\partial Z^*}{\partial t} = \frac{\partial Z^*}{\partial \tau} = 0 \qquad \text{(A.2)}$$

and that the determinants of the leading submatrices of the Hessian:

$$H = \begin{bmatrix} \dfrac{\partial^2 Z^*}{\partial t^2} & \dfrac{\partial^2 Z^*}{\partial t \partial \tau} \\ \dfrac{\partial^2 Z^*}{\partial t \partial \tau} & \dfrac{\partial^2 Z^*}{\partial \tau^2} \end{bmatrix} \qquad \text{(A.3)}$$

alternate in sign, the first being negative. We first set:

$$\frac{\partial Z}{\partial t} = \frac{\partial Z}{\partial \tau} = 0$$

This first-order partial derivatives are equal to:‡

$$\frac{\partial Z}{\partial t} = \frac{\partial P}{\partial t} t + P - P\frac{\partial c}{\partial t} - \frac{\partial K}{\partial t}$$

$$= \frac{\partial P}{\partial c}\frac{\partial c}{\partial t} t + P - P\frac{\partial c}{\partial t} - \frac{\partial K}{\partial P} \partial P \partial c \frac{\partial c}{\partial t}$$

$$= \frac{\partial P}{\partial c} (t - \frac{\partial K}{\partial P}) = 0 \qquad \text{(A.4)}$$

†∂Z^* ∂t denotes the value of the partial derivative of $Z(t, \tau)$ with respect to t evaluated at (t^*, τ^*).
‡∂c, $\partial t = 1$ and ∂c, $\partial \tau = v$.

$$\frac{\partial Z}{\partial \tau} = \frac{\partial P}{\partial \tau} t - P\frac{\partial c}{\partial \tau} - \left(\frac{\partial K}{\partial \tau}\right)^{\tau}$$

$$= \frac{\partial P}{\partial c}\frac{\partial c}{\partial \tau} t - P\frac{\partial c}{\partial \tau} - \left(\frac{\partial K}{\partial P}\frac{\partial P}{\partial c}\frac{\partial c}{\partial \tau} + \left(\frac{\partial K}{\partial \tau}\right)^{\mathrm{D}}\right)$$

$$= \upsilon\frac{\partial P}{\partial c}\left(t - \frac{\partial K}{\partial P}\right) - \upsilon P - \left(\frac{\partial K}{\partial \tau}\right)^{\mathrm{D}} = 0 \tag{A.5}$$

where:

$$\left(\frac{\partial K}{\partial \tau}\right)^{\tau} = \left(\frac{\partial K}{\partial \tau}\right)^{1\mathrm{D}} + \left(\frac{\partial K}{\partial \tau}\right)^{\mathrm{D}} \tag{A.6}$$

and:

$$\left(\frac{\partial K}{\partial \tau}\right)^{1\mathrm{D}} = \frac{\partial K}{\partial P}\frac{\partial P}{\partial c}\frac{\partial c}{\partial \tau} \tag{A.7}$$

Suppose that $\partial P \; \partial c < 0$, then solving the systems of equations $t = \partial K \; \partial P$ and $(\partial K \; \partial \tau)^{\mathrm{D}} = \tau P$ simultaneously with respect to t and τ we get (t^*, τ^*). With $\partial Z^* \; \partial t = \partial Z^* \; \partial \tau = 0$, the necessary condition for an extremum is satisfied. The second-order partial derivatives can be written as:

$$\frac{\partial^2 Z}{\partial t^2} = t\frac{\partial^2 P}{\partial c^2} + \frac{\partial P}{\partial c} - \frac{\partial^2 K}{\partial P^2}\left(\frac{\partial P}{\partial c}\right)^2 - \frac{\partial K}{\partial P}\frac{\partial^2 P}{\partial c^2}$$

$$= \left(t - \frac{\partial K}{\partial P}\right)\frac{\partial^2 P}{\partial c^2} + \frac{\partial P}{\partial c} - \frac{\partial^2 K}{\partial P^2}\left(\frac{\partial P}{\partial c}\right)^2 \tag{A.8}$$

$$\frac{\partial^2 Z}{\partial \tau^2} = t\frac{\partial^2 P}{\partial c^2}\upsilon^2 - \frac{\partial P}{\partial c}\upsilon^2 - \frac{\partial^2 K}{\partial P^2}\left(\frac{\partial P}{\partial c}\right)^2\upsilon^2 - \frac{\partial K}{\partial P}\frac{\partial^2 P}{\partial c^2}\upsilon^2 - \left(\frac{\partial^2 K}{\partial \tau^2}\right)^{\mathrm{D}}$$

$$= \left(t - \frac{\partial K}{\partial P}\right)\frac{\partial^2 P}{\partial c^2}\upsilon^2 - \upsilon^2\left(\frac{\partial P}{\partial c} + \frac{\partial^2 K}{\partial P^2}\left(\frac{\partial P}{\partial c}\right)^2\right) - \left(\frac{\partial^2 K}{\partial \tau^2}\right)^{\mathrm{D}} \tag{A.9}$$

and:

$$\frac{\partial^2 Z}{\partial t \partial \tau} = t\frac{\partial^2 P}{\partial c^2}v - \frac{\partial^2 K}{\partial P^2}\left(\frac{\partial P}{\partial c}\right)^2 v - \frac{\partial K}{\partial P}\frac{\partial^2 P}{\partial c^2}v$$

$$= \left(t - \frac{\partial K}{\partial P}\right)\frac{\partial^2 P}{\partial c^2}v - \frac{\partial^2 K}{\partial P^2}\left(\frac{\partial P}{\partial c}\right)^2 v \tag{A.10}$$

Evaluating (A.8), (A.9) and (A.10) at the (t^*, τ^*), we find:

$$\frac{\partial^2 Z^*}{\partial t^2} = \frac{\partial P}{\partial c}\left(1 - \frac{\partial^2 K}{\partial P^2}\frac{\partial P}{\partial c}\right) \tag{A.11}$$

$$\frac{\partial^2 Z^*}{\partial \tau^2} = -v^2\left(\frac{\partial P}{\partial c} + \frac{\partial^2 K}{\partial P^2}\left(\frac{\partial P}{\partial c}\right)^2\right) - \left(\frac{\partial^2 K}{\partial \tau^2}\right)^{D} \tag{A.12}$$

and:

$$\frac{\partial^2 Z^*}{\partial t \partial \tau} = -\frac{\partial^2 K}{\partial P^2}\left(\frac{\partial P}{\partial c}\right)^2 v \tag{A.13}$$

Expressions (A.11), (A.12) and A.13) are the elements of the Hessian (A.3). The determinant of the leading submatrix of order 1 x 1 is (A.11). A necessary condition for:

$$\frac{\partial P}{\quad}\left(1 - \frac{\partial^2 K}{\partial P^2}\frac{\partial P}{\partial c}\right) < 0$$

is:

$$\frac{\partial^2 K}{\partial P^2} > \frac{1}{\partial P\, \partial c} \text{ if } \frac{\partial P}{\partial c} < 0 \tag{A.14}$$

A sufficient one is:

$$\frac{\partial^2 K}{\partial P^2} > 0 \text{ if } \frac{\partial P}{\partial c} < 0 \tag{A.15}$$

The determinant of the leading submatrix of order 2 x 2 is:

$$|H| = -\left(\frac{\partial^2 K}{\partial \tau^2}\right)^{D}\left(\frac{\partial P}{\partial c} - \frac{\partial^2 K}{\partial P^2}\left(\frac{\partial P}{\partial c}\right)^2\right) - v^2\left(\frac{\partial P}{\partial c}\right)^2 \tag{A.16}$$

A necessary condition for $|H| > 0$ is:

$$\left(\frac{\partial^2 K}{\partial \tau^2}\right)^D > \frac{-v^2(\partial P/\partial c)^2}{\frac{\partial P}{\partial c} - \frac{\partial^2 K}{\partial P^2}\left(\frac{\partial P}{\partial c}\right)^2} > 0 \tag{A.17}$$

because the nominator and denominator are both negative.

Conclusion: a sufficient condition for (t^*, τ^*) to be a maximum of $Z(t, \tau)$ is:

$$\left.\begin{array}{l} t = \frac{\partial K}{\partial P} \text{ and } \left(\frac{\partial K}{\partial \tau}\right)^D = vP \\ \\ \frac{\partial^2 K}{\partial P^2} > \frac{1}{\partial P/\partial c} \\ \\ \left(\frac{\partial^2 K}{\partial \tau^2}\right)^D > -v^2 / \frac{1}{\partial P/\partial c} - \frac{\partial^2 K}{\partial P^2} \end{array}\right\}$$

References

van den Berg, L., Boeckhout, Sj., and Vijverberg, K. (1978), *Urban Development and Policy Response in the Netherlands*, Foundations of Empirical Economic Research, No. 2, Netherlands Economic Institute, Rotterdam.

van den Berg, L., Drewett, R., Klaassen, L.H., Rossi, A. and Vijverberg, C.H.T. (1981), *Urban Europe: A Study of Growth and Decline*, Oxford: Pergamon.

van den Berg, L. and Klaassen, L.H. (1978), *Financing Urban Systems*, Foundations of Empirical Economic Research, No. 2, Netherlands Economic Institute, Rotterdam.

van den Berg, L., Klaassen, L.H. and Vijverberg, C.H.T. (1975), *Evaluation of Governmental Welfare Policy by Means of a Social Welfare Function*, Rotterdam: FEER/NEI, 1975/7.

van Dam, F. (1981), 'Fare and ticket harmonization in the Netherlands', PTRC Summer Annual Meeting, August 1981.

De Langen, M. and Verster, A.C.P. (1976), 'Verband tussen bereikbaarheid en vestigingsgedrag', *Colloquium Vervoers-planologisch Speurwerk*, Delft: Institut voor Stedebouwkundig onderzoek.

Fitch, L., Eckman, A., Klaassen, L.H., Garden, J. and Rühl, A. (1981), *Service Levels of Urban Public Transport in the Netherlands*, Transportation Research Board, Washington.

Garden, J., Hoekert, M. and Rühl, A. (1981), *Public Transport – Level of Service and Financial Support*, PTRC Summer Annual Meeting, August 1981.

Hensher, D.H. (1976), 'The structure of journeys and nature of travel patterns', *Environment and Planning, A*, vol. 8, pp. 655–72; see also literature quoted there.

Institut d'Aménagement et d'Urbanisme de la Région Parisienne (1966), *Les Transports urbains et leurs usagers en région de Paris, Vol. 4.5, Déplacements isochrones. Diffusion des travailleurs dans Paris. Choix des moyens de transport par les usagers*, Paris, April.

Klaassen, L.H. (1969), *Voorkeuren in het personenvervoer, Verkeerstechniek*, The Hague: Koninklijk Institut von Ingenieurs.

Klaassen, L.H. (1979), *A Shopping Model*, FEER/NEI, 1974/3; in this report the supply side of shopping facilities is treated.

Klaassen, L.H. (1982), *The Proper Role of Subsidies for Public Transport*, PTRC Summer Annual Meeting, August 1981.

Klaassen, L.H., Molle, W.T.M. and Paelinck, J.H.P. (eds) (1981), *The Dynamics of Urban Development*, Aldershot: Gower.

Klaassen, L.H. and Otten, G.R. (1980), *The Valuation of Costs of Urban Public Transport and its Impact on the Distribution of the Subsidy Fund over Urban Public Transport Operators*, Netherlands Economic Institute, Rotterdam.

Klaassen, L.H. and Paelinck, J.H.P. (1981), 'Energy and transport', NEI paper presented at the Fourth International Transport Conference, Tokyo, 12–14 August.

Klaassen, L.H., Paelinck, J.H.P. and Wagenaar, S. (1979), *Spatial Systems*, Farnborough: Saxon House.

Service Levels of Urban Public Transport, a study commissioned by the Ministry of Transport and Public Works of the Netherlands; series of reports produced by the Ministry of Transport, Institute of Public Administration, Washington, DC/Netherlands Economic Institute, Rotterdam.

Steenbrink, P.A. (1974), *Optimization of Transport Networks*, New York: Wiley.

Transport and Road Research Laboratory (1980), *The Demand for Public Transport*.

5 The environment

5.1 The role of social equipment and environment in regional economic growth*

Introduction

As a result of developments in our society, environment and social factors play an increasingly important role in our economic thinking. When dealing with the impact of the development of social equipment on economic growth, it is not only desirable, but absolutely essential that the mutual relationships between milieu, social equipment and economic growth should be explored before the social infrastructure as such can be discussed. In view of the relatively complicated nature of these mutual relationships, the problem has been presented mathematically in an annexe. The main lines of thought reproduced in that annexe are as follows.

Mutual relationships between environment, social equipment and technico-economic capital

In order to reduce the problem to its essential terms and thus facilitate analysis, we introduce the concepts outlined below.

*See L.H. Klaassen, 'The role of social equipment and environment in regional economic growth' in A. Kuklinski (ed.), *Social Issues in Regional Policy and Regional Planning*, The Hague/Paris: Mouton, 1977.

Environmental capital By this we mean the quality of the natural environment as a whole: the flora, the fauna, the air, the water and the soil. We assume that human beings contribute to the reduction of the value of this capital by their productive activities and by all those activities which affect the diversity of the natural environment. We also assume, however, that humans are capable of so orienting their activities that the quality of this capital can be increased or improved. Consequently it is possible to avoid qualitative deterioration and to achieve improvement through well-directed human activity. At first sight, this statement may seem somewhat odd; what it is intended to convey is that humans must be regarded as capable of influencing nature – for example, by landscaping, reafforestation, the control of erosion and the prevention of natural disasters, and perhaps even by influencing the climate – in such a way as to increase the value of the natural capital. This point is often neglected in the emotional approach to environmental problems. For the purpose of our analysis, we must therefore emphasise that human activities do not only have an adverse effect on nature or simply prevent it from deteriorating; they may even help to increase the value of the natural environment.

Social capital We use the term 'social capital' to cover all the components of the social infrastructure, such as educational institutions, medical institutions, recreational facilities, the housing stock and cultural institutions, and social welfare institutions, such as old people's homes, institutions for handicapped persons, and so on. In general, it is probably true to say that the social infrastructure was for a long time regarded as unproductive; awareness of the fact that in the growth of society social equipment plays basically the same role as the environment and technico-economic capital is a recent phenomenon. We shall deal with this point more fully at a later stage.

Technico-economic capital This term covers all investments in industry, agriculture, trade and transport and in other activities not regarded as falling into the 'social' category. Obviously the borderline between the two categories cannot be very precise since, for example, social activities use the same transport infrastructure as technico-economic activities, even if often at different times. For the purposes of our general study, however, it will be assumed that the two categories can be kept quite distinct.

The three kinds of capital having thus been described, we now wish to introduce the realistic proposition that human beings are capable of influencing them. In the case of natural capital, this influence is known as environmental policy, and in the case of the other two it is called social policy and economic policy. We shall assume that these three policies are carried out in such a way that an optimal relationship between the three types of capital is obtained, a concept which requires further definition.

Before developing this idea, we must understand the mutual relationships between these three types of capital more clearly, always remembering that humans are capable of influencing each of these relationships. The analysis will have to show where and to what extent action is desirable.

The first relationsip is that between economic capital and environmental capital. Nothing much need be said about this. It is sufficiently well known that industrial and agricultural production, like transport, does much to spoil our environment. The effect on the environment of an increase in technico-economic capital is therefore negative. It is also clear that some activities contribute to pollution, with all its consequences, to a much greater extent than others and that any economic policy can and must take this into account. A region may refuse to permit certain activities and thus do something to reduce pollution. In many instances, however, the only result will be to move these activities to regions where environmental considerations play little part. This obviously means that the problem has merely been shifted. If we are really to take environmental policy seriously, we must go to the root of the matter; we shall revert to this point later.

The second relationship is that between social capital on the one hand, and environmental and technico-economic capital on the other hand. Unlike the first relationship, which is in fact a technical matter, this is a behavioural relationship which reflects the evaluation of elements of the social infrastructure. Any increase in technico-economic capital leads to higher incomes and hence to a greater demand for education, recreation, medical care, and so on. Economic growth thus results in a greater demand for, and therefore to a greater supply of, social infrastructure elements; consequently its influence is positive.

The same is basically true of the environment. At a given level of economic well-being, a superior kind of environment will attract people living in parts where the environment is less favourable and will thus lead to migratory movements. A very good example of such movements may be found in the Ruhr area, whose inhabitants, if they are financially in a position to do so, prefer to work elsewhere and therefore migrate to places where the environment is more favourable. In these places migrants thus strengthen the demand for social infrastructure elements.

The third and last relationship is that between technico-economic capital on the one hand and the environment and the social infrastructure on the other. The above remarks also apply, *mutatis mutandis*, to enterprises. For a modern industrial enterprise, not only will labour of a certain quality (the supply of which will depend on training and many other local facilities) be needed, but also facilities for staff recreation and relaxation. Here social and cultural facilities play an increasingly important part. An area with a high standard of social infrastructure will therefore be more attractive for the establishment of a new plant than one with a deficient infrastructure. The same is true of the environment. Not only are workers easier to find in areas with a favourable environment than in others, but the enterprise itself may, in areas with a good environment, create a better image for itself than it would have in a polluted milieu. Clearly, then, the influence is positive.

Final influences

The three relationships just described react upon each other, and it is therefore impossible to determine unequivocally whether the final influence exerted by a particular policy will be positive or negative. The diagram in Figure 5.1 may serve to clarify the situation. This diagram reproduces the relationships already described. All the influences are positive, with the exception of the impact of technico-economic capital on environment. It is precisely the negative factor which determines the overall influence of a given policy. The complicated nature of the problem appears most clearly when we consider environmental policy, which, on first analysis, has a favourable influence on the milieu itself. This improvement of the milieu leads to a strengthening of the social infrastructure and of the technico-economic capital. This last effect is in turn reinforced by an expansion of the social equipment. But the strengthening of the technico-economic capital has an adverse influence on environment. Even if all reciprocal influences are taken into consideration it does not appear

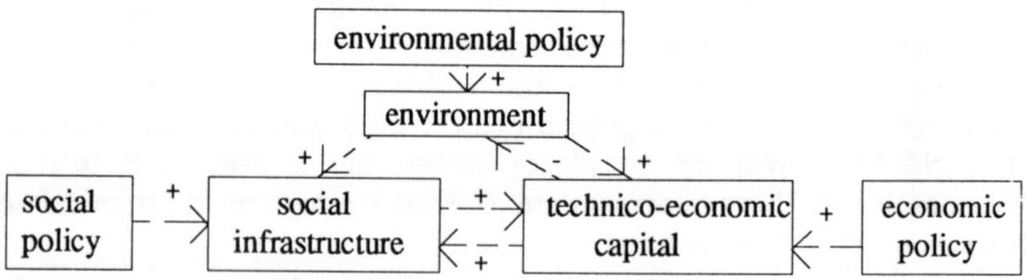

Figure 5.1 Interaction of policies

possible to determine, a priori, whether the overall influence of environmental policy is or is not favourable. The influence of such a policy is of course favourable as regards the social equipment and the technico-economic capital; but its final influence on the milieu itself remains uncertain.

In the mathematical appendix, all the influences of the three policies have been calculated; the conclusions are as follows:

1 The influence of an environmental policy on the milieu, and of an economic policy on the quality of the social equipment, is uncertain.
2 The influence of social policy and economic policy on environment is adverse.
3 All other influences are favourable.

The problem under discussion is therefore extremely complicated. Nevertheless, it is a fact that the influence of certain policies may confidently be described as uncertain or negative. Even a policy intended to strengthen the social infrastructure, a highly commendable purpose at first sight, could not be regarded as entirely positive on the above assumptions. It is clear, more particularly, that it will have adverse effects on the environment.

We thus know that the adverse and the uncertain effects arise because among all the effects an unfavourable influence emerges, namely the influence of economic growth on the milieu. It is therefore desirable to investigate what will happen on the assumption that this unfavourable effect is neutralised by administrative action, i.e. by the authorities' refusal to permit any but non-polluting activities. The diagram then assumes the shape as in Figure 5.2. The negative influence of economic growth on the milieu has disappeared and all the remaining effects are positive.

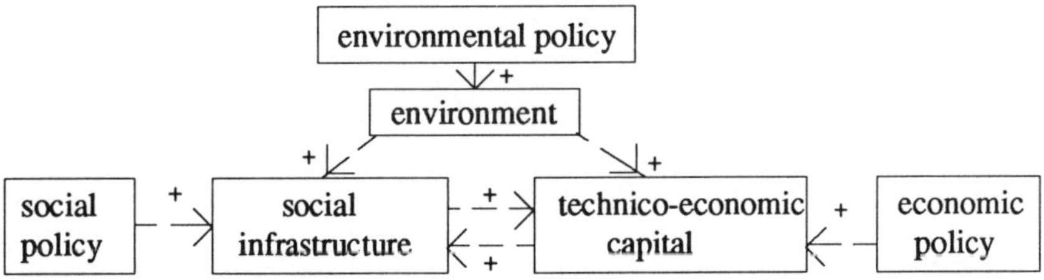

Figure 5.2 Corrected interaction of policies

The total effects are now as follows:

(a) social and economic policy measures have in the end no adverse impact on the environment;
(b) all other final influences are positive.

If we attempt to formulate this result comprehensively, it appears that the initial structure of the mutual relationships between the three factors studied implied an adverse influence of economic growth on the environment and this, in turn, led to a possible lack of coherence between social and economic policy on the one hand, and environmental policy on the other.

The objectives of the first two policies were therefore incompatible with those of an environmental policy. This external lack of coherence is avoided if economic growth is no longer allowed to affect the environment. All influences then become neutral or positive, and this re-establishes the coherence of the three policies.

Promotion of well-being

The foregoing considerations are a necessary introduction to the problem of the optimal distribution of the resources available for improving the environment, the social infrastructure and the economic capital. We shall make two assumptions in studying this problem. The first is that the milieu, the social equipment and the amount of technico-economic capital are the essential elements of our well-being. The second is that we have a certain amount available per unit of time in order to carry out our three policies – we assume that their relative importance is not yet known, but we know that in combination they are intended to promote well-being. We therefore have to determine how, having regard to the funds available, to the fact that well-being depends on three factors and to the reciprocal effects of these three factors, an optimal result may be obtained.

The analysis we have made leads us to the conclusion that, in using the available funds, allowance must be made for the indirect effects, so that when these effects are favourable, a smaller sacrifice of financial resources is required, and when they are not, the sacrifice will be larger. Formulated in terms of marginal utility, the principle may be expressed as follows: the relationship between two elements of the function of well-being – in terms of marginal utility – is not equal to the price ratio of these elements, but to the price ratio as corrected by the secondary effects caused by these elements. For example, the marginal utility of an environmental improvement is not equal to the value of the sum spent on it, but to that value less the favourable effects produced by the improvement on the social equipment and the technico-economic capital. Moreover, the marginal utility of an increment of technico-economic capital is not equal to the sums required for this purpose, but rather to this sum plus the value of the unfavourable effects on the environment and minus the value of the favourable effects on the social infrastructure. This means that we can no longer operate with the actual prices; instead we must use accounting prices, which represent the true social sacrifices required to achieve a certain improvement.

More detailed study of the role of social equipment

In what has been said above we arrived at the conclusion that to improve and expand social equipment is not merely an aim in itself, at least not if certain guarantees as regards the environment exist, but that such a policy also has a favourable effect on economic growth. This must be borne in mind as an additional advantage to be taken into account when the social infrastructure is programmed. Of late it has become customary in some quarters no longer to attach much importance to economic growth as such, but to assume that everything else takes precedence. In terms of our utility function, this would mean that the present situation is clearly sub-optimal, since the implication is that the technico-economic capital has been developed to such an extent that its marginal utility has become nil, whereas the marginal utility of the milieu and of the social infrastructure remains positive. It follows that the aim should be to reduce our economic well-being in favour of social and environmental well-being.

This theory may possibly be valid in the case of certain individuals, but to apply it as a general rule to countries or regions would seem to be a very strange proceeding. In many countries the level of economic well-being is so low that it would be absurd to tell their inhabitants that economic growth is devoid of meaning and that they had better think of values of a higher order. To do so would mean a complete failure to understand the problems of our fellow-men. For even within the confines of our Western world there are some regions where the level of economic well-being is clearly lower than in others.

After all, the feeling of well-being is purely relative and weakens when people find that by comparison others are more favourably placed. It might even be argued that it is the disagreeable awareness of lagging behind others, rather than the agreeable feeling of growth itself, which gives rise to the desire for growth. Even those who believe that God created humankind on entirely the wrong lines will have to accept humans as they are. And, such as they are, they desire a balanced state of well-being, where the environment, economic well-being and social circumstances are present in the right proportions. The means available to them for increasing their well-being must be distributed in balanced fashion among these three elements, so that progress is achieved in all fields. Such progress is an essential factor in the happiness of humans, and it is unrealistic to assume that people will suddenly decide no longer to improve certain essential features of their lives. By so doing, they would in fact be deciding to cease to be complete human beings. We therefore discard that possibility as not realistic enough.

The foregoing remarks do not mean that an improvement of the social circumstances in which humankind lives is important only if it leads to greater economic well-being. We merely wish to say that social improvements entail economic improvements as positive side effects, and because of this are even more important within the framework of an integrated welfare policy than they would be if taken in isolation. In the course of various field studies of social infrastructure, for example, it has been found that education and decent housing lead, in relation to their cost, to greater productivity on the part of those enjoying those benefits. This almost goes without saying in the case of medical care, except for a few very rare instances. Apart from this, the idea that better housing, a higher level of education and more advanced medical care are desirable in themselves because they make people healthier and happier is self-evident; that they may in addition be profitable from the economic point of view is a further advantage which places the equipment discussed here in the same category as other investments in technico-economic assets giving the same return. If therefore it is desired to strengthen the social infrastructure, this may be done in full knowledge of the fact that not only will certain essential positive effects be achieved on the social plane, but that a contribution will be made to economic growth. The effect is therefore twofold and has been included in our initial analysis as having a positive influence both on the social infrastructure and on technico-economic capital.

We have pointed out that any improvement in the social equipment may have a favourable impact on economic growth for yet another reason. In this case, the impact is external; it arises from the possibility of making a region more attractive, by means of improvements, to enterprises looking for a site and also to people seeking a place of residence which offers better facilities. Such people are as a rule financially independent or are at least able to take such a step in the certainty they will find suitable work at the new place of residence. The availability of such labour, which is often highly skilled, gives business new opportunities to expand its means of production in the places concerned.

The two influences together may have a considerable impact on economic growth and at a later stage may give rise to a further advance in social equipment.

The influence of distance on the utilisation of social equipment

In connection with the foregoing remarks, the question may be asked why the demand for recreational and educational facilities, medical care, and so on, should grow when the supply of such facilities is increased. This is not immediately obvious and calls for further analysis. In order to clarify this point we must, first of all, point out that in speaking of the utilisation of social equipment we are in fact speaking of services. Services are distinguished from goods by the fact that apart from a few exceptional cases, a service is consumed when and where it is provided. The reason is obvious: services cannot be stored and can be transported only to a limited extent with the aid of modern means of communication. This means that to use services the consumer must go in search of them. When the consumer goes to concerts or places of recreation, or attends educational institutions, it requires time and effort and often costs money. These three factors may be said to increase the price that has to be paid for the use of the actual service and thus affect the extent to which the service will be used.

The traditional theory of consumption often overlooks this point. Any analysis of the manner in which a consumer should act in order to obtain maximum satisfaction used to be based on the limitations imposed by income, and in most cases no explicit mention was made of the fact that two other very real limitations might in the long run form more effective barriers than income, namely the energy budget and the time budget. If we concentrate on the latter, we must admit that the time required to consume a particular service should be deducted from the total time available, and if the distance to be covered is great, this may reduce or totally eliminate consumption. At the other end of the scale, this means that consumption may be increased if the average distance of the consumer from the point of production is reduced. If the distance to be covered becomes smaller or the effort required to cover it is reduced, the consumer will tend to increase his/her consumption of the services supplied by social equipment. If an increase of such consumption is considered desirable – and in the light of the foregoing remarks it should be so considered, subject to certain reservations to be set forth later – then an increase in the density of the network of social equipment should be regarded as a contribution to social and economic growth.

In fact, as a result of economic growth itself, the effort required for the use of elements of social infrastructure is being substantially reduced. This is achieved through motorisation, the effect of which has not so much been to reduce distances as to reduce the energy and time needed. The influence of this development on the extent to which recreation is taken may be observed every weekend and in every holiday period. At the same time, measures are taken amounting to a reduction of the social distance that often still exists between the individual and elements of the social infrastructure, which are becoming more accessible through a reduction in the physical distance.

The first and most obvious measure is the creation of new elements of social infrastructure. If the places at which these new elements are set up are well chosen, they may be expected to have a considerable impact on consumption.

A second possibility is to induce people to move to places where the infrastructure is already available. This may, at first sight, seem rather dictatorial, but we must remember that people have for some considerable time been migrating to the towns (though in the case of the largest towns this migration is beginning to decrease) and this amounts to the same thing. In so far as the authorities are able, for example, by a growth-pole policy, to reinforce this trend to some extent, a situation will be created leading to a fuller utilisation of the social infrastructure than could be achieved without such measures. In many countries this growth-pole policy is already an essential ingredient of regional policy and it seems that other countries will take the same course. This will achieve a concentration of demand for the services of infrastructural equipment and hence make it possible to supply more of this equipment than could be supplied before. There will have to be a balanced combination of the two possibilities if an optimal result is to be obtained.

Some limitations

The foregoing remarks suggest that any reinforcement of the social infrastructure should be regarded as beneficial; we must, however, stress the fact that there are certain limitations.

If we take education as an example, it is clearly desirable that everyone should enjoy the highest possible level of education since they are thus given opportunities which they would otherwise not have had. Their lives become richer and more interesting, and these are aims worth pursuing. But it will also be clear that these advantages may have adverse effects when a person, on leaving a higher education establishment, finds that no other employment is available. In other words, it would be incorrect to consider the problem solely as one of supply and to disregard the question of the demand for the different levels of skill. It is quite possible that educational levels may be set too high in a particular country and that the result of the education would be disappointing, particularly for those who have invested time, energy and money in it. As education is extensively subsidised by the authorities, this applies, *mutatis mutandis*, to the authorities themselves. Bringing demand and supply into line may achieve substantial savings in the educational budget.

Other examples are the promotion of social housing and the creation of recreational and cultural facilities. Here, too, it will have to be borne in mind that every facility in itself stimulates demand, but that demand may not be sufficient to justify the existence of the new facility.

If the possibility of extending the social infrastructure is contemplated, it is necessary to calculate the advantages and disadvantages as precisely as possible and where feasible to quantify them in order to arrive at a rational decision.

Admittedly, such an analysis of costs and benefits is very difficult. Available techniques are gradually evolving, but we are still far from having reached a point where we can be satisfied with the results obtained. Elements which cannot be quantified will always be present and must be weighed in the final balance, just like quantifiable elements. This is clearly a task for policy-makers, but the decision must be carefully prepared by administrative and research staff.

It is only when this task has been given proper attention and has been carried out that policies designed to strengthen regions by the development of their social infrastructure will be successful. Success, it should be repeated, is not confined to the social plane, but is reflected in economic growth, particularly in backward regions. Taken in conjunction with strict measures to protect the environment, this is one of the most rewarding tasks for local authorities.

Mathematical annex

1 Let N = the amount of the environmental capital;
S = the amount of the capital invested in social infrastructure;
T = the amount of the capital invested in enterprises and in the technical infrastructure.

2 The following relationships will be found to exist:

$$N = N(T,N_A) \qquad \frac{\partial N}{\partial T} < 0 \quad \frac{\partial N}{\partial N_A} > 0 \tag{5.1}$$

$$S = S(N,T,S_A) \qquad \frac{\partial S}{\partial N} > 0 \quad \frac{\partial S}{\partial T} > 0 \quad \frac{\partial S}{\partial S_A} > 0 \tag{5.2}$$

$$T = T(N,S,T_A) \qquad \frac{\partial T}{\partial N} > 0 \quad \frac{\partial T}{\partial S} > 0 \quad \frac{\partial T}{\partial T_A} > 0 \tag{5.3}$$

where N_A = measures for the improvement of the milieu (environmental policy);

S_A = measures for the improvement of the social infrastructure (social policy);

T_A = measures for the expansion of the technical infrastructure and of the capital invested in enterprises (economic policy).

3 If $\frac{\partial N}{\partial T} = f_{nt}$, $\frac{\partial S}{\partial N} = f_{sn}$, etc.

and:

$$\frac{\partial N}{\partial N_A} = \frac{\partial S}{\partial S_A} - \frac{\partial E}{\partial E_A} = 1$$

then expressions (5.1)–(5.3) may take the form:

$$dN = f_{nt}dt + dN_A \tag{5.4}$$

$$dS = f_{sn}dN + f_{st}dt + dS_A \tag{5.5}$$

$$dT = f_{tn}dt + f_{ts}dS + dT_A \tag{5.6}$$

$$\begin{bmatrix} dN \\ dS \\ dT \end{bmatrix} = \begin{bmatrix} 0 & 0 & f_{nt} \\ f_{sn} & 0 & f_{st} \\ f_{tn} & f_{ts} & 0 \end{bmatrix} \begin{bmatrix} dN \\ dS \\ dT \end{bmatrix} + \begin{bmatrix} dN_A \\ dS_A \\ dT_A \end{bmatrix} \tag{5.7}$$

hence:

$$\begin{bmatrix} dN \\ dS \\ dT \end{bmatrix} = \begin{bmatrix} 1 & 0 & -f_{nt} \\ -f_{sn} & 1 & -f_{st} \\ -f_{tn} & -f_{ts} & 1 \end{bmatrix}^{-1} \begin{bmatrix} dN_A \\ dS_A \\ dT_A \end{bmatrix} \tag{5.8}$$

4 Formula (5.8) may take the form:

$$\begin{bmatrix} dN \\ dS \\ dT \end{bmatrix} = \frac{1}{|F|} \begin{bmatrix} 1 - f_{ts} f_{st} & f_{ts} f_{nt} & f_{nt} \\ f_{sn} + f_{tn} f_{st} & 1 - f_{tn} f_{nt} & f_{st} + f_{sn} f_{nt} \\ f_{tn} + f_{sn} f_{ts} & f_{ts} & 1 \end{bmatrix} \begin{bmatrix} dN_A \\ dS_A \\ dT_A \end{bmatrix} \tag{5.9}$$

where $|F| = 1 - f_{ts} f_{st} - f_{sn} f_{ts} f_{nt} - f_{tn} f_{nt}$ (5.10)

According to expressions (5.1)–(5.3), the following relationships exist:

$$f_{nt} < 0, f_{sn} > 0, f_{st} > 0,$$
$$f_{tn} > 0, f_{ts} > 0$$

The sign of $|F|$ is not invariable, but since both $- f_{sn} f_{ts} f_{nt}$ and $- f_{tn} f_{nt}$ are positive, it may be taken to be positive. The coefficients of influence are therefore the signs of the elements in matrix (5.9), or:

$$\begin{bmatrix} dN \\ dS \\ dT \end{bmatrix} = \frac{1}{|F|} \begin{bmatrix} \pm & - & - \\ + & + & \pm \\ + & + & + \end{bmatrix} \begin{bmatrix} dN_A \\ dS_A \\ dT_A \end{bmatrix} \tag{5.11}$$

where $|F| > 0$.

Measures for the improvement of the social and technical infrastructure have a negative influence on the environment. The effect of an expansion of the technical capital on the value of the social capital is not, a priori, certain. The other effects are positive.

Let us for one moment assume that $f_{nt} = 0$, in other words, that any impact of industrial production on the milieu is prohibited; then expression (5.9) becomes:

$$\begin{bmatrix} dN \\ dS \\ dT \end{bmatrix} = \frac{1}{|F'|} \begin{bmatrix} 1 - f_{ts} f_{st} & 0 & 0 \\ f_{sn} + f_{tn} f_{st} & 1 & f_{st} \\ f_{tn} + f_{sn} f_{ts} & f_{ts} & 1 \end{bmatrix} \begin{bmatrix} dN_A \\ dS_A \\ dT_A \end{bmatrix} \tag{5.12}$$

where $|F'| = 1 - f_{ts} f_{st}$

It will be found that:

$$\begin{bmatrix} dN \\ dS \\ dT \end{bmatrix} = \frac{1}{|F'|} \begin{bmatrix} \pm & 0 & 0 \\ + & + & + \\ + & + & + \end{bmatrix} \begin{bmatrix} dN_A \\ dS_A \\ dT_A \end{bmatrix} \tag{5.13}$$

where, again, the sign of $|F'|$ is not, a priori, known. If $|F'|$ is assumed to be positive, which implies that the effect of measures relating to the environment on that environment becomes positive in expression (5.11), then this effect also becomes positive in equation (5.13) and all the other signs in (5.13) are known. The effect of an improvement of the infrastructure on the environment has then become neutral. This also applies to the measures designed to improve the technical capital. All the other measures have positive effects.

5 The above system may be related to a welfare function and a budgetary restriction. If we assume:

$$\begin{bmatrix} 0 & 0 & f_{nt} \\ f_{sn} & 0 & f_{st} \\ f_{tn} & f_{ts} & 0 \end{bmatrix} = F \tag{5.14}$$

then:

$$\begin{bmatrix} dN \\ dS \\ dT \end{bmatrix} = F \begin{bmatrix} dN \\ dS \\ dT \end{bmatrix} + \begin{bmatrix} dN_A \\ dS_A \\ dT_A \end{bmatrix}$$

or:

$$\begin{bmatrix} dN_A \\ dS_A \\ dT_A \end{bmatrix} = (I - F) \begin{bmatrix} dN \\ dS \\ dT \end{bmatrix} \tag{5.15}$$

6 If the welfare function is:

$$\omega = \omega(N,S,T) \tag{5.16}$$

and the budgetary restriction:

$$Y = p_N N_A + p_s S_A + p_T T_A \tag{5.17}$$

it follows from expression (5.17) that:

$$dY = [p_N\ p_S\ p_T] \begin{bmatrix} dN_A \\ dS_A \\ dT_A \end{bmatrix} \qquad (5.18)$$

7 The maximum of ω in the case of equation (5.17) is achieved if:

$$d\omega = \lambda dY \qquad (5.19)$$

This follows from:

$$\frac{\delta\omega}{\delta N} = \lambda(p_N \frac{\delta N_A}{\delta N} + p_S \frac{\delta S_A}{\delta N} + p_T \frac{\delta T_A}{\delta N})$$

and similarly for S and T, which gives:

$$\begin{bmatrix} \frac{\delta\omega}{\delta N} & \frac{\delta\omega}{\delta S} & \frac{\delta\omega}{\delta T} \end{bmatrix} = \lambda [p_N\ p_S\ p_T] \quad (I - F) \qquad (5.20)$$

The three equations are:

$$\frac{\delta\omega}{\delta N} = \lambda(p_N - f_{sn}p_s - f_{tn}p_T) = \lambda p_N^S$$

$$\frac{\delta\omega}{\delta S} = \lambda(p_S - f_{ts}p_t) = \lambda p_S^S \qquad (5.21)$$

$$\frac{\delta\omega}{\delta T} = \lambda(p_T - f_{nt}p_N - f_{st}p_S) = \lambda p_T^S$$

8 To clarify this result, let us examine $\frac{\delta\omega}{\delta N}$ more closely. $\frac{\delta\omega}{\delta N}$ represents the marginal social utility of an improvement of the environment, at constant values for S and T. In order to ascertain what use must be made of the instruments in order to obtain this result (N variable, but S and T constant), it must be assumed that $dS = dT = 0$.

Equacion (5.15) then becomes:

$$\begin{bmatrix} dN_A \\ dS_A \\ dT_A \end{bmatrix} = (I - F)\begin{bmatrix} dN \\ 0 \\ 0 \end{bmatrix} = \begin{bmatrix} 1 & 0 & -f_{nt} \\ -f_{sn} & 1 & -f_{st} \\ -f_{tn} & -f_{ts} & 1 \end{bmatrix}\begin{bmatrix} dN \\ 0 \\ 0 \end{bmatrix} = \begin{bmatrix} 1 \\ -f_{sn} \\ -f_{tn} \end{bmatrix} dN \quad (5.22)$$

or:

$$\left.\begin{aligned} dN_A &= dN \\ dS_A &= -f_{sn}\, dN \\ dT_A &= -f_{tn}\, dN \end{aligned}\right\} \quad (5.23)$$

The substitution of expression (5.23) into (5.8) in fact gives $dS = dT = 0$ and $dN = dN_A$. As the cost of $dS_A = p_s dS_A$ and the cost of $dT_A = p_t dT_A$, the cost of an improvement of the environment dN is equal to $(p_n - p_s f_{sn} - p_t f_{tn})\, dN$, which is the cost calculated in equation (5.21).

9 This result, which may be obtained by a similar process for $\frac{\delta \omega}{\delta S}$ and $\frac{\delta \omega}{\delta T}$, may be interpreted as follows. An improvement of the environment of the order of dN costs $p_N dN$. This result may be obtained in the first place by a measure dN_A. However, dN_A not only affects N, but also S and T. The effect on S is $-f_{sn} dN$ and the effect on T is $f_{tn} dT$. The two effects are positive. This means that for the same amount $p_N dN_A$ not only is a change in N obtained, but also a (favourable) effect elsewhere. The 'real' cost of dN is therefore lower. The maintenance of S and T implies that $p_s f_{sn} dN$ less need be expended on S and $p_T f_{tn} dN$ less on T than if N had not been changed.

The above are in fact *accounting prices* which measure the *real sacrifices*, both direct and indirect. In the case of an environmental policy, these sacrifices are less than the price of an improvement of the milieu itself; in the case of changes in the technico-economic capital, it may well be that the sacrifice is greater than p_T since $f_{nt} < 0$. These relative preferences must be compared with the 'corrected' accounting prices rather than with the apparent prices.

5.2 Project evaluation and intangible effects: a shadow project approach*

Introduction

Many efforts made to assign values to elements of the environment have, up till now, been unsuccessful. This failure has had implications for, among other things, the development of cost-benefit analysis, which has been increasing in importance as an instrument for project evaluation.

In order to carry out an economic analysis of several reclamation projects in the Wadden Sea area in the Netherlands which stressed, in particular, the environmental effects (see Commission of Enquiry on the Third London Airport; Klaassen and Botterweg, 1974) it seemed advisable to set up a cost-benefit analysis which was more complete than usual and also to introduce the environmental elements in an unusual way. An analysis, where the net sum of the measurable effects is confronted with a verbal summing up of all imponderable effects, seemed in view of the attention which the natural environment has justly been receiving the last few years too broad as a basis for a judgement which is as objective as possible.

An approach which has recently received some attention is that of monetary compensation (Wadden Sea Commission, 1974). Here it is beyond our scope to delve into this compensation idea because the treatment of its theoretical aspects, in particular, would require too much space. A few words on the subject would not be inappropriate, however. Neither could we resist the temptation to expose the essential weakness of the compensation idea by giving a brief account of its background. The idea is, in principle, that when any nuisance is experienced, he who causes the nuisance should extend pecuniary compensation to him who experiences it. The latter then returns to the same state of welfare as before the nuisance was experienced.

The amount of the compensation represents, then, the assessment of the damage to the environment. A little reflection soon shows that such an approach to the matter overlooks the essence of the problem. A compensation in no way guarantees that no damage is done to the environment, while it is precisely this which should be the fundamental requirement of any method. The following short narrative illustrates the situation that can occur as a result of the compensation idea.

*See L.H. Klaassen and T.H. Botterweg, 'Project evaluation and intangible effects: a shadow project approach' in P. Nijkamp (ed.), *Environmental Economics*, Leiden: Martinus Nijhoff, 1976.

There were once, not so long ago, two fathers with two sons who lived at some distance from a large town. Each of the sons had a motor-bike which he had to start early in the morning in order to get to work, in town, on time. Both fathers were rudely awakened every morning by the devastating din, and even began to show signs of nervous disturbance. But since they were wise men, they did not quarrel with each other, but discussed their common problem calmly over a glass of good wine. They soon reached the conclusion, however, that their own knowledge was not sufficient to solve the problem satisfactorily, and it was quite natural for them to pay a visit to the local library the very same day in order to deepen their knowledge in this field. They found an abundance of British literature which gave a detailed account of the principle of compensation. If noise nuisance was experienced, they read in profound scientific papers, monetary compensation should be given. Any deterioration in the quality of life would thus be undone.

Both men absorbed this advice, and being completely satisfied, acted accordingly. Over a second glass of good wine, they agreed that the value of the noise nuisance, expressed in money, would amount to about 100 pennies per day. So they arranged that the first father would pay this sum to the second father to compensate him for the annoyance caused to him by the first father's son. The second father undertook to make an offering of equal size to compensate the first father for the annoyance caused by the second father's son.

Although the noise nuisance after this agreement was no less than beforehand and their financial position was neither strengthened nor weakened, they lived together happily ever after, quite convinced that they both received full compensation for the nuisance caused to them by each other's son. Needless to say, they now had an even deeper respect for economic science than they had, as wise men, already.

This narrative is intended to show how little trust the authors of this article have in the compensation idea. In its stead, another approach, that of the shadow project, seems to be more fruitful. This approach, which was originally formulated for the purpose of evaluating possible reclamations in the Wadden Sea area, can, in principle, have a much wider application within cost-benefit analysis.

We start from the assumption that nature (particularly in the Netherlands) must not be degraded any further and that it must be stipulated that for any proposed project which is detrimental to the natural environment, provision be made for the realisation (or the financing) of a shadow project. This shadow project should prevent or compensate any damage to the environment not by means of payment of a sum of money, but by an addition to the environment at least equivalent to the environmental damage incurred. The theory is that the cost–benefit analysis is not based on the value possessed by nature or the environment, but on the sum of money required, i.e. the costs which have to be made, to maintain the environment in its present state. Although we have been discussing shadow projects as a possible means of avoiding problems of the valuation of nature, we must add, probably superfluously, that the shadow project concept is of course also applicable in cases where there are imponderable effects, e.g. of a social or cultural nature.

No further deterioration of nature

In recent years it has become increasingly apparent that natural areas have an indispensable function within the process of town and country planning in the Netherlands. By various regulations, the qualification 'natural area' is made increasingly difficult to obtain, while the purchase policy is aimed at insuring long-term preservation (including the possibility of proper control). On the other hand, the use made of natural areas has assumed such proportions that in various instances the quality has suffered. There are many kinds of natural areas; there are also many different reasons for a natural area to be given a protected status. Although we will not be dealing with this point in any detail, the following brief observations may be made.

Most of the reasons are concerned with the use we can make of it, e.g. provision of water and air, but also of foodstuffs, genes sources and the possibility that nature signalises poisonings, etc. Besides these resources, there is also a large group of social motives. It can, for instance, be desirable to grant a protected status to natural areas from an ethical or aesthetic point of view. A richly varied nature is also of paramount importance for education and science; science being concerned not only with nature as a study object, but also with the possibility of its use as a reference for other studies. When enumerating the functions of the natural environment we often tend to make an extremely long list. This is probably justified, for there are an infinite number of reasons for wanting a 'well-functioning nature', this being in fact directly related to the possibility of 'life'.

It is, however, incorrect to attribute all these functions simultaneously to all natural areas – smaller or larger areas, with or without a protected status – in which the natural processes or old cultural patterns are preserved. The functions of nature are infinite; those of natural areas are clearly limited.

The protection of natural areas has the specific aim of preserving nature in spite of everything. This means that the use of the natural area must be in accordance with the specific policy principles. The purchase of a plot of land as a breeding-place for the purple heron means that it cannot, at the same time, have a positive recreation value.

As we have observed previously, the valuation of functions of nature is a risky undertaking. With natural areas it is even pointless since the aim for which the status is granted – which may already be dubious to the outsider – indicates the value of the land. The degree to which this aim, which can materialise in a specific plan, is substantiated, will determine the value of the land. If the purpose of the natural area is of a strictly scientific kind, then this automatically determines the value. The fact that it is not given a function in the recreation sphere is a result of the specific aim and will not therefore have a negative influence of the assessment of the natural area.

The value of a natural area cannot therefore be deduced from a list of general functions of nature. There is no point in determining the extent of the contribution of one natural area to all the functions of nature. The value of a natural area is bound up with the proposals made for that area, these being based in particular on ecological insights.

First and foremost, we must recognise that the protected natural areas in a country do not by any means represent the whole natural wealth of that country. There are in fact quite a lot of valuable areas which owe their character to human differentiation of activities through the ages, up to the beginning of the twentieth century. The rich meadow bird areas, the vast moors, the pools adjoining the great rivers, the old peat diggings, the remains of primitive reclamations, etc. are undeniably the results of human activities in the past. These activities were followed, however, by a natural development, in which man played an extremely modest part. There are also certain areas where human influence has been negligible such as coastal wetlands, estuaries, dunes and moors.

The variation in countryside to which we have become accustomed is being threatened by the adaptation to new norms and techniques. In the interest of both a 'well-functioning nature' and the preservation of the greatest possible variety of natural areas and countryside, we cannot accept any further reduction of natural areas. With this in mind, we will consider the following aspects in more detail.

Some developments in cost–benefit analysis

If in a cost–benefit analysis all the effects are discussed, then we are dealing with a social cost–benefit analysis. In such an analysis all social effects of a certain project for the whole community[1] are weighed against each other in order to make an assessment of the project. The principle behind such an analysis had already been accepted during the last century but, partly because of an imperfect set of instruments and incomplete statistical material, could only be applied in a more or less intuitive way. The result, i.e. the ultimate assessment, was therefore partly dependent on the qualities of the supervisor of the project, whether this was the government or a private company.

For several decades now attempts have been made to bring certain – particularly social – imponderable effects into account in project evaluations. In some cases, efforts to quantify these effects by means of the determination of shadow prices have been successful. For some years now, there has been a growing awareness that environmental factors should also be taken into account, when space-devouring or highly polluting projects are being evaluated. Moreover, not only is increasing attention being paid to threatened biological entities and ecological processes, but it is being suggested increasingly often that certain rural and socio-cultural assets, such as unique polder (reclaimed) countryside and certain qualities of inner towns, must not automatically be sacrificed to projects which on other grounds seem acceptable. This development ensures that increasingly more aspects of our society are being included in any significant project evaluation.

In the introduction we have given two examples of fairly recent analytic methods. We paid particular attention to the methods used to determine as objectively as possible the compensation to be paid to those incurring damage from a project. Examples of the application of such methods are the Delta works in the Netherlands and the Third London Airport (Tinbergen, 1960; Commission of Enquiry on the Third London Airport). In both cases, the cost-benefit analyses included the costs of financial compensation, for instance, to certain categories of fishermen, who would no longer be able to fish in the Delta area, and to those living in the neighbourhood of a new airport, who would experience noise nuisance and would therefore be obliged to move to somewhere else.

It should be apparent from the short narrative in our introduction, that these methods are unacceptable to the present authors. The reason is that when people inflict injury on each other, a reciprocal compensation is useless since it can hardly prevent any further injuries from happening. There would, at most, be something to say for this principle when there is an obvious, one-sided infliction of damage. In that case, there are two possibilities. The first is that the costs to be paid for the damage are less than the costs of preventing the damage to the environment. In this case, the destruction will just continue. The second is that the price of paying for the damage is higher than the 'corrective' costs; it would then have been cheaper to prevent the damage in the first place. The method is therefore either ineffective or too expensive. If compensation is too expensive, a potential offender will presumably ensure that the damage does not occur, thus dispensing with the necessity of paying out compensation. In that case, the obligation to provide compensation has proved an effective means of preventing damage to the environment. However, the question then arises: what is in fact our present relationship with the environment? Figure 5.3 is intended to illustrate that relationship.

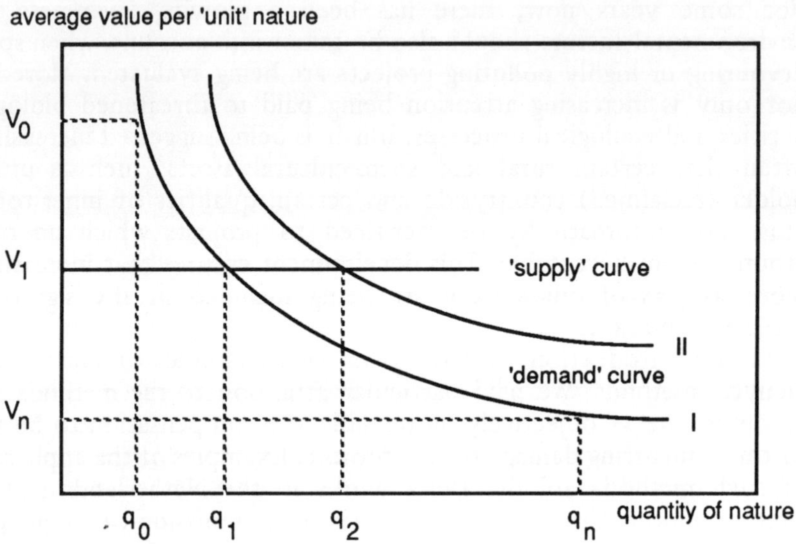

Figure 5.3 'Demand' and 'supply' of nature

In the diagram the 'amount' of nature available is set out on the horizontal axis and its value per 'unit', unknown in fact, is set out on the vertical axis. The downward-sloping curve represents the 'demand' for nature. It is assumed that nature was once so abundant that the average value of a 'unit' of nature was, for humans, very small (V_n). For a long time this value remained practically the same, until the amount of nature was depleted by deforestation and reclamation (of waste land) to such an extent that the average value of nature began to rise. If this development were to continue further, then the time would come when there is so little nature left (q_0) that its value is extremely high (V_0). Each further decrease of nature results in an even more rapid increase in value. The value will finally become infinitely high. It is clear that, in this last stage, a monetary compensation for the detrimental effects of a certain project is no longer possible. Every project involving environmental damage becomes socially unremunerative.

In the following we assume that in the Western world, and certainly in the Netherlands, apart from certain local or regional exceptions, we have reached a point on the demand curve that corresponds with an amount of nature q_1 : nature has become so scarce that we do not appear to be very far from the point at which the value of nature becomes infinite.

The ever increasing number of efforts to prevent a further decrease in the amount of nature and even to enlarge this amount indicate that we have now reached the point q_1. This would mean that we have already overstepped a certain mark and that a greater 'amount' of the good 'nature' is generally considered to be desirable. If we imagine a horizontal supply curve through V_1, which means that we are capable of 'producing' nature at a cost per unit of V_1, then a further encroachment on nature from that point would be societally pointless. This is because the value lost is greater than the cost of avoiding the damage or providing compensation in some other way by means of effective measures.

An increasing appreciation of nature will reveal itself in an upward movement of the demand curve. The amount of nature required will then increase and the supply curve will intersect the demand curve at a point more to the right. This means that the cultivation of nature becomes a socially significant matter until point q_2 on the horizontal axis is reached. A downward shift of the supply curve means an increase in knowledge about and efficiency of 'nature cultivation'. Since the value of nature is not known, but the fact that no further damage to nature will be permitted is, we will assume in the following that the point of intersection of demand and supply curves has been reached (or perhaps even passed), and for that reason, compensation in nature will have to be given for every imminent infringement.

The shadow project and the project evaluation

Because of the limitations of the methods of cost-benefit analysis discussed in the previous section, and the view that we have, at least in the Netherlands, arrived at a situation in which the amount of nature has reached or passed its lowest level, a summary of the shadow project idea will now be presented.[2]

Suppose we are to evaluate a proposed project which has on the one hand certain technico-economic and social advantages and disadvantages, and on the other hand certain environmental disadvantages. It is of course quite conceivable that the project is environmentally neutral or that its effects on the environment are positive. We will return to these positive effects later on. Suppose also that both the technico-economic and the social effects are positive and when combined have a volume of $(dT + dS)$.[3] It is not just enough for this sum of net effects $(dT + dS)$ to be positive. If the project – excluding environmental effects for the moment – is to be profitable, then its investment and other costs (C) must be offset. The following must therefore apply:

$$dT + dS = KC \tag{5.1}$$

where $K \geqslant 1$. In this equation K is the socio-economic benefit-cost ratio. If the sum of the net effects of the project $(dT + dS)$, as well as the investment and other costs are now known, then the socio-economic benefit-cost ratio can be determined, the criterion being that this ratio is at least equal to unity since the project would not otherwise be profitable.

However, the fact that the project will encroach on nature to a certain degree (dN) has yet to be taken into account. Therefore, instead of expression (5.1), the following equation should be applicable:

$$dT + dS + dN = K^{*}C \tag{5.2}$$

where $K^{*} \geqslant 1$. If K^{*} – the social benefit-cost ratio, with a wider scope than K – were measurable, then we could ascertain whether or not the project is socially profitable. Damage to the environment is, however, not quantifiable, and K^{*} is therefore not measurable. Thus no conclusion can be made regarding the social productivity of the project. The following solution, already hinted at in the foregoing and based on the assumption that the environment must not be spoiled any further, now becomes possible. This means that one or more shadow projects, whose task it is to remove or avoid those consequences of the project which are detrimental to the environment should be carried out at the same time as the original project, desired on economic and social grounds. Since $dN = 0$ in that case, given the costs of these shadow projects, we can calculate K^{*} in expression (5.2). Investment and other costs involved in the shadow projects are added to the investment costs of the project in this calculation. Total investment costs are therefore higher, and the unavoidable result is that $K^{*} < K$. The social benefit-cost ratio of the project will therefore be lower than the socio-economic benefit-cost ratio. Only if the project does not have any environmental effects will $K = K^{*}$. In sum, the foregoing implies that if a project has adverse effects on the natural environment, these disadvantages will have to be compensated by executing shadow projects simultaneously. As a result of this action however, the socio-economic profitability of the basic project will become lower than when there is no need to carry out shadow projects because the costs of the shadow projects have to be charged to the basic project.

If we apply the shadow-project idea, we clearly reduce the problem of quantifying the non-quantifiable. Moreover, since the non-quantifiable detrimental effects are offset by shadow projects, the greatest possible care is taken that nature is not spoiled any further, or in any case that the loss is replaced as much and as well as possible. The use of the shadow-project idea in the cost-benefit analysis represents therefore an improvement on the method of monetary compensation discussed earlier, which could not guarantee that the expected damage would be removed. Perhaps needlessly, we repeat that the shadow-project idea was not just devised as an analytical instrument and that shadow projects should be set up as compensation for certain losses.

Three additional remarks form a fitting conclusion to this section. First, it is of course not essential that the supervisor of the initial project undertakes the shadow project as well. In many cases, that could even be undesirable, particularly if the basic project and the shadow project are of such different characters that it is impossible for one supervisor to have insight into the specific problems attached to the execution of both projects. It is of course essential that the promoter of the initial project provide the finances necessary for the execution of the shadow project(s) accompanying this initial project.

Secondly, we could question the soundness of our basic assumption. Is it correct to contend that, in the Netherlands at least, nature must not be spoiled any further? In the section 'No further deterioration of nature' we have attempted to show that this assumption is justified.

The concern shown by experts, such as biologists and ecologists, for the environment could even arouse the impression that too much nature has been lost already, so that even shadow projects 'in arrears' would have to be carried out. This would imply that in future every project with effects detrimental to the environment should be accompanied by the appropriate shadow projects. In the Netherlands such a shadow project 'in arrears' has already been proposed in one instance. Conservators have declared themselves in favour of the realisation of a new sand bar with dunes and a briny pool off the Voorne coast, to compensate for the recent loss of the natural area 'De Beer'. This natural area was sacrificed to the construction of

Europoort, the new seaport area near Rotterdam. If such a harbour project had been submitted for approval today, instead of ten years ago, then 'De Beer' would at least have had to be replaced by an equivalent – newly created – natural area. This would have been a good example of a shadow project!

Our last comment is of a more general nature. We must not forget that the shadow-project idea is not necessarily concerned only with the avoidance of damage to nature or the replacement of nature which has been destroyed, but can also be concerned with, for example, the preservation of old town centres, the preservation of rural scenery, the avoidance of noise nuisance to people, in short, the preservation of all sorts of cultural, natural, social and even technico-economic entities – such as windmills and other old industrial establishments – which for the sake of new projects are threatened by destruction. They are in danger of being sacrificed not exactly because one forgets to include such impending losses in the evaluation, but rather because they are often so difficult to quantify that one is wary of including them. We have already shown that the shadow-project idea can be of great help here since, instead of including in the calculations the value of what has been lost, the cost of avoiding the loss or of replacing it can be added to the cost of the proposed project.

The problem of the non-interchangeability of shadow projects

In the foregoing, we have avoided giving a definition of a shadow project, since we are faced with an almost endless number of possible ways of spoiling the natural environment. A requirement of a shadow project designed to replace nature which has been lost to us is that the replacement resemble the original as closely as possible. In view of the numerous possible ways of spoiling nature, it is obvious that this requirement can cause problems. It is hardly possible, certainly for economists, to predict the problems related to the specification of a suitable series of shadow projects pertaining to a specific project. However, we believe that, in practice, there will indeed be possibilities of defining the environmental damage as accurately as possible and then finding suitable shadow projects. The nature of the shadow project is of course closely bound up with the nature of the environmental damage. In order to define our views in more detail, it seems sensible to classify all possible kinds of environmental degradation under a number of main headings. We distinguish, among others:

1 noise nuisance;
2 air pollution;

3 water pollution (by both solid and liquid wastes, thermic pollution);
4 surface pollution;
5 visual pollution;
6 the loss and destruction of natural areas.

It is clear that for each of these groups of infringements, choosing one or more shadow projects requires a different approach. For each group we will now indicate briefly, using some simple examples, which shadow projects could be considered as possibilities.

1 If the production of sound causes damage to the environment (for instance, by disturbance to people or by disturbance of a bird sanctuary) the only solution seems to be to specify a shadow project in such a way that the expected noise nuisance is avoided or is rendered harmless. It is, for instance, conceivable that if a motorway is to be constructed in a sound-sensitive area, sound absorbent installations (e.g. an earth bank) be built at the side of the motorway. If this is not possible, then this particular motorway must be projected further away from this area. The higher investment costs which this requires come under the costs of the shadow project and should therefore be paid by the initiator of the project.

The shadow project attached to noise nuisance caused by aeroplanes is made up of two elements; a restriction of flying and the use of low-noise motors. Here, too, the cost of the shadow project consists of the resulting extra costs for the airline companies and their passengers.

2 It is difficult to imagine that an air-purifying installation would be projected away from the source of pollution as compensation for a certain degree of air pollution. At specific points in different towns, where traffic causes an excess of air pollution, however, they are being tested.

If we wish to eliminate the problem of air pollution by shadow projects, then elimination at the source of pollution – i.e. an 'avoiding' shadow project – seems a good solution. All sorts of filter systems have been and are being designed to limit air pollution. The problem is, however, that the air pollution caused by, for example, an industrial process, can never be 100 per cent eliminated. Moreover, with continually improving purification, marginal costs rise with increasing speed.

If a certain level of air pollution must not be exceeded and a certain new activity can purify only 80 per cent of its emission, then the remaining 20 per cent will have to be taken care of by a further limitation of air pollution of the same kind in other activities, until this 20 per cent is compensated. Certain injustices are probably unavoidable here – should one activity have to purify more than other, older, activities? Problems concerning the 'import' and 'export' of air pollution will also arise. Assessment of the costs of purification, if and as much as possible, seems the appropriate solution here.

3 The specific problems attached to air pollution, arising from the non-local character of this form of pollution, apply in many cases to water pollution also. The most important difference is that, contrary to polluted air, polluted water can be collected at a central point. The purification of water can therefore occur away from the source of pollution.

4 As was the case with air pollution and surface pollution, shadow projects for water-polluting processes should be sought in the form of avoidance of damage.

5 It is difficult to estimate the extent to which visual pollution is detrimental to nature.[4] Visual pollution does of course infringe upon the possibilities of enjoying nature. Shadow projects can also be defined for visual pollution, aiming at avoidance of disfiguration. It is, for example, possible to lay high-voltage cables underground, although this is of course relatively expensive.

An increasingly intensive search is being made for ways of avoiding disfiguration of the countryside by elements such as cooling-towers, switch stations, etc. They could, for instance, be constructed underground, camouflaged by green areas or given an attractive exterior. Once again, the costs of the damage-avoiding shadow projects have to be added to the costs of the initial project.

6 While the shadow projects related to the above pollution categories had a damage-avoiding character, it is conceivable that if natural areas are threatened (with destruction) as a result of a certain project, the corresponding shadow projects should have a replacing character.

Before considering these replacing shadow projects further, we will first give some examples of this type of shadow project. A motorway which has been projected through a natural area not only reducing the total area, but also dividing it into two smaller parts, could be made to go around the natural area and not through it. Sea defences are often improved by straightening out sea dikes. Because of the lower investment costs, this is usually done on the sea side. The obvious objection to this is that natural areas, such as mud flats, are thereby threatened with destruction. The dikes can, however, also be straightened on the landward side in order to preserve the mud flats. An objection to this alternative approach is that land must be expropriated, and that certain areas of cultivated land threaten to become isolated and are not well-protected against floods. The costs of remedying these drawbacks should therefore be regarded as the costs of the shadow project.

In some cases, it will be quite impossible to find a damage-avoiding shadow project for a certain basic project. The shadow project will then have to be of the replacing kind. An example of such a basic project is the construction of Europoort near Rotterdam, previously referred to, which necessitated the sacrifice of the natural area 'De Beer'. As we have already noted, a (partial) replacement of De Beer off the Voorne coast is now being considered. This project can be regarded as a typical replacing shadow project.

Because of their unique character, certain natural elements are irreplaceable. It would be correct to decide in such cases, proceeding on the assumption that no further degradation of nature may be allowed to occur, that however urgent the initial project, a natural area of this kind must not be sacrificed. Higher investment (or exploitation) costs will have to be accepted, so that the project can be realised elsewhere – i.e. on a less suitable site.

If the natural objects involved are not, in principle, irreplaceable, shadow projects can certainly be defined to replace that nature which has been lost as a result of the construction of the initial project. In many countries where a large proportion of 'nature' is not really nature since it arose in the past largely as a result of human actions, it seems quite conceivable that large sections of this nature are replaceable.

A biological policy concerned with the replacement of existing nature has, however, one noteworthy aspect. It takes time to make 'nature'. A new natural area often takes many decades and perhaps even centuries to develop into a stable system. Moreover, developments of this kind should, particularly at the outset, be accompanied by (costly) measures of control. The drawback that there is a period of many years during which the nature that has been sacrificed no longer exists and the nature replacing it is not yet available should not be forgotten in the evaluation. Determining the extent of this drawback produces difficulties, since it is impossible to give an opinion on the value of nature.[5]

This is not, however, the greatest problem. Although the transition period can be lengthy, the requirement that nature is not endangered in the long run will in any case be satisfied. The most important problem is the design of suitable replacing projects. The problem of the valuation of nature in money terms would seem to present itself again here. The difference with the money compensation idea, however, lies in the fact that in the shadow project approach it suffices to define a shadow project corresponding in value to nature which has been lost, while in the compensation idea a valuation in money of that which has been lost would have been necessary. This means that solving the problem is simplified by replacing the need for a quantification by that for a classification of values.

There is a general rule that for each basic project for which only shadow projects with a replacing character come into consideration, a large number of possibly suitable shadow projects must be designed which may be used to replace, wholly or partially, nature that has been lost to us. From these, ecologists and others can choose those projects which between them provide just enough compensation for the nature which is to be sacrificed. This group of shadow projects should of course be chosen in such a way that the total cost remains as low as possible.

It appears, therefore, that possibilities for defining shadow projects of a replacing character do indeed exist. However, since the specification of suitable replacing shadow projects will be a difficult and lengthy procedure, it seems desirable to introduce a supplementary requirement. This is that shadow projects with an avoiding character should take priority over shadow projects with a replacing character unless avoidance involves so much money and effort that these costs are higher than those of replacing shadow projects.

Only when it appears that neither avoidance nor replacement is possible will we be unable to satisfy the basic requirement that nature must not be spoiled any further. The question whether the project under consideration is so urgent that it should be carried out in any case should be answered within the framework of the democratic decision-making process.

Some supplementary comments

Some comments to supplement the foregoing seem to be appropriate here. First, it should be emphasised that a project which has features which are detrimental to the environment can also have features which are favourable to the environment. It is, for instance, conceivable that although the construction of a new road from A to B results in an increase of road traffic from A to B, thus causing extra air pollution, the new connecting road is not only shorter, but has abolished traffic congestion. The increase in air pollution as a result of the preference for the new road instead of, for instance, the train, is counterbalanced by a decrease in air pollution due to a more efficient traffic flow. In this case, compensation by means of a shadow project only has to be provided for the net increase in air pollution.[6]

A second example is concerned with replacing shadow projects. If during the construction of an open-air recreation area a part of the natural environment has been violated, but has been replaced according to the requirements described earlier, then overcompensation could arise, e.g. if the recreation project itself possesses natural qualities. This is quite conceivable because open-air recreation areas are often laid out in a more or less 'natural' way, so that when the trees and shrubs are full-grown and when extensive recreative use has been made of parts of the recreation area, 'nature' can arise. This nature can only be called overcompensating if the condition laid down earlier that this new nature be equivalent to the value of the (part of) nature that has been destroyed, is satisfied. In that case, provision for the new nature can be taken account of in the definition of the shadow projects of the initial recreation project in such a way that no overcompensation takes place. Thus a saving in the investment costs of the shadow projects will be effected.

It is possible that the new nature mentioned in the previous example is not of the same kind as the nature which has been lost. This takes us on to the following point. If we require that nature is not depleted any further but do not require at the same time that nature must if possible be extended, it could possibly represent a saving in costs if shadow projects were designed for groups of initial projects. The theory is that the overcompensation resulting from a certain project can be used as a shadow project for another project, if the kind of nature that is overcompensated is appropriate.

Although this view places high demands on the exchange of information, it is conceivable that a central controlling organ, probably necessary anyhow for the assessment and approval of combinations of initial-project /shadow projects, could also function as a 'shadow'-project bank'. Overcompensations of completed projects are 'stored' here, and if possible, brought out again to serve as a shadow project of other projects. All this would of course be accompanied by a monetary clearance, which would also proceed through the shadow-project bank. An advantage of such a system is that there is no discrimination between individual enterprises and the government. With an internal clearance of shadow projects pertaining to governmental initial projects, the government could have the advantage over individual enterprises. Since an individual enterprise is concerned with only one or few initial projects, it will have no or few possibilities of exchanging shadow projects.

Another possibility presented by a shadow-project bank is the clearance of other advantages which shadow projects offer. A shadow project which serves to create nature can, for example, offer both social and economic benefits simultaneously. These benefits can then again be included among the benefits of the basic project or can compensate the social and economic disadvantages of other projects if these are of the same kind as the extra social and economic benefits of the shadow project in the environmental sphere.

Another problem is that although we have continually been assuming that there are still 'voids' where the shadow project can be realised, this is true only to a very limited degree. New sandbanks which rise out of the sea or new islands which are growing slowly in the Wadden Sea are indeed areas which can replace land which has been forfeited elsewhere. In most other cases, we will not be able to find land where there is 'nothing'. Many of these areas, which we have indicated above by the term 'natural area' may have a completely natural vegetation, but can also have an old agrarian structure. According to the earlier formulation of our basic assumption in this section, such areas of land are not suitable as sites for a shadow project because they do not add to the amount of nature already available. Even so, a somewhat less narrow interpretation of the term 'shadow project' is possible. We could say that the extension of a good protective status to areas which are threatened with destruction, or the avoidance of a seemingly unavoidable menace to an area, can also be regarded as a project in the sense described above.

For instance, if the construction of a very controversial road can no longer be avoided, compensation could be found by cancelling a connection somewhere else, sound in itself but just as harmful. This kind of compensation can solve the problem of no land being available for the realisation of shadow projects.

One last comment remains to be made. As we have suggested above, the shadow-project idea can also be applied to other non-quantifiable values. This application makes sense if rare things are involved, which are faced with imminent destruction if certain new projects are carried out. One of the most spectacular examples of this is the construction of the Assuan Dam. Expensive operations were carried out to spare historical buildings or to remove them elsewhere. Here, too, the shadow projects must be of the same nature as the objects that have been lost to us. And here, too, we can consider both avoiding and replacing shadow projects. An example of an avoiding shadow project is the construction of an underground railway along a financially less favourable route, so that a certain asset will not have to be spoiled. The reconstruction (perhaps elsewhere) of a valuable property is an example of a replacing shadow project. This reconstruction should take place in appropriate surroundings.

Conclusion

The shadow project idea is founded on the non-quantifiability of certain values. Because of this non-quantifiability, not every project which is accompanied by certain negative external effects is tested exhaustively for its social productivity. If they had indeed been tested, many projects which have been given the green light in the past, would have been rejected. No one can be blamed for past mistakes. Instruments for determining the social effect of all kinds of human activities did not even exist at the time the decisions were made.

In our opinion, the shadow project concept creates a possibility of evading the decay of all sorts of assets. If we are really concerned about our environment in the broadest sense of the word, application of the shadow project concept can certainly provide a way out. However, this means that more exacting demands will have to be made on every project with external effects. Either the project will become less profitable because extra investments will be needed to avoid certain effects, or it will become less productive because the investment costs of shadow projects to be carried out to replace certain forfeited values have to be included in the costs of the basic project.

The price of caring about a really acceptable social development is therefore that projects involving extensive external effects – in relation to the other advantages and disadvantages of the project – will not be chosen. If we are indeed prepared to pay this price, then the shadow-project idea can, as we have already seen, be the answer. In that case, it would be worthwhile developing this idea in more detail as soon as possible, paying particular attention to the problem of defining shadow projects. For this purpose, we could, for example, take a number of test objects and at the same time carry out a complete cost-benefit analysis which includes the shadow projects that will have to be carried out. If such a test were in any way successful, then we should have moved a step forward in the direction of a more acceptable society.

Notes

1 Effects which influence not only the national community, but also the international community come to mind here.

2 Readers are referred to titles in the References for a more detailed account.

3 *dT* represents the net change in technico-economic capital and

dS a change in social capital, both occurring as a result of the project.

4 Visual pollution, formed for instance by old buildings, may sometimes be a help to nature since they provide homes for animal species such as bats and barn owls.

5 The longer the transition period, the more difficult it can be for flora and fauna threatened with extinction to acclimatise to the new, specially adapted environment.

6 This applies only if one's aim is the elimination of any further increase in air pollution. If one's objective is more stringent, then more than the net increase of air pollution should be eliminated.

References

Commission of Enquiry on the Third London Airport; Papers and Proceedings; inter alia, Vol. VII, para. 20.3, p. 366.

Klaassen, L.H. (1972), 'Growth poles in economic theory and policy' in A. Kuklinski and R. Petrella (eds), *Growth Poles and Regional Policies*, Paris/The Hague: Mouton, CEUCORS Ser., Vol. 3.

Klaassen, L.H. (1973), 'Economic and social projects with environmental repercussions: a shadow project approach', *Regional and Urban Economics*, vol. 3, no. 1, pp. 83–102.

Klaassen, L.H. and Botterweg, T.H. (1974), 'Evaluating a socio-economic and environmental project', *Papers of the Regional Science Association*, vol. 33, pp. 155–75.

Klaassen, L.H. and Paelinck, J.H.P. (1973), 'Maatschappelijke Baten-Kosten Analyses; enkele Kwalitatieve Beschouwingen', in *Economie dezer Dagen*, Rotterdam: Rotterdam University Press.

Klaassen, L.H. and Verster, A.C.P., assisted by Botterweg, T.H. (1974), *Kosten-Baten Analyse in Regionaal Perspectief*, Groningen: Tjeenk Willink.

Report Wadden Sea Commission (1974), The Hague: Ministry of Transport.

Tinbergen, J. (1960), *De Economische Balans van het Deltaplan*, Report Delta Commission, The Hague: Ministry of Transport.

6 Welfare policy

6.1 Prosperity and well-being*

Introduction

When certain economic concepts suddenly enjoy a revived interest, it is often worthwhile to forget actuality for the time being and revert to the classic writings of economy. Doing so, one often finds in older writings more fundamental reflections on such concepts than many a modern publication can provide. This is particularly true of the concepts of prosperity and well-being.

Let us, therefore, ponder for a while on the attention that three economists of earlier times paid to the complexities of prosperity and well-being. The shortest and clearest definition is perhaps that of Carl Menger (1968), who in his *Principles of Economics* of 1872 described the importance of goods as: 'The importance, which specific goods or specific quantities of goods attain for us because we are conscious of the fact that we depend upon them for the satisfaction of our needs.'

A more concise definition of the significance of individual or collective goods is hardly imaginable. Rightly, the author emphasises

*See L.H. Klaassen and T.H. Botterweg, 'Prosperity and well-being' in *Report of the Tokyo Transport Conference*, Tokyo: Department of Transport, 1975.

the importance of being conscious of the need for goods. We will dwell at length on this later.

A somewhat more concrete definition of the value of goods to us is given by Pierson (1912):

> If a value is put on air, on sunlight, drinking water, friendship, art, then one simply states that these things must be classified as goods. To attach value to something means that one is unwilling to miss such an article and being pleased to acquire it. However, this expression 'value' can also be used in another context so that it does not refer to kind or species, but to a certain quantity of goods. For instance, when one thinks that water and air have no value, then no doubt one refers to the latter; one states not that water and air are superfluous, but that one attaches no importance to a gallon of water, to a cubic yard of air. We often attach great value to a kind of goods, but nothing to a certain quantity of the kind. The reverse cannot occur; if the kind is useless then any amount of this kind is useless as well. But when an article is in such great supply that it can be classified as non-economic, then a kilogram, a litre or a cubic meter of the article is equally worthless. (p. 54)

Marshall (1938) is, if possible, even more concrete and, at the same time, more concise. After speaking of 'desirable things', classifying these as 'material' and 'immaterial', he says:

> *material goods* consist of useful material things, and of all rights to hold, to use, or derive benefits from material things, or to receive them at a future time. Thus they include the physical gifts of nature, land and water, air and climate; the products of agriculture, mining, fishing, and agriculture buildings, machinery, and implements; mortgages and other bonds; shares in public and private companies, all kinds of monopolies, patent rights, copyrights; also rights of way and other rights of usage. Lastly, opportunities of travel, access to good scenery, museums etc. are the embodiment of material facilities, external to a man; though the faculty of appreciating them is internal and personal. (p. 54)

It is a good thing to find that basically economists have always had the well-being of mankind at heart. True, these early writers regarded the supply of material goods as a genuine part of that well-being, on a level with material collective goods and immaterial goods. No economist in his right mind will ever have denied that the environment is important to our well-being, though in the situation often found in developing countries, where environmental goods are plentiful in relation to other material goods, he may have emphasised the need to concentrate on the supply of the latter kind. But in all other cases environmental goods play exactly the same role as the other material goods. They form one of the factors that determine human well-being, and as such are essentially a part of the field covered by economic science. The above quotations show that it has been like that from the start.

Perhaps these quotations were not even needed for the argument. No responsible economist would ever be prepared to say that environmental goods are irrelevant to well-being, that it is not well-being, but prosperity that matters. Nevertheless, that is precisely what many people believe economists think. They accuse economists of thinking only of profit and disregarding the environment, which is nonsense and shows a complete ignorance of economics. Apparently these people confuse the one individual manufacturer who tries to charge the cost of the unpleasant external effects of his production to the community, with the scientific economist, who studies the totality of all effects and for whom such external effects are just as important as the primary production that causes them. So, let us once and for all discard those incorrect notions about economists and economic science.

Economic and non-economic goods

When attempting to analyse somewhat deeper the problem of prosperity and well-being, it is perhaps wise to take a look at the difference between economic and non-economic goods, a difference that has been recognised, after all, for more than a hundred years. Economic goods are those that participate in trade, non-economic goods are those that because of their abundance do not participate in trade. The air we breathe is often mentioned as an evident example of non-economic goods. As a kind, air is essential, but a certain volume of air is not important since normally speaking it does not make sense to offer a volume of air for sale. But a non-economic good will become an economic good the moment anybody cannot make use of it without hindering someone else in his attempt to do the same. A manufacturer who is polluting the air that we breathe is hindering us in our consumption of clear air, thus making of clear air an economic good. He is using air in such quantities that scarcity results and economic loss is sustained. The early history of industrial development shows plenty of examples of environmental pollution on a large scale; such pollution occurs to this day, and is even intensified by the development of the manufacturing industry. We have here clear examples in which such greedy use is made of environmental goods that the value-added created by industrial activities is no longer a faithful representation of the increase in well-being.

It is not so that environmental pollution reduces that increase to nil, but at any rate the total increase is less than is suggested by the money income created. However, this statement is not new. We have already said that well-being does not depend on money income alone. It is true that we use income as a yardstick for well-being, for lack of a better one, but all economists agree that this yardstick, for all that politicians are fond of using it, is an extremely defective tool for comparing the level of well-being in the wealthier countries. One cannot lay down in absolute terms that it should never be permissible to sacrifice non-economic goods in such a way that they become economic goods, but one *can* say that it is permissible only if and as far as an adequate quantity of economic goods becomes available as a compensation. Damage to the environment should be considered acceptable if compensated by a comparable gain in other goods.

We are strengthened in our view if we try to establish more precisely what non-economic goods are. Clean air is not really a very good example; the open country is probably a better one. We can enjoy the open country without directly paying a price. But not without sacrificing something. To reach the open country, we have to make sacrifices of efforts and time, and often, though indirectly, of money. Few people have open country, in all its variety, next to their own homes. Open country demands space, so to enjoy it one must bridge distances. The effort, time and cost needed to do so constitute the price to be paid for enjoying the countryside.

If we look at it that way, damage to our environment means that we shall have to go farther to enjoy the open country, and pay more in time, effort and cost. So, strictly speaking, damage to the environment does not change the 'open country' from a non-economic into an economic good; it was already an economic good, the enjoyment of which demanded sacrifices. These sacrifices become greater, but greater material prosperity can enable us to make them, and then open country elsewhere comes within our reach. Suburbanisation has proved that it is even possible to achieve a compromise between sharing in the increase in material prosperity by working in the city and enjoying open country by living in cleaner, pleasanter suburbs.

If only we were more aware of what has just been said, and in particular if we could look at the problem less emotionally, we should find it easier to realise that it is ourselves who will determine whether or not a balance will be struck between keeping the environment inviolate and acquiring other material goods. Then we shall also see that we need not profess an absolute preference either for the preservation of the environment or for the acquisition of material goods. A realistic objective would rather be the provision of environmental and other goods in such a combination that well-being, which depends on both kinds of goods, becomes as great as possible.

The essence of well-being

What we want therefore is a balanced supply of goods, of which environmental as well as other goods form part. This formulation might perhaps create the impression that the problem allows a static solution; in other words, that a certain level of supply of environmental goods and other goods represents a prosperity level that will remain constant as time goes on. Nothing is further from the truth and, once more, we revert to what Menger (1968) stated so clearly. Our well-being concerns not only the goods we possess and can effectively enjoy, but also and especially the ratio between them and all the goods that we know could contribute to our well-being. In other words, it is not the quantity of goods in our possession, but that quantity *in relation to* the possible quantity that determines our degree of well-being. The degree of well-being is the ratio between the goods we have to satisfy our needs and the needs themselves, or, formulated in yet another way, it is the degree to which our needs can be satisfied by the goods that are available to us.

The point just made, though sometimes minimised, is a fundamental one. It is relevant to our problem, for our well-being will decrease the very moment we become aware that we need more things than before to satisfy our needs, whereas the actual availability of goods is not keeping pace with our increasing needs. So our well-being does not depend so much on what we have or can afford, as on what we can afford as compared to what we should like to be able to afford.

It is certainly not a new statement that has just been made. On the contrary, it is as old as economics itself, and the problem is probably as old as the world. It arises in various forms. We may well wonder if not the intensified contact between the developed and the developing world has increased enormously the dissatisfaction among people in developing countries about their own level of existence by enabling them to compare it with that in developed countries. The reason for that dissatisfaction could well be that the gap in well-being could not be bridged by an adequate improvement of material prosperity. People have become conscious of what they might possess much too fast in relation to the rate of growth of their income, and a growing dissatisfaction was the unavoidable result. Even moderate people in the developing countries, who are keenly aware that the prosperity level of the developed world can only be attained at long term, are slowly made dissatisfied by the planning philosophy of many economists, which is deliberately to set very high targets for the future growth of prosperity in the countries concerned, targets that cannot be attained practically anywhere with the exception of the

Far East. Even when this kind of planning results in higher achievements than would otherwise have been possible, there will still be an increasing dissatisfaction, plainly because the targets always appear to have been set too high.

The process just described is by no means limited to developing countries. In the Western world, too, dissatisfaction is purposely stimulated in two respects: in relation to our supply of material goods, and in relation to our environment. Technical progress and advertising are responsible for ever higher targets for the provision of material goods; the leaders of the environment lobby, using the same communication as the manufacturers, see to it that we develop an increasing sense of dissatisfaction with our environment. The more successful they are in their endeavours, the unhappier we become. And that means no more and no less than that our well-being decreases, or at any rate increases considerably less than without their activities.

The more effective this communication is, the stronger the influence of the 'dissatisfactors' in our society, and the more useless our efforts will appear to be. However, if an increased supply of environmental and other goods does really enlarge our well-being because our demands continue to rise, why then that perseverance and all that toil to meet these demands? Why do we not simply drop them all? Then we do not have to slave and can still be as happy as we were before.

The answer is quite simple. Human beings have always strived to make progress. It is inherent in humans to try to raise their living conditions to a higher level and he will do this to a greater extent as his educational level rises.

It is quite true that contentment can also be attained otherwise. We could aim at a condition such as existed in the Netherlands in some industrial regions in earlier times and which was described by cynics as follows. The priest kept the people ignorant and the manufacturers saw to it that they remained poor. Because they were ignorant, they did not notice that they were poor and therefore remained content with the circumstances under which they had to live. But this does not seem the right aim for us to pursue. Bliss born from ignorance is not a suitable basis for real happiness; it is a dumb complacency that is unaware of further and higher objectives.

Of course, the Belgian who without higher aspirations is enjoying his holiday in the Ardennes, or the Dutchman who feels quite happy on the beaches of the Wadden Islands, is basically a happier man than he who during his holiday in Italy feels frustrated because he cannot afford to go on Safari in East Africa. But is that a valid reason to deny these people all information about potential enjoyment elsewhere in the world? Is it not possible for people to experience happiness in the knowledge that for them, too, the future may bring greater opportunities?

Should we take no action against the increasing pollution of our environment, not try to keep our cities fit to live in and our countryside peaceful and varied? Should we prevent manufacturers from providing us with better and cheaper products that can make our lives more comfortable?

Put this way, all those questions seem rather unrealistic. Defining the future development in this manner, we are perhaps setting our aims too low, whereas in the world of today we are often setting them too high. It would be wisdom to find a compromise between an extreme conservatism, which promises us easy satisfaction, and an extreme progressiveness, which leads to an equally extreme aversion to the present society.

Could it be that the standards which are now being evolved in environmental policy will show a way out of our dilemma? It is certainly worthwhile considering.

Physical planning and well-being

Let us now turn to what has been said about well-being. We have seen that the degree of well-being is the ratio between the goods we have to satisfy our needs and the needs themselves. While in the foregoing section we concentrated on the denominator of the degree of well-being, namely our needs in the widest sense of the word, we now deal with the nominator of the degree of well-being, namely the goods we have to satisfy our needs.

We have seen that the totality of these goods is built up of all kinds of material and immaterial things. Many of the material things are immobile, and mostly distributed unequally over the world or, on a smaller scale, over a country. People who live in a region where there are no woods, but would nevertheless like to enjoy them, have to travel to get what they want. Some people can afford to travel, others whose income is not high enough will be denied that pleasure, unless woods are created in their own neighbourhood. The immobility of many goods together with the need for these goods is the reason why in many countries physical planning has been introduced as an instrument to bring the immobile goods within reach of those who need them in such a way as to minimise the consumer costs (i.e. generalised transportation costs).

Scheme 1 will show that the urgency to introduce physical planning in a region may depend on the density of population and on the relative level of income in that region. A higher level of income results in greater needs of the inhabitants in the region, which means that because of an increasing need of land for economic and social purposes, such as for example unspoiled land for recreation, the scarcity of land does increase, as does the urgency of introducing physical planning.

The tragedy, however, is that, at the moment that physical planning becomes urgent, the environmental situation is mostly so bad that an improvement of the situation is attainable only with the utmost exertion and at extremely high expenses. It is evident that the long-term result of the development of a country would be much better if the same relative urgency is given to the problems mentioned in scheme 1 (see Figures 6.1 and 6.2). Scheme 2 gives some examples of the areas distinguished in scheme 1.

		Very urgent	Urgent	Not very urgent
A	Thinly populated, low-income areas	Economic development	Social development	Physical planning and environment
B	Densely populated, low-income areas	Economic development	Social development	Physical planning and environment
C	Densely populated, high-income areas	Social development	Physical planning and environment →	← Economic development
D	Very densely populated, high-income areas	Physical planning and environment	Social development	Economic development

Figure 6.1 Scheme 1: Hypotheses on the degree of urgency given to different kinds of problem of human society

A	Many rural areas in large, relatively thinly populated low-income countries
B	Urban regions in developing countries
C	Rural regions in small, densely populated countries; urban regions in large, relatively thinly populated developed countries
D	Very large cities and their agglomerations in developed countries (e.g. New York, Tokyo, Paris)

Figure 6.2 Scheme 2: Examples of the areas distinguished in scheme 1

Physical planning on a national scale seems a good instrument to provide people with a great variety of immobile goods within or near their neighbourhood such as parks, schools and swimming-pools. It also seems a good instrument to prevent a country's unique pieces of nature from falling victim to land-hunger for economic or social purposes. So physical planning on a national level may be able to take care of irreplaceable stocks of capital in a country, or a region within a country. It seems not to be a fit instrument, however, to take care of the irreplaceable stocks of capital on a world level. In today's world it is still possible that estuaries with a unique kind of biological life are being destroyed in favour of the construction of harbours. Still it is possible that a unique mountain valley is destroyed by the construction of a four-lane highway, and that a virgin area with unique recreational potential is destroyed by the construction of an oil refinery in the neighbourhood.

Often one cannot simply blame national authorities for this bad management of world-unique parts of land, because one cannot always expect national governments to think on a world level, while trying to find a solution for their pressing national economic and social problems. Nor can one expect of governments in extensive, thinly populated countries where 'waste' land is abundant that they will exercise great care in selecting land that they need for urban growth or infrastructure.

Looking at the long-term needs of the world's population, on the one hand, one cannot but feel convinced that an international authority in matters of physical planning is badly needed to save the world's stocks of capital from being spoiled or destroyed. On the other hand, one immediately realises that introducing such an authority is extremely difficult.

First, the activities of such an authority will certainly be frustrated by problems of finding proper criteria for an internationally integrated programme on physical planning. These criteria should be based on a rather complete view of the worldwide effects of physical planning on economic, social and natural capital. This view, that should be based on a complete and (on behalf of this) a complicated, empirically tested and spatial model must still be considered as wishful thinking. Secondly, the activities of an international authority on physical planning will mainly be impossible because of the difficulties that will rise in achieving international co-operation.

In regard to the difficulties mentioned, it should, for the time being, be advisable to induce national physical planning authorities to concentrate on the development of national, long-term planning for the sake of a better distribution and a better care of stocks of capital on a world level. This very long-term planning is not only important from an international point of view, but may at the same time be advantageous on a national level because it may prevent what may be called a 'boomerang-effect' of a lack of long-term physical planning.

For example, in some tourist countries, such as those around the Mediterranean and Caribbean seas, decision-makers, anxious to 'develop' the regions that were attracting tourists, have failed to realise that by such development they were robbing those regions of their attractiveness and have forced tourists to start looking for other, still virgin beaches in even more remote countries in Africa and on the Pacific coast. It is sad to see how the new tourist countries fall into this same trap, and are continuing to develop tourist regions through lack of long-term considerations of the disadvantageous effects of these developments on the physical environment, and consequently on economic and social development.

Our examples seem to suggest that nowadays particularly the coastal regions of the world are in danger of being completely spoiled. That inference may be correct, for it is precisely the coastal regions that can fulfil many recreational and economic functions and are therefore much in demand for development. It is, however, those very coastal regions that often provide the most important pieces of nature – e.g. tidal marshes, estuaries, mangrove forests and cliff coasts, all full of wildlife and often with unique ecological systems.

These countries should, then, concentrate their development efforts on those coastal stretches that are *not* unique. The location of an industrial complex should not be chosen just because it is the cheapest from the business–economic point of view. From the world-level, societal and national long-term point of view, a more expensive location for that particular industrial complex may well be preferable to the unthinking destruction of a unique seashore.

As we have seen, a national or regional adaptation of human activities to the totality of physical entities of that nation or region is not enough to ensure the optimisation of well-being. To achieve that, a world-wide, long-term equilibrium between human needs and the totality of world stocks of natural capital is needed. We are convinced that at the national level for the optimisation of well-being rational thinking *internationally* is essential, for it may safely be accepted that the establishment of an international authority that could take care of this international optimisation of well-being is impossible.

Of course, long-term physical planning on a national level as suggested here also needs to establish criteria or standards for bringing about an acceptable environmental policy. One might remark that, since an international authority will be unable to define internationally consistent standards, a national authority will have even less capacity to define such standards. Our opinion, however, is that as long as standards are being defined and lived up to in a serious way on the national level, then a great deal will also have been gained on the world level. There still remains the general question, stated in the foregoing, of the ability of standards to increase well-being by curbing our needs.

Standards and shadow projects

At first sight, the answer to the question raised at the end of the previous section does not seem very difficult to find, at least not as far as environmental factors are concerned. More and more, we are introducing, or trying to introduce, fixed standards for the quality of the waters of our rivers, the air, the historical hearts of our cities, the scenery and the ecology. We are adapting certain rules and constraints in order to ensure a level of quality in the environment as a whole that is acceptable in terms of the actual situation. Whether or not these are to be considered fixed and stable is a question that deserves some further attention, particularly in the light of the foregoing sections, where we have stressed the tendency towards ever increasing demands in almost all fields of human activity. We will give that some attention in the next section.

Now let us, first, consider the importance of standards, particularly as to their consequences for the economy.

In the existing national accounts a number of items are not, unlike others, recorded at their market value. Many government services have in fact no price at all. Defence is an example. The solution that has been found for these goods and services is to put their value equal to the costs that have been made for producing them. In principle, the value of the services of a civil servant equals, or so it is assumed, his/her salary including social charges paid by the government. The value of the service of a government department equals the total costs of this department, including salaries and social charges.

The question occurs to us if the same procedure could not be applied to other elements of our well-being, elements that so far have not been accounted for in our national accounts? To that end, we could define nature, in the widest sense, as a stock of valuable elements. In the course of time, this stock has decreased considerably, and there is a general feeling that it has sunk below an acceptable minimum. Now if we call this stock 'natural capital',* we can state

*If we attach value to nature as such, 'natural capital' seems a better word than 'environmental capital', which suggests that nature is important only so far as it functions as an environment for humans.

that we have been consuming natural capital without accounting for it in the form of depreciation in the national accounts. The same reasoning holds for the stock of raw materials, which is also steadily decreasing without any explicit consequence for our national economic calculations.

For the sake of the argument, we will for the moment confine ourselves to the natural capital, and suggest as a basic assumption that natural capital can be created by human beings. Many will hesitate to accept this assumption; it is to be expected that biologists, in particular, will be rather sceptical. The idea of humanity creating nature is, as experience in Holland has taught us, accepted more readily by agricultural engineers. Still, even biologists are coming round, in view of the successes achieved by agricultural engineers in the new polders.

Once admitting that nature can be created by human effort, one has to accept as well that natural stock that has got lost can be replaced, with the exception perhaps of some unique areas of natural beauty. Now as soon as standards set for nature (for the quality of the ecology, water, air, etc.) become effective, the implication is that no further damage to nature is to be permitted. Or, to put it otherwise, from the moment the standard becomes effective, any economic project, however profitable, would cause more damage to the environment than the value added it produces. It follows, then, that the introduction of standards implies that the value of bits of nature lost through economic projects is put at zero until the standard is reached, and at an infinitely high amount of money from that moment onwards.

But even though the value of nature from a certain point onwards is infinitely high, as long as nature can be reproduced damage to nature can be avoided simply by replacing any natural capital that is lost. For if the value of the nature lost through an economic project were to be extremely high, then so would be the value of the nature reproduced; the only factor really relevant is the cost of the (re)production of natural capital.

The above considerations lead to the conviction that any standard for nature can be fully maintained if all economic projects are accompanied by environmental projects (to be called 'shadow projects') which compensates for the environmental damage caused by the economic projects.

An example may be instructive. For the construction of Europoort in the harbour area of Rotterdam a bird reserve of great value was sacrificed. At the time, this was accepted as an inevitable consequence of the city's industrial expansion, and the damage to nature was not accounted for. Now a new bird sanctuary is being 'constructed' on an island some thirty miles to the south. The costs involved represent the value of the productive forces needed to reproduce the lost part of the natural-capital stock. Had the two projects been integrated at the time, the total costs of the economic project, including those involved in compensating for the decrease in value of nature would have been accounted for in the national bookkeeping system, as representing the real total costs of the economic project to society.

Under the assumptions made earlier, it would be a logical decision to attach to any licence for carrying out an economic project the condition that no net harm is done to nature, implying that the entrepreneur shall be responsible for carrying out a corresponding nature project. Of course, industrialists are not, in general, experts of landscaping, their contribution will be in most cases simply one of financing the nature project.

The consequences of a procedure as outlined above are twofold. First, economic projects will become more expensive, thus less attractive. Only economic projects profitable enough for the shadow project to be financed out of its revenues will be carried out. Quite rightly so, for projects that can hold their own only if no shadow project need be paid for, may be profitable from an economic point of view, but from a societal point of view they are not. Secondly, with shadow projects the national accounts will reflect that no net damage is caused to nature, whereas in the conventional approach the economy is treated as something entirely separate from the rest of society.

But what to do in those cases where natural capital has already been impaired to such an extent as to fall below the standards set? The answer is that, in those cases, nature projects will have to be undertaken for their own sake. In our terminology, the costs of producing nature would be lower than the value attached to it, in which case it is perfectly rational to increase the stock of natural capital to the point where its value equals the costs. That point represents equilibrium, and shadow projects are then sufficient to maintain it.

With respect to the stocks of raw materials, an entirely analogous situation prevails. Wherever it is possible to increase such stocks, reproduction by means of shadow projects is to be encouraged. The stock of timber can be prevented from decreasing, or even be increased, by reafforestation. In many countries it is a rule that for every full-grown tree that is felled, a new young tree must be planted, a rule that is completely in accordance with the shadow-project approach, by which the originator of an economic project is bound to compensate for damage done to nature. Of some raw materials there are infinitely large stocks, e.g. sun energy and tidal energy.

These can safely be used without shadow projects being undertaken, for in such cases one cannot speak of diminishing stocks.*

There are also raw materials that cannot be reproduced at all. To compensate for their use, two courses lie open. The first is to recuperate them from the products in which they have been worked up, the users of the raw materials being held responsible for the recycling. The second course, indicated for materials that cannot be recycled, is to find shadow projects in the production of substitutes, the cost of the necessary research being imputed to the users of the raw materials.

Here, as with shadow projects, to compensate for nature losses, the consequences of the procedures suggested are twofold. First, stocks are kept from being depleted; and secondly, the national accounts reflect much more accurately than before what is actually happening.

It would be erroneous to imagine, however, that thanks to the introduction of shadow products to keep up the stocks of natural capital and raw materials, the national accounts would give a faithful account of all the values in society. It is the cost of preventing damage to nature that is recorded, but by no means the real value of bits of nature destroyed or created. No more can the value of human lives lost through traffic accidents be accounted for, neither by conventional reckoning nor by the shadow-project approach. Still there is a difference, which we shall try to illuminate by the following example.

Suppose a project is carried out which has the effect of increasing traffic, and would therefore carry the danger of an increase in accidents. Without a shadow project, the scheme in Figure 6.3 would be set up. The decision-makers would be confronted with the proposition to weigh the net benefits of 50 against 5 human lives and the environmental damage. Under the shadow-project approach, the project would be considered permissible only if the number of accidents would not increase, which could be achieved by perfecting the roads and/or the vehicles. The scheme would then be as shown in Figure 6.4.

It is now plain that the basic project is really a profitable one. The external effects have been taken care of by shadow projects at a cost of 40, and there is still a positive net benefit of 10. The *value* of human lives or of nature has not been in discussion, for it is obviously untrue that this value would, in the case presented, equal 40. The only conclusion is that 40 is needed to *prevent* their sacrifice, and

*Of course, the constructions needed to gather the sun energy or tidal energy may harm nature quite severely, so for this decrease of natural capital shadow projects should be undertaken.

Benefits		Cost
200		150
	Net benefits	50
200		200

Note: Non-quantifiable external effects: (a) environmental damage; and (b) 5 human lives annually.

Figure 6.3 Scheme 3: Project without shadow project

Benefits	Costs	
200	For basic project	150
	For shadow project	40
	Net benefits	10
200		200

Figure 6.4 Scheme 4: Project with shadow project

that is all that is needed for a rational decision if we have the courage to say that henceforth no more damage to nature or sacrifice of human life is to be tolerated.

Of course, there may be those who still want to express the value of nature and human lives in money terms so as to find more elegant solutions to the problems. We are not among them, contenting ourselves with a solution that is essentially the same as the one applied of old to many activities of the civil service. We do not express in money the value of defence, of education, of care for the aged, for invalids or for handicapped children. We just define what is necessary or tolerable, and from that conclude to what extent we shall build up defence or give assistance, thus expressing that the defence of the realm or help to those in need is worth at least the amount spent on them.

Accepting that line of thought, one is at once freed from the unpleasant and impossible duty of measuring the immeasurable; the immeasurable will always remain immeasurable. However refined the analysis, no one will be able to translate into money terms human suffering, the loss of a bird reserve, the harm done by a polluted river or noise nuisance. What we *can* do is to calculate how much it costs to prevent an accident, to preserve nature or to clean a river, and whether or not these costs are higher than the benefits to be gained by our economic projects. How much higher is irrelevant. The method enables us to change a cardinal problem into an ordinal one; as long as we are convinced that what is preserved is more valuable than the costs of preservation, we know all we need to make rational decisions.

It would seem that in adopting the ideas exposed above, we can still remain faithful to our national accounts. After all, those accounts are not to blame for the wrong ideas about the development of our well-being that we have derived from them. It is because we were so late taking proper measures in the environmental field that our national accounts gave us a false picture. They did not register wrongly what we did right, but registered rightly what we did wrong.

Standards as a relative concept

The previous section seems to suggest that the maintenance of certain standards presents more of a problem than their definition. The present section concerns the theoretical and practical problems of finding that definition.

Some authors in the environmental field seem to think that environmental standards are quite a novelty, that they have never before existed. That view is both erroneous and arrogant; it suggests that we have introduced a new idea, a breakthrough in environmental thinking resulting from a completely new outlook on society as a whole; and that standards are to be set now once and for ever, and that they are the exponents of a drastic change in all fields of human thinking, notably in economics and more particularly in capitalist societies.

In fact there have always been environmental standards, and they are a function of the income level in the country where they are applied. All developed countries have their sewage systems, drinking-water systems, garbage collection, nature reserves, laws concerning noise nuisance, etc. Such amenities increase in number as the country becomes richer and as more money becomes available to provide them to the public. Additional standards are regularly being introduced; the present wave of new standards represents, at most, the accelerated introduction of regulations that had been postponed too long. The introduction as such follows a trend that has been followed for centuries.

When we look at standards in this way, it also becomes clear that future standards will be different from present standards. Not only because in spite of what some people say, our incomes will continue to rise, but also because we have become conscious of the damage we are doing to nature in trying to obtain ever higher incomes.

Our preferences are shifting and consequently our standards are shifting too. In view of what happened in past periods, this is not unacceptable, it may even be rational. The question is, however, how fast we are raising our standards and how fast we can raise up society to the desired level of well-being.

The problem is, then, no longer one of finding shadow projects for new economic projects so as to prevent further damage to nature, but one of adjusting existing activities and their impact on the environment. Our concern is no longer one of maintaining the quality of the environment, but of rapidly improving that quality at the expense of the economy. But then the question arises to what extent, if at all, are these things possible. How fast can we increase the expenditure to comply with environmental claims without serious repercussions in the economic, consequently in the social, field? This question becomes even more urgent when we realise that we have obligation not only to our environment, but also to the two areas endangered by environmental claims, namely the economy and society.

'Attainable ends'

We now arrive at the quintessence of the conflict situation in which we find ourselves, i.e. the incompatibility of the aims we are pursuing or that others are making us pursue, with the means and instruments at our disposal within the boundaries of the period that we are mentally allowing ourselves, perhaps unconsciously, to accomplish these aims. We simply cannot wait to buy a bigger car, a colour television set, a motor-boat or a holiday in Thailand. But even less are we prepared to wait for our environment to become quite clean again, for noise nuisance to disappear completely, for our cities to become almost insufferably perfect models of liveability and for the water of our rivers to become fit for drinking. We want to see the poorer countries developed instantly, and not fifty years hence. Everything has to happen now, totally and without delay.

One does not need all that much understanding of economics to realise that all those aims cannot be accomplished simultaneously. The possibilities for the future are limited, and it is no use setting targets which can be realised only in the very long term, unless we fully appreciate just how long that period is going to be. Otherwise the extremely scant successes achieved in relation to those targets, even in the medium run, are bound to lead to tensions, and those tensions will become frustrations as large as life when, moreover, we insist on regularly raising our aims. We shall then be like a man who is pursuing a phantom which glides away whenever he approaches.

It must be admitted that planning for the medium long term is not very well possible without the background of a long-term plan. Something that seems desirable and possible in five years' time will be really desirable then only if it fits into the framework of what we want after ten years, and if that again fits into our picture of twenty or thirty years hence. The only function of our long-term wishes should thus be to serve as a framework for medium-term targets. The moment we make ourselves familiar with a structure of society for the year 2000 we want to make that structure into a reality. But that cannot be done in a few years' time, the less so because in ten years' time we shall have replaced the alluring picture of the year 2000 by an even more alluring one of the year 2010!

To break this vicious circle, we shall have to translate our long-term plans into plans attainable in the medium term, and therefore we must learn to look upon these realistic aims as the real aims, as tasks the realisation of which practically all of us will witness. That we shall set ourselves new targets the moment the present targets have been realised goes without saying, and it is even healthy. But these targets will also have to meet the demands of attainability. Striving for a good cause makes sense, but it should be accompanied by the feeling that one has the power to attain one's aim and to set oneself new targets. Perhaps there are those who reproach us for being conservative, notwithstanding our endeavour to strike a neutral position. Perhaps they are right. But conservatism can be founded on realism, and as long as that is true, being conservative does not to us appear objectionable.

To set an unattainably high target for underdeveloped countries, and to point to dangers for world peace if that target is not met, is to us pernicious and neither more nor less than a kind of macro-blackmail; with this difference, however, that real blackmail produces at least something for one of the parties. The discussion about environment is moving in the same direction. People exert themselves to give reaons why one ought to be concerned about one's environment, and then everything done to actually improve the environment is scornfully typified as a drop of water falling on a red-hot plate. That the fire is kept burning by nervous fuelling escapes attention. It is the same with television advertisement producers. With the most primitive means – some good and witty 'spots' excepted – the viewer is enticed into buying products in which he/she is only marginally interested. However, the need conjured up decreases a sense of well-being, and it is hoped that thus stimulated he/she will wish to restore the original balance. The effect is negative if he/she is not in a position to buy. The artificially created aim is then unattainable and frustration and decreased well-being are the only results.

In the Netherlands, in some political parties, there appears to be the beginning of a breakthrough with regard to the above-mentioned problem. Unfortunately we are still at a far cry from a situation in which – as Professor P. de Wolff once suggested – each political party will add to its election programme an estimate for the coming term of office, translating the party's wishes in a consistent system of income and expenditure. But there is, at any rate, a discussion about figures, so far rather confused and certainly not very clear to the voter but a start. And if the leaders of political parties would realise that it is also in their own interests that such a procedure is adopted, then a great deal would have been gained. Later they will probably understand that the voters too – and that means all of us – will experience the benefit.

However, the programmes should be well considered and prepared on the basis of realistic forecasts. This is possible on the basis of medium/long-term programmes, which of course should not be designed at the last moment with the object of winning an election. Another condition is that a system of feedback is used, so that after a party's term in office a balance-sheet can be drawn up of initial targets together with the degree of their realisation by the governing parties. Here lies, perhaps, a first, fundamental task for the office of a national ombudsman: to check how far political promises have been kept.

6.2 Some considerations about the productive capacity of consumption expenditures*

> The mathematically precise economic growth models that have been in vogue since the 1940s seldom take explicit account of the notion of investment in human beings. Increases in tomorrow's income are assumed to result primarily from today's additions to material capital, and since consumption displaces capital investment, it becomes an enemy of growth, not a handmaiden. (Alan Berg, *The Nutrition Factor, its Role in Natural Development*, Washington, DC)

Introduction

In the existing economic literature a sharp difference is still made between consumption expenditures on the one hand, and investments

*See L.H. Klaassen and W. Eizengen, 'Some considerations about the productive capacity of consumption expenditures' in Martin S. Feldster and Robert P. Irnman (eds), *The Economics of Public Services*, London: Macmillan, 1977.

on the other hand. This is done in spite of the fact that, in actual government policy, although implicitly, a different position is often taken.

The rationale of the distinction is that it is assumed that investments contribute to the increase of the capital stock and through this, via an increase in production, to a further increase in consumption potentials. With consumption, however, the end of the productive chain is reached. As Marshall already expressed it, 'consumption is the end of production'.

By putting the problem in this way, a number of important statements made by classical authors is neglected. These authors pointed out repeatedly that the physical and psychical well-being of human beings is decisive for their productive capacity and that this well-being is influenced to a considerable extent by the level of their consumption. We might quote a few of these statements:

> A plentiful subsistence increases the bodily strength of the labourer, and the comfortable hope of bettering his condition, and of ending his days perhaps in ease and plenty, animates him to exert that strength to the utmost. (Adam Smith, 1869)

Marshall indicates that the 'necessaries of an ordinary agricultural or of an unskilled town labourer' consist of:

> a well-drained dwelling with several rooms, warm clothing, with some changes of underclothing, pure water, a plentiful supply of cereal food, with a moderate allowance of meat and milk, and a little tea, etc., some education and some recreation, and lastly, sufficient freedom for his wife from other work to enable her to perform properly her maternal and her household duties. (Marshall, 1952)

And Rothschild states:

> Only workers who can afford certain 'semi-luxuries', like better and quicker forms of transport, better housing, holidays and entertainment, will be able to stand up fully to the nerveracking atmosphere of modern factory life. (Rothschild, 1954)

These statements indicate two important things. First, it is assumed that a certain level of consumption is needed to enable the worker to maintain a certain level of productivity, and secondly, that a higher level of productivity requires a higher level of consumption.

The last statement is particularly interesting since the reasoning is usually the other way round, namely that a higher consumption level can be attained only through an increase in production or productivity. Of course, this is true but the point is that an increased productivity can be maintained only if supported by a higher level of consumption. This means that in fact each level of performance requires certain inputs in the human being, be it physical or psychical, in order to maintain this level in the longer run.

This statement is obvious in so far as physical labour and food is concerned. A certain amount of food is needed for a physical performance during a longer period of time. But it is no less acceptable to assume that, with increasing psychological tensions in an occupation, inputs of a higher order, such as recreation, proper medical care, further training, etc., will also be needed in order to guarantee that the performance will not decrease in the longer run.

The foregoing seems to justify an attempt to introduce the productive capacity of consumption expenditures into economic models. It may be assumed that such a procedure, particularly for growth models, could contribute to our insight in growth processes as well as to the effectiveness of government policy. This does not hold only for models of Western economies, but maybe even more so for those to be used in developing countries. An attempt to construct a very simple model incorporating the above considerations is undertaken in the next section.

A simple alternative growth model

Let us start from the usual simple Harrod–Domar model. The well-known principle of this model is:

$$\Delta Y = \frac{1}{\kappa}(Y - C) = \frac{1 - a}{\kappa} Y \qquad (6.1)$$

resulting in:

$$g = \frac{1 - a}{\kappa} \qquad (6.2)$$

This expression holds under the conditions that:

$$Y = C + I \qquad (6.3)$$

and

$$C = aY \qquad (6.4)$$

where Y = income;
C = consumption;

κ = capital output ratio;
a = consumption ratio;
g = rate of growth.

The most essential objection to this model is that income growth reaches a maximum if the savings ratio is unity, which means that the consumption ratio is zero. This evidently erroneous assumption stems from the more basic assumption that income can only grow as a result of net additions to the capital stock and consequently consumption is unproductive. The latter assumption implies that consumption may be reduced to zero without influencing the productive capacity of labour. If we drop this last assumption the model changes drastically and makes it, at the same time, considerably more realistic.

We make two basic assumptions:

1. A certain level of consumption is needed to keep the productive capacity of labour just constant (to be indicated as *regenerative* consumption).
2. A consumption higher than this level contributes positively to the growth of productivity (income), although at a decreasing rate with growing income.

The first assumption is analogous to the one used concerning investments. In order to maintain the productive capacity of capital, reinvestments in capital goods have to take place. A certain level of gross investment is therefore needed for 'replacement' purposes. Only to the extent that gross investments exceed this level can we speak of an increase in the capital stock or rather of an increase in the productive capacity of the capital stock. In equation (6.5), I therefore represents the degree to which gross investments exceed the level of investments needed to maintain the productive capacity of the capital stock.

In fact the assumption with regard to consumption is completely analogous to this. If the productive capacity of labour depends upon the level of training, physical health, nutrition, the quality of housing, etc., then it is clear that a certain amount of all these things is needed to maintain the productivity of labour at a given level. Housing is needed, nutrition and medical care are needed, etc. Also in a macro sense education is needed as a result of the fact that elderly people leave the active population and are being replaced by younger people entering the active population. The latter need education in order to maintain the average educational level of the active population as a whole.

Furthermore, it follows from this last example that the level of consumption needed is not independent of the income level. A higher level of income necessarily will be linked to a higher level of education of the population in general, and the active population in particular. In order to maintain this higher level of education, the expenditure for education will have to be higher than in case where the level of education is lower. The other categories of expenditures for consumption show a similar picture. The higher the strain on labour, the higher will be the need for medical care, for recreation, etc.; in other words, the higher the level of consumption will have to be in order to prevent a decrease in productive performance.

The second assumption logically follows from the first one. This assumption is that, if consumption exceeds the level required according to the first assumption, a positive contribution to labour productivity is given, be it, with increasing consumption, to a decreasing extent. As a matter of fact, the same elements play a role here. Better housing and nutrition, better medical and recreational possibilities, more education, etc., all contribute in principle to an increase in the potential performances of the active population.

If we incorporate both assumptions in a simple growth model, the following results:

$$\Delta Y = \beta_0 (C - \bar{C})^{\beta_1} I^{\beta_2} \tag{6.5}$$

where I represents net investments, and $\bar{C}$ is regenerative consumption. It should be remarked here that according to equation (6.5) an additional assumption has been made, namely that if $C = \bar{C}$, net investments do not contribute to an increase in income. This means that net investments are ineffective if the productive capacity of labour is not simultaneously raised. This assumption expresses the idea that an intensified capital stock sets higher requirements on labour and, if these are not met, investments will show no return.

An additional assumption should be made. It is assumed, as stated before, that the level of the regenerative consumption is a function of the existing level of income. The most simple hypothesis would be that:

$$\bar{C} = \bar{a} Y \tag{6.6}$$

which completes the model.

The solution of the model is:

$$\Delta Y = \beta_0 (a - \bar{a})^{\beta_1} (1 - a)^{\beta_2} Y^{\beta_1 + \beta_2} \tag{6.7}$$

or:

$$g = \beta_0 (a - \bar{a})^{\beta_1} (1 - a)^{\beta_2} Y^{\beta_1 + \beta_2 - 1} \tag{6.8}$$

The optimal value of a, i.e. the value of a that maximises g at any level of Y can be derived from:

$$\frac{\partial g}{\partial a} = \left(\frac{\beta_1}{a - \bar{a}} - \frac{\beta_2}{1 - a}\right) g = 0 \tag{6.9}$$

or:

$$a^{OPT} = \frac{\beta_1 + \beta_2 \bar{a}}{\beta_1 + \beta_2} \tag{6.10}$$

For the optimal savings ratio, write:

$$\sigma^{OPT} = 1 - a^{OPT} \tag{6.11}$$

then we find:

$$\sigma^{OPT} = (1 - \bar{a}) \frac{\beta_2}{\beta_1 + \beta_2} \tag{6.12}$$

If σ exceeds $(1 - \bar{a})$, a decrease in income will result. $1 - \bar{a}$ thus may be defined as the maximum savings ratio (and consequently $\bar{a}$ as the minimum consumption ratio). We thus may write:

$$\sigma^{OPT} = \frac{\beta_2}{\beta_1 + \beta_2} \sigma^{MAX} \tag{6.13}$$

The preceding equations express the importance of $C - \bar{C}$ and I (which in fact has been defined as $I^G - R$, as gross investments minus the necessary replacements). The higher β_2 is in relation to the sum of β_1 and β_2, the higher the optimal savings ratio is and correspondingly lower the optimal consumption ratio.

Note that β_1, β_2 may be regarded as elasticities. For example, β_2 is the elasticity of the increase in income with respect to net investment. Similarly, β_1 is the elasticity of the income increase with respect to 'excess-over-minimum' consumption $(C - \bar{C})$.

Theory and policy

Contrary to the Harrod–Domar model that concentrates solely on savings, the preceding model would indicate that an increase in the level of consumption, in so far as the optimum level of consumption not yet has been reached, contributes more to economic growth than savings (investments) could do. From this, it follows that for countries with a very low income level, aid in the form of stimulation of consumption may make much more sense than aid in the form of investments. In practice, this fact has been recognised, if not explicitly, by many governments. The desirability of better training, improvement of medical care and recreational possibilities, better housing, and so on, stressed by almost any government, is certainly not a recent phenomenon.

No doubt, the significance of these objectives always has been that each of them is desirable as such, even without taking the consequences for productivity into account; but implicitly it also has been stated that they all are needed to meet the requirements of the development of society. It does not seem unrealistic to state that economists initiated thinking in this direction and afterwards (but not necessarily consequently) governments started to pursue a policy of stimulation of certain consumption categories. In the meantime economists stopped considering these things as important.

It is evidently not true that governments have been inclined to stimulate *all* sorts of consumption. They discriminate clearly between different groups of expenditures and promote consumption more strongly if the assumed influence on well-being (and through this on productivity) is supposed to be larger. The extremes run from compulsory consumption (primary education) via the subsidisation of secondary and higher education, medical care and recreation to the taxation of alcoholic drinks and tobacco, and even the prohibition of some sorts of consumption (certain drugs). This clearly means that governments intend to decrease the level of certain forms of consumption and increase others, according to the assumed influence on well-being. Through this the effect of consumption on productivity is implicitly maximised. It does not seem unlikely that governments in behaving like this anticipated the development of economic theory. This conclusion can be drawn not only with regard to the macro level of government policy, but also concerning the micro level of business management.

The importance of the human factor in organisation has in recent years been emphasised more and more in management. The willingness to incur costs for the acquisition and development of human resources is therefore understandable.

However, it seems that in this field, too, theory is lagging behind the factual developments. This is true, in particular, for accountancy procedures as usually applied. According to conventional accountancy procedures, expenditures for human development are registered as expenses. This implies that only a relationship between expenditures and revenues in the current year is assumed. Nevertheless, a part, and sometimes even a large part of those expenditures, often relates to returns in future years. In so far as this is the case, conventional accountancy theory cannot be regarded to be a useful basis for long-term management of human assets.

In so far as expenditures in favour of human resources are related to the current period only, it will be more difficult for a manager to justify funds for building human assets than for building physical assets. According to conventional accountancy, operating expenses are overstated, and net income understated when an organisation is investing more in human capabilities than they are being consumed. On the other hand, conventional accountancy understates operating expenses and overstates net income when human capabilities are being liquidated faster than they are created. One should keep in mind that write-offs of human resources are not recorded. Besides that, investment in human resources is not included in the measurement of the net return for evaluating current and future projects.

In this framework it is very interesting to mention the Human Resource Accounting research at the University of Michigan. This project in co-operation with business is directed towards developing a human resource accounting system. It deals with questions like how expenditures for recruitment, training, and on-the-job learning should show up on balance-sheets in order to serve the management not only with regard to physical assets, but also with regard to human assets. As a result, it is learned to what extent costs of acquirement, recruitment and training on the job are related to future years. (Examples of investments in human resources recognised in one firm can be found in William C. Pyle, 'An accounting system for human resources', *Innovation*, no. 10, 1970.)

It has become evident in this section of our study dealing with government policy and business management that, at least with regard to the impact of certain types of consumption on productivity, theory is lagging behind reality. It can be added that similar remarks can be made concerning consumer behaviour. Certain types of consumer spending are regarded as productive by the operating units themselves, i.e. contributing to working capacity. One can think of expenditures made for further schooling, in the form of tuition, books, a study. Considering the choice of devoting the evening to study or leisure, one has to take into account future revenues. The same might apply to other expenditures; for instance, regarding medical treatment and housing. As Katona puts it: 'The sum total of skills and education . . . as well of their health, represent economic assets' (in *Michigan*

Business Review, July 1961). And it really does not matter whether the government, business or consumer units pay for it. It will be clear that disregarding the impact of certain types of consumer expenditure on production can lead to miscalculating and might prevent us from making the right decision.

A cost-benefit approach

The question arises in how far the foregoing considerations could contribute to a more effective government spending. It seems that the answer is to be found in the application of a general cost-benefit approach in which all effects of the different government expenditures are considered. Basically cost-benefit analysis, although applying certain principles of economics, does not discriminate between consumption and investment expenditures. As the word says, it occupies itself solely with benefits on the one hand, and costs (in whatever form) on the other hand. The formal procedure is as follows. Write:

$$\mathbf{x} = A\mathbf{x} + B\mathbf{z} \qquad (6.14)$$

where $\mathbf{x}$ = the vector of variables influenced;
$\mathbf{z}$ = the vector of the elements of a given project.

The matrix B represents the primary effects of $\mathbf{z}$ and the matrix A the mutual influences between the $\mathbf{x}$s. The solution runs:

$$\mathbf{x} = [I - A]^{-1} B\mathbf{z} \qquad (6.15)$$

The total benefits of the project are:

$$B = \mathrm{i}' \hat{\lambda}\mathbf{x} = \mathrm{i}' \hat{\lambda} [I - A]^{-1} B\mathbf{z} \qquad (6.16)$$

where i = the unit vector;
$\hat{\lambda}$ = diagonal matrix of the (money) weights to be attached to $\mathbf{x}$.

Total costs equal:

$$C = \mathrm{i}' \hat{c}\, \mathbf{z} \qquad (6.17)$$

where $\hat{c}$ represents the diagonal matrix of the unit costs for $\mathbf{z}$.

The project considered is to be carried out if $B > C$, or if:

$$i' \left\{ \hat{\lambda} \, [I - A]^{-1} \, B - \hat{c} \right\} \mathbf{z} > 0 \qquad (6.18)$$

It appears that in this procedure all effects are taken into account regardless of the character of **z**. This means that no distinction is made between the **z**s that represent investment costs and those that represent other costs. This is in fact in complete accordance with reality. If the project is a road project, not only are investment costs of the road considered, but just as well other (e.g. maintenance) costs. If the procedure is applied to an educational project, higher incomes in the future belong to the x-variables since the interaction coefficients represent *all* effects initiated by the project.

The foregoing means that the application of cost-benefit analysis forces us to consider not only the conventional effects of income creation by investments, but the effects of all sorts of expenditures on any variable considered to be relevant in a societal context. This implies that the effects of expenditures for consumption are explicitly taken into account.

Since cost-benefit analysis does not, a priori, exclude certain effects, it may be said that in this sort of analysis a wider approach to expenditure problems is followed than in conventional economic theory. The latter starts from an a-priori structure of the A and B matrices, dictated by mere convention. Cost-benefit analysis, although not a theory but merely a method of estimating the effects of a given expenditure, does not exclude certain interactions and consequently considers all possible direct and indirect effects in order to enable the judgement of the viability of the project.

Apart from the fact that conventional economic theory only considers the effects of investments on income and not effects of so-called consumption expenditures on income, still another basic difference is to be mentioned: **x** represents *all* variables that are influenced by **z** not only economic variables, but also environmental, social and other variables. The theory that has to underlie cost-benefit analysis is thus considerably wider than economic theory. If properly applied, its application forces us to reconsider economic theory, make it more general and incorporate it into a much wider theoretical framework in which all elements that are relevant for human well-being are properly taken into account. It should be noted that the studies that have been performed in the field of testing theories on the assumed interaction between the variables, in principle, all make use of some sort of cost-benefit approach, although not always in the general sense indicated above.

Statistical evidence

From the foregoing it follows already that it might not be expected that, apart from a number of cost-benefit analyses, much research has been done to analyse the productive effect of certain kinds of consumption. Some studies have been mentioned in 'Social amenities in area economic growth' by L.H. Klaassen (OECD, Paris, 1968). The most well-known study in this area is probably the one by Leland S. Burns, 'Cost-benefit analysis of improved housing: a case study' (UCLA, 1965), in which for a number of regions in the world residential housing projects have been analysed with regard to their productivity effects. This study was a part of the International Housing Productivity Study to which B.K. Tjioe, of the Netherlands Economic Institute, made important contributions. In this study the net revenue of a subsidised residential housing project was observed in the Indian Pine Ridge reservation in South Dakota, USA. Two-thirds of the revenues consisted of indirect productivity effects and of savings in the medical and educational field; 45 per cent of the total revenues was due to productivity effects. The interesting study by H. Correa, 'The economics of human resources' (The Hague, 1962) should also be mentioned; this author emphasises the statement 'that labour is to some extent also subject to deliberate transformation and that it therefore makes sense to speak of a production function of labour' (p. 13). The various inputs of this production function, human beings and the social-economic factors that affect their productive power, are the object of his study.

Also in this framework, several studies can be mentioned in the nutritional field, dealing with the relationship between calorie intake and physical and psychological conditions that determine the capability to work. Dealing with this matter, it is useful to quote Harvy Leibenstein's study on *Economic Backwardness and Economic Growth* (New York/London, 1957, p. 63):

> The wage-productivity relationship can best be examined if it is broken up into two parts: (1) the relation between income (= wages) and nutrition and (2) the relation between nutrition and productivity. A 1936 study by Lord Boyd Orr shows clearly that in England the value of the nutritive components of diet (that is, calories, proteins, fats, calcium, iron, etc.) are monotonic increasing functions of income. Similar studies reported by the League of Nations' Committee on Nutrition gave similar results for a number of other countries. It is also evident from the Food and Agriculture Organization estimates of calorie consumption in various countries that low calorie consumption, generally speaking, goes with the low income per capita countries and high calorie consumption with high per capita income countries. Also, it is clear from a number of detailed studies of workers in

various underdeveloped countries that for the groups studied, the calorie intake per man per day is, in these cases, considerably below that designated by nutrition authorities as adequate for the maintenance of health, of normal body weight, and for the carrying out of a full day's work at 'normal' speed.

For further references in this field, see *Nutrition and Working Efficiency*, no. 5 in the basic studies series Freedom from Hunger Campaign, by the Food and Agriculture Organization of the United Nations (Rome, 1962), 2, 'Relation between diet and working capacity'. This study gives much evidence with regard to the positive relationship between dietary improvement and health and production in different countries; see also chapter IV, 'Income distribution, nutrition and working efficiency' in David Turnham, *The Employment Problem in Less Developed Countries: A Review of Evidence* (OECD, Paris, 1971), Employment series, No. 1. Similar evidence is in H.A. Kraut and E.A. Muller, 'Calorie intake and industrial output', *Science*, vol. 104, no. 2709 (29 November 1946). See also H. Kraut, *Uber die Deckung des Nahrstoffsbedarfs in West Deutschland*, Bibl. 'Nutricio et Diets' (Basle/New York, 1960), particularly the graph on page 46 clearly suggesting a positive correlation between calorie intake and production in Germany during the period 1936–52. And Alan Berg, *The Nutrition Factor, its Role in National Development* (Washington, DC, 1973). Under some circumstances, nutrition may be a 'precondition to the advancement of the other factors and a propellant to many forms of production. In short, not only is malnutrition a consequence of underdevelopment, but it is also a contributing factor, a drag on the potential from which better nutrition might be provided' (p. 195).

In G.C.M. McGonigle and J. Kirby, *Poverty and Public Health* (London, 1936), chapter VII is of interest: on the basis of human field research this shows that increased mortality was associated with dietary deficiencies. Because people moved to better housing with higher rent, not enough money was left to buy the necessary calories in order to maintain health and working capacity. This study emphasises the importance of generating adequate quantities of housing within the financial reach of relocatees. A similar conclusion can be drawn from Michael W. Pozen *et al.*, 'Evaluation of housing standard of families within four years of relocation by urban renewal', *American Journal of Public Health and the Nation's Health*, vol. 58, no. 7 (July 1968). In K. Rodahl *et al.*, 'Physical work capacity', *Archives of Environmental Health*, vol. 2, no. 5 (May 1961) it is concluded that although physical characteristics between groups of schoolchildren in Philadelphia, Germany and Sweden, in general were quite comparable, 'Swedish children were superior to both in work capacity, supposedly as a result of greater physical activity' (see also Editorial by Oscar J. Balchum).

In James M. Hundley *et al.*, 'Height and weight of first-grade children as a potential index of nutritional status', *American Journal of Public Health and the Nation's Health*, vol. 45, no. 11 (November 1955), on the basis of data concerning height and weight (as indicators of health and working capacity) of first-grade children in Philadelphian public schools for the periods 1925–7, 1932–4 and 1947–9, it was concluded:

> The data indicate that children from economically favoured areas were taller and heavier than children from economically underprivileged areas. Both economic groups of children showed a secular increase in growth. During the depression years, 1932–34, children from the lower economic areas showed no interruption in their secular trend. On the other hand, children in the economically favoured areas during the depression did show a significant deviation from their secular trends. This deviation was statistically significant for height in boys and for stockiness in both boys and girls.

In the educational field, P. de Wolff and R. Ruiter have contributed studies in their paper for the Vereiniging voor de Staathuishoudkunde on the economics of education. In this study (The Hague, 1968), a cost-benefit analysis was made on higher education. The results of the methodology that they discussed are characterised by the authors as being meagre. At best, this study provides a minimum quantitative indication of the contribution of expenditure for education to economic growth. Similar conclusions are derived by M. Blaug in *An Introduction to the Economics of Education* (London, 1970).

References

Marshall, Alfred (1938), *Principles of Economics* (8th edn), London: Macmillan, p. 54.

Marshall, Alfred (1952), *Principles of Economics, an Introductory Volume* (8th edn), London: Macmillan, p. 58.

Menger, C. (1968), *Grundsätze der Volkswirtschaftslehre*, Tübingen: Mohr.

Pierson, N.G. (1912), *Leerboek der Staathuishoudkunde* (3rd edn), Haarlem: De Erven F. Bohn, pp. 58–9.

Rothschild, K.W. (1954), *The Theory of Wages*, Oxford: Blackwell, p. 31.
Smith, Adam (1869, new ed. 1970), *The Wealth of Nations*, Harmondsworth: Penguin, Books I–III.

7 Government policy

7.1 Optimum governmental welfare policy for regions and cities*

Introduction

The welfare of a country's population is given concrete form in smaller geographical units such as regions, cities, etc. Here an attempt to give substance to the concept of regional or urban welfare, and to find out to what degree improvements of regional or urban facilities contribute to the people's welfare. By means of the concept of a potential a social welfare function will be defined in the second section. One of the problems of such a function is the determination of the various coefficients, and a method is briefly presented which can be used for measuring those coefficients and thus, indirectly, regional welfare differences. In the third section the concepts of the potential and the social welfare function are used to obtain a better insight into the regional and urban welfare policy of the government. Some factors will be discussed which determine the spatial and functional allocation of public expenditure, to be treated here as one of the instruments of a welfare policy used to influence the level of regional potentials and thus the regional welfare level. A model is

*See L.H. Klaassen, L. van den Berg and C.H.T. Vijverberg, 'Optimum governmental welfare policy for regions and cities' in *Papers of the Regional Science Association 1976*, Regional Science Association, Department of Regional Science, University of Pennsylvania, USA, 1978.

presented in the fourth section for the optimum allocation of welfare investments according to the ideas of the foregoing sections. The first part of this section presents an approach for two facilities and n regions, and the remainder is dedicated to the solution of the system (see van den Berg, Klaassen and Vijverberg, 1975).

Potentials and social welfare function

The concept of a potential The concept of a potential, or accessibility as it is called in most English literature, is closely connected with the so-called *gravity*-models, which try to explain a series of spatial interaction phenomena between two points by an analogy with physical phenomena. Gravity theory pivots around Newtonian physical law, which says that the attraction exerted by two bodies upon each other is proportional to their masses and inversely proportional to the squared distance between those bodies. In its traditional form the spatial gravity model, based upon the law of Newton, can be written therefore as:

$$T_{ij} = K \frac{W_i^{\,1} W_j^{\,2}}{c_{ij}^{\,n}} \tag{7.1}$$

where T_{ij} is the amount of interaction between two zones i and j, $W_i^{\,1}$ and $W_j^{\,2}$ are measures of the 'masses' belonging to zone i and zone j, and c_{ij} represents the distance, or in more general terms the generalised transportation costs, between i and j. K is a constant of proportionality and n a parameter to be estimated.

A.G. Wilson (1971) has shown how a whole family of spatial interaction models can be constructed from the above relation by using additional information of the total interaction between area of origin i and area of destination j. As an example, Wilson mentions a study of the spatial location of purchases in shopping centres, in which the distribution of population and of the purchasing power of the people were given. In that case, the interaction variable T_{ij} is defined as the flow of money from zone i to shops in zone j. The mass term for zone i is taken to be the total purchasing power of inhabitants of i ($e_i p_i = \Sigma_j T_{ij}$), defined as the average volume of purchases per inhabitant of zone i (e_i) multiplied by the population of zone i (p_i). The mass term belonging to zone j is measured as the size of the shopping centre in j on the assumption that size gives a good approximation of attractiveness. The model is:

$$T_{ij} = (e_i p_i) \frac{W_j^2 f(c_{ij})}{\sum_j W_j^2 f(c_{ij})} = P_{ij} (e_i p_i) \tag{7.2}$$

in which:

$$P_{ij} = \frac{W_j^2 f(c_{ij})}{\sum_j W_j^2 f(c_{ij})} \tag{7.3}$$

For the correct derivation of expression (7.2) from the traditional model in (7.1), we refer to Wilson. Here we are mainly interested in the interpretation of P_{ij}. Wilson interprets P_{ij} as the probability of an inhabitant of zone i visiting shops in zone j, and also as the relative utility, obtained by an inhabitant of i by shopping in j.

Elsewhere we adopted the interpretation of probability introducing, at the same time, the concept of a potential, defined as:

$$P_{ij} = \frac{W_j^2 f(c_{ij})}{\sum_j W_j^2 f(c_{ij})} = \frac{\Pi_{ij}}{\Pi_i} \tag{7.4}$$

in which Π_i represents the potential of zone i for a certain service or facility (see Klaassen and Verster 1974). In the context of the shopping model, mentioned above, Π_{ij} is interpreted as the absolute quality which an inhabitant of i attaches to the shopping facilities in j. The choice to buy in a certain shopping centre is determined, however, not only by the absolute quality of j, but also by the quality of shopping centres in all other zones, which compete with zone j for the favour of an inhabitant from i. The quality of the shopping facilities in j is weighed against the totality of shopping facilities potentially available to inhabitants of i by taking the ratio between the absolute quality Π_{ij} and the shopping potential of zone i ($\Pi_i = \sum_j \Pi_{ij}$). From this, it follows that Π_{ij}/Π_i is the relative attractiveness or quality of shopping facilities in j as perceived by inhabitants of i. This factor of relative attractiveness determines the probability that an inhabitant of i visits shops in j; or in other words, it determines the percentage of total purchasing power of inhabitants of i spent in shops in zone j.

On the basis of the foregoing we define the potential of region i for a certain facility in a general sense as:

$$\Pi_i = \sum_j x_j \exp(-\delta c_{ij}) = \sum_j q_j s_j \exp(-\delta c_{ij}) \tag{7.5}$$

in which x_j = size s_j such as the area or a similar measure of size of the facility concerned, weighted by some quality index q_j;

$\exp(-\delta c_{ij})$ = a specification of the distance function $f(c_{ij})$, in which c_{ij} represents the generalised transportation costs, determined as the weighted sum of all costs (money, time and effort) of bridging the distance; and δ is a coefficient for the sensitivity to distance, which represents the strength of the influence of the generalised transportation cost on the interaction between i and j.

It appears, then, that a potential is the sum of the value of a specific variable in all regions considered, weighted by distance and quality. It is interpreted as the degree to which region i is provided with a certain service or facility within region i itself as well as in all other subregions of the whole research area. In other words, Π_i represents the degree to which facility concerned is within the reach of the inhabitants of region i (hence the concept of accessibility).

Social welfare function Welfare is essentially immeasurable. In general, the concept of welfare represents the degree to which an individual or a group of individuals is of the opinion that their needs are satisfied by the available means. Needs as well as means include material and immaterial, measurable and non-measurable items. However, though welfare as such is not measurable, it is possible to say whether or not an individual or a group of individuals prefers situation A to situation B. In such a case, it is commonly said that welfare in A is greater than welfare in B, but the correct meaning is that the individual or the group, if given the choice, would choose A rather than B; see, for example, Graaff (1967). The preference ordering of the population as a whole is described in a *social welfare function* or collective preference function, a concept analogous to the utility function in the theory of consumer behaviour. Such a function gives a definition of welfare. The arguments of the welfare function are all the factors which can be considered determinants of welfare. Naturally there are not only economic determinants, but also social, cultural and psychological ones. Not all of them are quantifiable by the same method, some are not or only in an indirect way quantifiable. We find ourselves compelled to choose the most important determinants, in the hope that with their help we shall be able to develop a sort of functional definition of welfare. Of course, such a definition cannot escape being somewhat biased.

Reference can be made to studies about migration and migration motivations in selecting the determinants (see, for example, Schouten, 1975, and Ter Heide, 1965). Every decision to migrate is based upon the evaluation of interregional differences in the quality of life, differences which Ter Heide discerns in four spheres:

1 the economic sphere or sphere of work;
2 the sphere of housing (relates to the house itself);
3 the sphere of facilities (the geographical environment of the house);
4 the sphere of social relations (the social environment of the house).

In the following we will make use of three of these spheres, namely the spheres of housing and facilities, and the economic sphere. The more recent term 'livability' has more or less the same meaning as Ter Heide's housing factors. As facilities are counted medical care, education, culture, recreation, social servicing, etc. These variables will be formulated as potentials in the way described before, for we are interested not only in the physical presence of a facility and its size (and, perhaps, its quality), but also in the place where that facility is located and in the sacrifices (in money, time and effort) required for using them. Using a potential, one can do justice to these spatial aspects; that idea will now be elaborated further.

Let us assume that it is possible to construct potentials for all factors relevant to the social welfare function and for each regional or urban area distinguished. Let there be $v = 1, \ldots, V$ facilities, and $i = 1, \ldots, I = J$ regions, then the potential of facility v is defined as:

$$\Pi_i^v = \sum_j x_j^v \exp(-\delta^v c_{ij}^v) \tag{7.6}$$

in which the meaning of the symbols is the same as before.* These potentials can be used to construct a social welfare function. Let us assume, as before, that welfare is determined by three potentials, for instance, a housing potential, a facilities potential and an employment potential. The social welfare function of region i can then be represented by:

$$W_i = W(\Pi_i^\lambda, \Pi_i^c, \Pi_i^{ic}) \text{ for } i = 1, \ldots, I \tag{7.7}$$

*The potentials are defined as weighted sums of x_{ji}, regardless of the number of people using the facility. For comparison of potentials over regions we should bring in the number of users, but that aspect is left out for reasons of simplicity.

which implies that the welfare of region i is a function of all the distinguished components of economic and socio-cultural infrastructure.

The specification of the function is assumed to be such that different combinations of housing, working and facilities can lead to the same welfare position (principle of substitution), and also that the continued rise of one of the potentials, *ceteris paribus*, will cause a decreasing rise in welfare (declining marginal rate of substitution or decreasing marginal returns). As a frame for thinking we tentatively take a Cobb–Douglas-like function:

$$W_i = (\Pi_i^{\,h})^{a^h} (\Pi_i^{\,v})^{a^v} (\Pi_i^{\,w})^{a^w} \tag{7.8}$$

The form of this function satisfies the conditions required if:

$$\frac{\partial W_i}{\partial \Pi_i} > 0 \text{ and } \frac{\partial^2 W_i}{(\partial \Pi_i)^2} < 0 \tag{7.9}$$

which is the case if $0 < a^h, a^v, a^w < 1$.

But expression (7.8) also shows some typical characteristics. Under the potentials approach the welfare in region i appears to depend not only on the availability of facilities in region i itself, but is equally influenced by facilities in all neighbouring regions as far as they are accessible. In the next section this interregional interdependence will be treated further.

A second element which complicates expression (7.8) is the possible interdependence of the potentials that are arguments in the welfare function. It will be clear that some potentials are mutually dependent; their relationships can be positive or negative. When that is true, a change in a potential $\Pi_i^{\,v}$, as a consequence of a conscious governmental policy, will influence all the other potentials that are functions of $\Pi_i^{\,v}$. Formally the foregoing can be represented by:

Let:

$$W_i = (\Pi_{1i})^{a_1} (\Pi_{2i})^{a_2} \tag{7.10}$$

then:

$$\frac{\partial \Pi_{2i}}{\partial \Pi_{1i}} \gtreqless 0 \tag{7.11}$$

If expression (7.11) represents a *positive* relationship, then both the direct and indirect effects of governmental policy ($\partial\Pi_{1i}$ and $\partial\Pi_{2i}$ respectively) are positive, so that the positive change of welfare becomes extra great. In addition, these effects are passed on to surrounding regions owing to the interregional interdependence. Such a situation of positive influence could occur, for example, if the regional stimulation policy of the government, meant primarily to create employment, via the construction of social infrastructure should increase the recreational potential as well.

In a *negative* relationship the welfare benefit to be gained from a rising potential will be reduced by the decline of one or more other potentials. That could happen if extension of employment were damaging to the environment. In short, it follows that an understanding of the relatedness of potentials and of interregional interdependence is of great importance in determining the welfare effects of government measures. Before we continue this subject, a few more short comments on function (7.8) will be given.

The αs in this function represent the weights of each of the determinants of regional welfare. It will be noticed that (7.8) assumes that the same αs apply to all regions and to all groups of population. Seemingly we assume that regions are homogeneous in the demographic and social structure of their population. Generally, however, preferences for the various welfare determinants depend on age group and social group, so that for each relevant group a separate welfare function must be defined. If, on the other hand, we may assume that people belonging to the same group will react essentially in the same way, irrespective of the region where they live, then we may also assume that for such a group the αs will be the same in each region and that they will not be region-specific. That implies that the demographic and social structures of the population in a region are seen as important variables for explaining the regional differences in preference orderings and the changes therein over time. At a later stage, different welfare functions will have to be defined per group in each region. This aspect will not be treated in detail here.

Little attention was paid so far to possible differences in the preferences of the population on the one hand, and the government on the other hand. But there are arguments to distinguish between social welfare functions representing the preferences of the population and such functions representing the priorities of the government (see, for example, van den Berg, Klaassen and Vijverberg, 1975). A difficult problem with welfare functions is the determination of the α-coefficients. Because it is impossible to make a direct measurement of W_i, it is also impossible to make a direct estimate of the αs with, for example, multiple regression analysis. Elsewhere it was suggested that the problem can be solved with either an explicit method using results of public opinion polls of relative preferences; see, for example, Schouten (1975), or an implicit method for estimating the as on the basis of ex-post 'revealed preferences' in Klaassen and Verster (1974), Nijkamp (1970, 1975) and Hordijk, Mastenbroek and Paelinck (1974). In the next subsection we shall also give a short description of an implicit method in which the preferences of the population are seen as expressed in internal migration movements.

Measuring welfare differences We shall assume that the distribution of migrants among possible areas of destination corresponds to the relative differences in regional welfare. In other words, we shall assume that the internal migration flows reflect the interregional differences in welfare. Every migration decision is preceded by an appreciation of the relative welfare level of the possible area of destination and account is taken of the distance barrier due to financial and socio-psychological factors.

The foregoing remarks mean that we postulate a welfare function for the population which has the same form as the welfare function in expression (7.8):

$$W_i = (\Pi_i^b)^{\lambda^b} (\Pi_i^v)^{\lambda^v} (\Pi_i^w)^{\lambda^w} \qquad (7.12)$$

Taking this as a basis, we can define the relative attractiveness of area j to an inhabitant of area i as:

$$\frac{A_{ij}}{A_i} = \frac{(\Pi_j^b)^{\lambda^b} (\Pi_j^v)^{\lambda^v} (\Pi_j^w)^{\lambda^w} \exp(-\beta d_{ij})}{\sum_j (\Pi_j^b)^{\lambda^b} (\Pi_j^v)^{\lambda^v} (\Pi_j^w)^{\lambda^w} \exp(-\beta d_{ij})} = \frac{W_j \exp(-\beta d_{ij})}{\sum_j W_j \exp(-\beta d_{ij})} \qquad (7.13)$$

where A_{ij} = the attraction of j for the average inhabitant of i;
A_i = the sum of the attraction of all areas for an inhabitant of i;
d_{ji} = the total generalised (financial and social) costs of a move from i to j;
$\lambda^b, \lambda^v, \lambda^w$ = relative weights of the attraction potentials;
β = distance sensitivity.

On the ground of our hypothesis of migration behaviour, namely that the flow of migrants from i to j is a function of the relative attraction of region j weighted by the generalised migration costs, we can write, following Klaassen and Verster (1974):

$$m_{ij} = \frac{A_{ij}}{A_i} m_{i\cdot} = P_{ij}\, m_{i\cdot} \tag{7.14}$$

where m_{ij} = the flow of migrants from i to j;

$P_{ij} = \dfrac{A_{ij}}{A_i}$ = the probability that an inhabitant of i will migrate from i to j;

$m_{i\cdot}$ = the total flow of migrants from i to all other regions ($m_{i\cdot} = \Sigma_j\, m_{ij}$).

We note that expression (7.14) holds for all i and j, therefore also for m_{ii}. This last symbol represents the number of people who do not migrate but go on living in i. Their number has also been incorporated in $m_{i\cdot}$, which therefore equals the number of people who stay in i, plus those who move either from i to j or somewhere else. By definition, this equals the total population of i, which implies that expression (7.14) can also be written as:

$$m_{ij} = P_{ij} p_i = \frac{(\Pi_j^h)^{\lambda^h} (\Pi_j^v)^{\lambda^v} (\Pi_j^w)^{\lambda^w} \exp(-\beta d_{ij})}{\sum_j (\Pi_j^h)^{\lambda^h} (\Pi_j^v)^{\lambda^v} (\Pi_j^w)^{\lambda^w} \exp(-\beta d_{ij})}\, p_i \tag{7.15}$$

In words, expression (7.15) expresses that the flow of migrants from i to j is determined by the relative weighted attraction potentials (or the relative regional welfare) of j with regard to i, and is proportional to the total population of i. If we succeed in quantifying all potentials and distance functions, it will become possible to estimate by some statistical regression method the λ-coefficients, which are the weights attached by the population to the determinants of its welfare. With the help of the λs we can identify the preferences of the population and make use of them in the social welfare function.

Government expenditure and welfare

Governmental welfare policy The concepts of the potential and the social welfare function developed earlier can be used to obtain a better insight into the regional or urban welfare policy of the government. It is the central government's responsibility to promote welfare in the whole country by means of the instruments of regional policy at its disposal. Because the welfare of a country's population is given concrete form in smaller geographical units, the government, in its policy towards the various regions of the country, will try to make the regional welfare differences as small as possible, or at any rate to ensure to every region a certain minimum level. One of the instruments available to the government is the amount of money spent on the components of economic and socio-cultural infrastructure; in other words, the public expenditure directed towards the increase of the various potentials that are determinants of regional welfare.

The foregoing does not imply that the government should realise in all regions exactly the same combinations of components of the regional welfare function. It does mean that the government should try to influence the level of relevant potentials in such a way that the resulting combination brings the social welfare in every region up to a certain desired standard. That statement implies that all elements of the welfare function are, in principle, substitutable and that different combinations can represent one and the same welfare level. The specification of function (7.8) corresponds with this implication.

If the government has a certain annual budget at its disposal for increasing potentials, it is confronted with a two-sided selection problem: (a) to decide upon the spatial allocation of governmental funds to the various regions, giving priority to regions with a relatively low welfare; and (b) to decide upon the functional allocation of funds within each region to the various welfare components, giving preference to components with the highest contribution to welfare.

The regional as well as the functional allocation of public funds is determined according to the priorities of the government, embodied in its social welfare function. In this governmental selection function which relates to the welfare of all regions together, the total welfare of all regions will be weighed as well as the various welfare components within each region. Both sorts of weighing are directly related to the actual regional situation. The increase of welfare in a lagging region contributes most to national welfare, and the rise of a relatively low potential within a region has extra priority.

In the last section it was argued that the selection process is complicated by different forms of interdependences between potentials and between regions. In the next subsection attention will be paid to the interregional interdependences and the relations between potentials and governmental expenditure will be dealt with.

Potentials and government expenditure Government expenditure is taken here as an instrument to increase potentials. The various ways in which a potential can be increased by means of public expenditure are evident from the potential formula:

$$\Pi_i = \sum_j q_j s_j \exp(-\delta c_{ij}) = \sum_j x_j \exp(-\delta c_{ij}) \qquad (7.16)$$

which indicates that public outlays for a certain facility can be related to: (a) the quality of the facility, the size remaining the same; (b) the physical size of the facility at equal quality; and (c) the quality of the transport infrastructure.* Government expenditure is divided into current expenditure and capital expenditure or investments. In the following we shall restrict ourselves to public investments for net expansions of the physical size of facilities at equal quality. In that case, the increase of a potential equals:

$$\Delta\Pi_i^v = \sum_j \Delta x_j^v \exp(-\delta c_{ij}) \tag{7.17}$$

Let:

$$\Delta x_j^v = k_j^v I_j^v \tag{7.18}$$

in which k_j^v represents the additional size of facility v that can be produced in region j with a unit-of-investment amount I_j^v. It follows that:

$$I_j^v = \frac{1}{k_j^v} \Delta x_j^v = p_j^v \Delta x_j^v \tag{7.19}$$

in which p_j^v represents the price of a unit added to the size of facility v in region j in terms of governmental capital outlay needed.

From expression (7.17) it also appears that the potential of region i is determined not only by public expenditure in that area but also by the corresponding public expenditure in all other (relevant) regions, since Π_i^v is the sum of all Π_{ij}^v's. Such a spillover or interregional interdependence is essential for a potentials approach. For instance, when region i invests in educational facilities, not only will the educational potential in i, and thus the welfare level of i, increase, but the educational potentials and thus the welfare of all other regions will also be influenced by those investments, though only to the extent to which the educational facilities of region i are accessible to other regions. Conversely, the welfare of i is influenced by investments in, for example, recreational facilities in another region, provided that the costs of transport from i to that region are not prohibitive. The picture would be very complicated if attention should also be paid to the mutual dependence of potentials. For the sake of clarity, we shall ignore this sort of interdependence.

*In the foregoing sections no mention was made of a transport potential. The omission was deliberate: the influence of transport facilities on regional and urban welfare had been accounted for in each separate potential.

In principle, the government can spend the total net amount of investments on all potentials in all regions, so that, using the same terminology as in expression (7.7) we may write for the government's budget relation:

$$\bar{Y} = \sum_j (I_j^h + I_j^v + I_j^w) \qquad (7.20)$$

or:

$$\bar{Y} = \sum_j p_j^h \Delta x_j^h + \sum_j p_j^v \Delta x_j^v + \sum_j p_j^w \Delta x_j^w \qquad (7.21)$$

Simplified, it can be stated that unit investment prices in all regions are identical per facility, so that equation (7.21) becomes:

$$\bar{Y} = p^h \sum_j \Delta x_j^h + p^v \sum_j \Delta x_j^v + p^w \sum_j \Delta x_j^w \qquad (7.22)$$

We will investigate the problems of the governmental welfare policy in greater detail in the next section.

Optimum allocation of welfare investments

Approach for two facilities and n *regions* Assume that the welfare function for the ith region consists of two elements Π_{1i} and Π_{2i}, defined (as before) as:

$$\Pi_{1i} = \sum_j x_{1j} \exp(-\delta_1 c_{ij}) \qquad (7.23)$$

and:

$$\Pi_{2i} = \sum_j x_{2j} \exp(-\delta_2 c_{ij}) \qquad (7.24)$$

The values for Π_{1i} and Π_{2i} at the beginning of the year under consideration are indicated by $\Pi_{1i}^{(0)}$ and $\Pi_{2i}^{(0)}$ respectively. In the analysis it is assumed that the attraction element in each region j is defined by x_j, regardless of the number of people using the facility. Obviously this assumption restricts the validity of the analysis but enables us to keep the argument relatively simple. A more complete analysis could be made by assuming that the attractiveness of x_j declines (or increases) with the number of people attracted by it.

We now assume that the government divides a given sum of money among the regions and the (two) facilities in such a way that the increase in the welfare of all regions together is maximised. Write:

$$W_i = (\Pi_{1i})^{a_1} (\Pi_{2i})^{a_2} \tag{7.25}$$

and consequently:

$$\psi = \Delta W_i = (\Pi_{1i}{}^{(0)} + \Delta\Pi_{1i})^{a_1} (\Pi_{2i}{}^{(0)} + \Delta\Pi_{2i})^{a_2}$$
$$- (\Pi_{1i}{}^{(0)})^{a_1} (\Pi_{2i}{}^{(0)})^{a_2} \tag{7.26}$$

from which it follows that:

$$d\psi_i = a_i \frac{W_i^{(1)}}{\Pi_{1i}{}^{(0)} + \Delta\Pi_{1i}} d\Pi_{1i} + a_2 \frac{W_i^{(1)}}{\Pi_{2i}{}^{(0)} + \Delta\Pi_{2i}} d\Delta\Pi_{2i} \tag{7.27}$$

Write:

$$\Delta\Pi_{1i} = \sum_j v_{1j} \exp(-\delta_1 c_{ij}) \tag{7.28}$$

and:

$$\Delta\Pi_{2i} = \sum_j v_{2j} \exp(-\delta_2 c_{ij})$$

in which $v_{1j} = \Delta x_{1j}$ and $v_{2j} = \Delta x_{2j}$ (7.29)

Then:

$$d\psi_i = a_1 \frac{W_i^{(1)}}{\Pi_{1i}{}^{(0)} + \Delta\Pi_{1i}} \sum_j \exp(-\delta_1 c_{ij})$$
$$+ a_2 \frac{W_i^{(1)}}{\Pi_{2i}{}^{(0)} + \Delta\Pi_{2i}} \sum_j \exp(-\delta_2 c_{ij})\, dv_{2j} \tag{7.30}$$

and:

$$d\psi = \sum_i d\psi_i = a_1 \sum_i \frac{W_i^{(1)}}{\Pi_{1i}{}^{(0)} + \Delta\Pi_{1i}} \sum_j \exp(-\delta_1 c_{ij})\, dv_{1j}$$
$$+ a_2 \sum_i \frac{W_i^{(1)}}{\Pi_{2i}{}^{(0)} + \Delta\Pi_{2i}} \sum_j \exp(-\delta_2 c_{ij})\, dv_{2j} \tag{7.31}$$

An alternative approach would be to assume a 'government' welfare function in which the national welfare is a function of the welfare levels of each individual region:

$$\psi = \psi(\psi_1, \ldots, \psi_n) \tag{7.32}$$

so that:

$$d\psi = \sum_i \psi'_i d\,\psi_i \tag{7.33}$$

in which the weight ψ'_i would be a declining function of the welfare level of the ith region. We will continue the argument with the simple assumption that $d\psi = \sum_i d\psi_i$, in which all weights are equal to unity.

Now assume a budget restriction:

$$\bar{Y} = p_1 \sum_j v_{1j} + p_2 \sum_j v_{2j} \tag{7.34}$$

in which $\bar{Y}$ is the sum of money the government is willing and able to spend freely (i.e. after deduction of the running costs of the facilities already existing at the beginning of the year). We now write:

$$d\bar{Y} = 0 = p_1 \sum_j av_{1j} + p_2 \sum_j dv_{2j} \tag{7.35}$$

and can derive the following first-order equilibrium conditions:

$$\frac{\partial\psi}{\partial v_{1j}} = a_1 \sum_i \frac{W_i^{(1)} \exp(-\delta_1 c_{ij})}{\Pi_{1i}^{(0)} + \Delta\Pi_{1i}} = \lambda p_1 \tag{7.36}$$

$$\frac{\partial\psi}{\partial v_{1k}} = a_1 \sum_i \frac{W_i^{(1)} \exp(-\delta_1 c_{ik})}{\Pi_{1i}^{(0)} + \Delta\Pi_{1i}} = \lambda p_1 \tag{7.37}$$

$$\frac{\partial\psi}{\partial v_{2j}} = a_2 \sum_i \frac{W_i^{(1)} \exp(-\delta_2 c_{ij})}{\Pi_{2i}^{(0)} + \Delta\Pi_{2i}} = \lambda p_2 \tag{7.38}$$

$$\frac{\partial\psi}{\partial v_{2k}} = a_2 \sum_i \frac{W_i^{(1)} \exp(-\delta_2 c_{ik})}{\Pi_{2i}^{(0)} + \Delta\Pi_{2i}} = \lambda p_2 \tag{7.39}$$

The unknowns in these equations are the v_{1j}'s, the v_{2j}'s and λ, together $2n + 1$ in number. The number of equations equals $2n$ plus the budget restriction, i.e. also $2n + 1$. This means that the unknowns can in principle be determined as functions of the existing levels x_{1j} and x_{2j}, the distances c_{ij}, the two prices p_1 and p_2, and total government expenditures $\bar{Y}$. Although the equations look rather daunting, it may be remarked that the analysis results in a twofold optimisation procedure; first, finding the optimum distribution of new facilities over the regions, and secondly, finding the optimum expenditure on each facility. The first result may be written as:

$$\frac{\partial\psi}{\partial v_{1j}} = \frac{\partial\psi}{\partial v_{1k}}$$

and alternatively:

$$\frac{\partial\psi}{\partial v_{2j}} = \frac{\partial\psi}{\partial v_{2k}} \tag{7.40}$$

indicating that the marginal utility of the additional facility in j should equal the marginal utility of the additional facility in k. The second may be written as:

$$\frac{\dfrac{\partial\psi}{\partial v_{1j}}}{\dfrac{\partial\psi}{\partial v_{2j}}} = \frac{p_1}{p_2}, \ \forall_j \tag{7.41}$$

This is a well-known formula, which indicates that the ratio of the marginal utilities of facilities 1 and 2 should equal the ratio of their prices.

The solution of the system The first-order conditions allow for the following solution procedure. Write:

$$z_{1i} = a_1 \frac{W_i}{\Pi_{1i}} \tag{7.42}$$

$$z_{2i} = a_2 \frac{W_i}{\Pi_{2i}} \tag{7.43}$$

Then expression (7.36) may be written as:

$$\sum_i z_{1i} \exp(-\delta_1 c_{ij}) = \lambda p_1, \forall j \tag{7.44}$$

or, in matrix notation:

$$z'_1 D_1 = i' \lambda p_1 \tag{7.45}$$

in which D_1 is the matrix of distance elements.

Similarly, we write for the second facility:

$$z'_2 D_2 = i' \lambda p_2 \tag{7.46}$$

From expressions (7.45) and (7.46) we derive the values for z'_1 and z'_2

$$z'_1 = i' D_1^{-1} \lambda p_1 \tag{7.47}$$

$$z'_2 = i' D_2^{-1} \lambda p_2 \tag{7.48}$$

We proceed by rewriting expressions (7.42) and (7.43) as:

$$\frac{W_i}{\Pi_{1i}} = \Pi_{1i}^{a_1 - 1} \Pi_{2i}^{a_2} = \frac{z_{1i}}{a_1} \tag{7.49}$$

$$\frac{W_i}{\Pi_{2i}} = \Pi_{1i}^{a_1} \Pi_{2i}^{a_2 - 1} = \frac{z_{2i}}{a_2} \tag{7.50}$$

or as:

$$\ln \frac{z_{1i}}{a_1} = (a_1 - 1) \ln \Pi_{1i} + a_2 \ln \Pi_{2i} \tag{7.51}$$

$$\ln \frac{z_{2i}}{a_2} = a_1 \ln \Pi_{1i} + (a_2 - 1) \ln \Pi_{2i} \tag{7.52}$$

From these i sets of equations all Π_{1i} and Π_{2i} may be derived. Since the $\Pi_{1i}^{(0)}$ and $\Pi_{2i}^{(0)}$ are known, all $\Delta\Pi_{1i}$ and $\Delta\Pi_{2i}$ can be computed. Since furthermore:

$$v'_1 D_1 = \Delta\Pi'_1 \tag{7.53}$$

and:

$$v'_2 D_2 = \Delta\Pi'_2 \tag{7.54}$$

we find:

$$v'_1 = \Delta\Pi'_1 D_1^{-1} \tag{7.55}$$

and:

$$v'_2 = \Delta\Pi'_2 D_2^{-1} \qquad (7.56)$$

It appears that the values of the vs can be derived in a fairly straightforward way from the first-order equilibrium conditions. It should be noted, however, that the solution of the system has one important restriction, namely that all $v \geqslant 0$. This should of course be taken into account by rewriting expressions (7.36)–(7.39) as Kuhn-Tucker rather than as Lagrange-conditions.*

Final remarks

We have dealt here with the problems of developing a governmental welfare policy for regions or cities on the basis of a social welfare function. The introduction of potentials into this welfare function makes for a genuinely interregional treatment. It is our opinion that the concept of potential offers a realistic criterion for the distribution of government funds among the lower administrative units such as regions and municipalities. On the basis of the potentials the government could pursue a sort of redistribution policy for social welfare, in which public expenditures are divided among regions and social groups in order to spread welfare more evenly over the country. The optimum allocation of welfare investments depends on the measurement of regional welfare differences. It is our opinion that the proposed (implicit) method of measuring these differences by means of migration movements offers good possibilities. However, it is necessary for the ideas outlined here to be elaborated. That is why we present them for discussion.

7.2 Some thoughts about the limits to government power†

Introduction

In 1956, Professor J. Tinbergen wrote his eminently instructive book (Tinbergen, 1956) on the principles of economic policy, a book that has greatly influenced the practice of economic policy both in the Netherlands and elsewhere. It stated some very clear principles:

*The equality sign should be replaced by the inequality sign $\leqslant$.

†See Klaassen, L.H. and Eizenga, W., 'Some thoughts about the limits to government power' in S.I. Cohen, P.A. Cornelisse, R. Teeken and E. Thorbecke, *The Modelling of Socio-Economic Planning Processes*, Aldershot: Gower, 1984.

1 There are unequivocally defined objectives of economic policy.
2 There are instruments that, through a known interdependent system of education, can contribute positively to the realisation of these objectives.
3 The order of magnitude of the influence of these instruments is known.
4 The government uses its own insight to decide about the application of the instruments, and is capable of realising the objectives under certain conditions.

How far are these principles still valid now that society has changed so much? The following arguments are intended to give some insight into that question.

Extension of the system

Tinbergen's (1956) system was essentially an economic system, instruments and objectives being strictly economic variables, as such it may still be valid. But can this essentially economic macro-system be adjusted – and how can that be done – to accommodate non-economic subsystems, with non-economic variables? Tinbergen himself has been concerned with that problem on more than one occasion. Before taking it up here, let us present the concepts and terminology we shall use to describe and assess policy measures (Klaassen, 1973). A policy tends to be judged[1] by its consistency and efficiency; it is deemed consistent if its objectives are not conflicting among themselves (internal consistency), or with the objectives of other policies (external consistency). It should be pointed out at once that in economic policy, complete internal consistency can never be achieved, and that it is highly doubtful that any policy, economic or other, could be fully consistent with all others. We shall indeed use the expressions 'internal' and 'external' consistency in a limited sense. A policy will be considered internally inconsistent if its explicit objectives cannot be achieved by any combination of instruments; analogously a policy will be considered externally inconsistent if its explicit objectives cannot be reached by any combination of all the instruments that can be envisaged to serve the totality of policies.

A policy is efficient if, in relation to the cost, its instruments make a significant contribution to the objectives of that policy. It is internally efficient if the instruments achieve many of its direct goals; its is externally efficient if they also contribute to the objectives of other policies.

Many combinations of consistency and efficiency can be envisaged.

A measure may contribute to industrial growth and thus be internally efficient, while being inconsistent, in that it pushes up the price level; moreover, if it stimulates the kind of industry that worsens pollution, it is externally inefficient and inconsistent.

The question that concerns us here is: is it still possible to judge by the four principles of economic policy, stated above, whether a policy meets the demands of efficiency and consistency? If we can convince ourselves and others that it is not – at any rate at our present state of knowledge – we shall have begun to answer a more general question, namely is government still as simple as it used to look?

The first thing to consider is that since the Second World War the world has become much more complicated. Just after the war, when it seemed as if nothing could stop the economy from growing, when environment, space and exhaustible deposits of raw materials were not yet matters of concern, and when there was full employment, there was no reason to think twice about the effects of measures of economic policy outside the economic field. Things are very different now; we have woken up to the fact that virtually every problem has economic, social, environmental, labour market and still other aspects, and that any tool wielded on behalf of any policy has so-called side-effects in all other policy areas, so that the desirability of that tool cannot be ascertained without the study of many different segments of society.

The same phenomenon is observed in agriculture, road construction, re-allotment plans, health care and the labour market; it has indeed penetrated the whole of our society. We are discovering all the time how our cherished projects have unwittingly trespassed into other fields, sometimes with positive effects but more often to their detriment, making the outcome we had envisaged seem far less attractive now. The Delta Scheme was hailed at the time as a blessing for the Netherlands, especially by those who had lived through the 1953 floods. Now that other matters are pressing for attention, doubts are expressed on all sides: should not other solutions have been considered besides the one ultimately chosen for safety reasons alone? Of the hundreds of regional hypermarkets that have sprung up, especially in Belgium and Germany, to serve car-driving consumers, many people now ask themselves if the advantages weigh up against the traffic nuisance they cause, the violation of scenery, the erosion of urban centres and the loss of provisions for non car-owners. In other words, we are now wondering whether the monodisciplinary approach should not gradually be replaced with a multidisciplinary approach, taking account of the effects – quantified or otherwise defined – in other fields.

With all such social developments undeniably on the march, what can scientists do? From the above, one task emerges at once: the important task of quantifying all economic and non-economic effects of a certain policy measure, expressing them if at all possible in the same units. For quantification makes it possible to combine a growing number of effects and compare their costs and benefits. Attempts in that direction come under the heading of 'policy analysis'.

If on the basis of positive knowledge completed by intuition, we set ourselves to list and preferably quantify the advantages and disadvantages of a project with a view to appreciating its economic and social merits, we are indeed studying relations between aspects, and therefore relations between disciplines. We try to assess the effects of labour market tension on sickness leave, those of the layout of roads on the nature of traffic accidents, the influence of better medicine against gastric complaints on the patients' productive days, of growing air traffic on the functioning of the auditory organs of those living around the airfield, of working in shifts on the number of divorces, of boating holidays on the quality of the water in the areas reserved for such leisure activities, and so on. Highly important investigations all of them, tending to bring scientists of various disciplines together and pressing them, as it were, into co-operation. It is no longer possible for a scientist skilled in one discipline to do this kind of research – and hence his own work – without calling in the help of researchers from one or more other disciplines involved in the problem under study. An economist can no longer afford to be just that, a sociologist fails if he is no more than that, and a technician will fail to make his projects acceptable to society by their technical merits, be they ever so great. Similar reasonings hold for the scientists of other disciplines. However, calling in the help of other disciplines, while undeniably widening the scope of scientific research, is still no more than one step twoards a truly interdisciplinary approach to social problems. Characteristically, cost-benefit analysis takes into account that the execution of a given project will affect other fields than the one traditionally associated with it. But the analytical framework ought to be extended still further, as the following example may illustrate.

Suppose a large new project is considered for an area already industrialised. A cost-benefit analysis is undertaken, taking into account, as it should, the new project's effect on the environmental quality of the region, especially on the pollution of air and water. However, the analysis would be incomplete, and no proper basis for a decision, if it would be left at that. From investigations in the Ruhr and Rhine estuary we know that large segments of the population have grown so sensitive to the environment as to deem the lack of environmental quality a proper reason for emigration from industrial areas or for not settling there. Should people with a certain grade or kind of skill be specifically involved, then the structure of the labour market would be affected, and thus the set of locational conditions that attracted the industry in the first place. It was precisely such developments that in the Ruhr area helped to create the need for a multitude of foreign workers, especially in the metal industry. The social problems that entailed are well known: a different cultural background and 'foreign' behaviour are conducive to ghetto-building and other segregation phenomena.

We could continue the chain of causes and results – with its many cross-connections – just described, but even the incomplete chain may have made our point, which is that subareas of science are closely interwoven and that therefore a cost–benefit analysis cannot be limited to the study and evaluation of the direct effects of a certain project, but should include as many as reasonably possible of the indirect (or circular) effects, effects that may involve several disciplines. Only then are we really venturing on an interdisciplinary approach, for the disciplines enlisted will be looked upon as a system of closely related subareas of science, none of which can claim priority for as long as the study is in progress. It depends on the nature of the problem which disciplines will ultimately carry the greatest weight when it comes to decision-making, but it will rarely be possible to spot them beforehand. Only after the integral analysis will it become certain which effects are more important than others. At this point, two significant statements can be made:

1 To assess a policy's consistency and efficiency, the principal final effects caused by its instruments in all other areas of society must be known.
2 The system of disciplines is so complicated and so little analysed – being singularly inaccessible to analysis and quantification – that the effects may never be fully known.

Unequivocally defined objectives?

It follows from the above two statements that the developments of the recent past have made it more unlikely that the government is capable of conducting a consistent and efficient policy, and that indeed the second and third principles of economic policy presented in the introduction have devaluated somewhat. But have the arguments developed in the previous sections also shed some light on the presence of unequivocally defined objectives? It would be interesting to find out whether such objectives can still be found at all in the reality of today, but we will content ourselves with the assumption that they exist for a certain period of administration. However, with the expansion of the relevant interdisciplinary system the number of objectives has increased considerably. Environmental aims, various social goals, and many objectives of spatial planning are among the recent additions, a satisfactory development in itself, but increasing the danger of internal inconsistency because of the multitude of instruments required. Lack of understanding of the interdisciplinary system may also cause inconsistency: it is easy to overlook one or two items as the numbers of tools and objectives go on to increase.

Land policy is a good example of a policy that is as regular as clockwork in creating political difficulties. If one states that land should be used so as to yield maximum benefit to society, one is still safely on neutral ground. A concrete proposition about the payment to be made to landowners who are (for good societal reasons) dispossessed, however, is already more hazardous. Must one attach the greatest weight to the market value, thus letting the interests of present owners (a societal group) prevail, or to the consumption value, thus favouring the future users (a larger societal group). If the land is expropriated at the consumption value (present value of net returns, selling price of arable land or selling price of land set apart for the expansion of existing or establishing of whole new plants?), town expansion will become relatively cheaper because the houses to be built on the sites thus acquired will have relatively low rents, and because public parks, common greens, sportsfields as well as infrastructure will require fewer means to be laid out than elsewhere in the town. However, that reasoning only holds for land at the periphery of towns; the validity of the same principle for land in town centres now used for offices but wanted for housing is questionable. If the principle could be extended to inner cities, land for housing would be relatively cheap on the outskirts of cities and more expensive in the inner city where it would have to be taken from other destinations. In view of their tight financial situation many municipalities would then prefer to go on using land in their inner cities for office purposes and land at the periphery for housing, a tendency that is directly opposed to the one now generally favoured.

The conclusion can be drawn that, though there might be unequivocally defined objectives, their number is so large as to make their consistency uncertain. Even less can be known about the effects and successes scored by the instruments used to attain those objectives.

Freedom in the use of instruments

The next question is how far the fourth principle, the government's freedom[2] to use instruments at its discretion, can still be upheld. An implicit answer to that question was already given in establishing that lately the essentially economic system has expanded into an interdisciplinary one. Groups who are mainly desirous of having their economic interests served by government policy have been joined by others who formerly used to keep themselves outside the political sphere. These common interest groups can roughly be divided into three categories. First, there are the groups that concentrate their efforts on a single aspect of social life, advocating for instance the decrease of car traffic, accelerated introduction of environmental protection, prevention of electricity production in nuclear plants, etc. They keep their objective firmly in mind and try to make and defend their point at all possible places and all possible times and by all possible means. Characteristically, they tend to isolate their objectives from the social context in which it belongs. Their vigorous and single-minded pursuit of one single aspect of society may have its usefulness.

The second category makes a point of emphasising the interests of certain groups of people. Women, senior citizens, pedestrians, cyclists, car drivers, employers, employees, etc., they all have their own associations which, vigorously or timorously, proclaim and defend their own interests, which may run parallel or opposite to those of the former category.

The actions of the third category, finally, are oriented towards a certain region, be it large or small (a quarter of a large town, for example). Groups of this kind aim to safeguard or raise the well-being of their own subsociety, and to that end plead their cause with the authorities. The emphasis they lay is slightly different from those of the two other categories, but there are obviously points of contact and overlaps.

What makes these categories remarkable is not so much that their objectives should clash with those of the government as that they give so much weight to specific interests. The government, compelled to weigh up these interests and pronounce, so to speak, Solomonian judgments all the time, finds itself hampered in its freedom of action. The stronger the so-called pressure groups are, the harder it becomes for the government to ignore their wishes. Indeed pressure groups can achieve success by their actions in shifting the accents of government policy from those the government would have placed, had it been free to make its own decisions together with Parliament. Pressure groups may even compel the authorities to take measures which but for that pressure would not have been taken at all, the result being that insufficient funds are left for objectives of the government's preference. As an example we may mention the police protection that has to be provided to air passengers and aeroplanes as a direct result of actions undertaken by mainly political groups cherishing views that deviate from the accepted pattern. Already the mere financial implications of the police activities may disrupt the financing of other necessary measures.

A group formally belonging to the third category is that of such international organisations as the UNO, IMF, OECD, EC, and NATO. These 'actors' also influence national policies to varying degrees, limiting to some extent the central authorities' freedom of action. National governments often find themselves bound by agreements whose conclusion is largely out of their control, agreements from which they can hardly if at all withdraw. On the other hand, the growing 'pluralism' of power seems to be making it increasingly difficult for national governments to respect international agreements.

This, then, is the picture that emerges: Parliament and the political organisations it represents find themselves joined or opposed by a host of other groups and organisations, influencing government policy with varying success and actually claiming part of the governing authority. Hearing procedures have become routine, and have no doubt had a considerable influence on government decisions.

It is clear from the foregoing that governing is no longer the well-arranged and transparent activity it seemed to be when the consensus on objectives and instruments was greater. The new developments have also led to lengthy, cumbersome procedures with unpredictable outcomes. In the Netherlands, for example, it has long been uncertain if and how the Oosterschelde was to be closed, and even now, after years of squabbling, it is uncertain that the solution eventually chosen does not leave large groups of the population unsatisfied. The zeal with which individual points of view are defended and maintained makes it well-nigh impossible to arrive at a considered, well-balanced decision acceptable to the general public. Yet it is not the general objective that is contended – everybody agrees that the ultimate aim should be the promotion of general welfare – but the weight to be attached to each of its elements. Until the weights have been determined, the outcome remains open and subject to attacks from groups who invariably attribute the highest weights to their pet aspects.

Pluralism of power

In the previous section we have seen that in our present Western civilisation numerous associations are formed for the express purpose of serving certain (group) interests. They vary in legal and societal status and membership and cover very nearly all facets of social existence, pleading such varied causes as the levelling of incomes, optimum spatial planning, optimum distribution of responsibility, equity in the administration of justice, etc. Belinfante's typology of the Western state and its decision power comes to mind; he describes the state as an exchange where various spheres of influence, weighing up their respective powers, set 'exchange rates' for them which, in turn, determine the power of the state (Prakke, 1974). Or in Prakke's terminology, 'The State may no longer possess the monopoly of power, but its invested official status has enabled it to develop into a platform on which and by which interests vying for priority may be confronted and weighed. It has become a clearing house for societal pressure and counter-pressure, and the means to give social equilibrium legal status.' (p. 11)

It is true that government policy can be called successful only if the different pressure groups can be made to accept common objectives, or if at least the policy objectives are widely accepted by society.

All this is highly relevant to the problem which concerns us, because it shows how and to what extent the power of the state has been limited. In the past we have seen how political parties, after vigorously pushing their programmes during election time, were compelled and prepared to make considerable concessions for the sake of forming a coalition cabinet. Now we are witnessing every day how the government programme agreed upon by the political parties is curtailed, bent and otherwise changed. The fact is that the Cabinet's programme represents only one (sometimes modest) segment of the total oligopolistic supply of policy proposals. The government's limited political power will be the more manifest as the government coalition is weaker,[3] as witness the frequent government crises in several West European countries.

A dynamic system

The system we have attempted to describe above is in fact dynamic. Sets of government objectives are subject to constant change, for governments will always try to meet the altered preferences prevailing in our society and continuously voiced by pressure groups. Much the same thing happens, for that matter, in the bosom of the interest groups themselves, who are also required to adapt their objectives to the wishes of their rank-and-file. To keep up the fiction of a controllable 'macro-system' (the model of total society), it is of course essential that the signals from the ranks are correctly interpreted by the relevant policy bodies; correct interpretation is in fact a precondition for the proper adjustment of policy objectives at the right time. On the other hand, lack of consensus among the 'followers' with respect to the 'worthiness' of certain objectives may seriously injure the (sub-)system's controllability.

We will not go deeply into the causes of the continuity of societal processes; suffice it to point out that in a world full of uncertainty it is to be expected that the results of actions fall short of the expectations. The very tensions between hope and reality may then give rise to new actions, oriented not only to the aims to be achieved, but also to the means by which they are to be achieved. Instruments are not likely to be replaced until the old ones have been proved ineffective. Both the setting of objectives and the choosing of instruments involves a learning process.

Societal developments as well as long-term effects of government measures may generate new insights which, in turn, will influence what is going to happen next and what measures will be taken in the next stage. Thus the whole system moves up to the next stage, whose features have been generated in the previous one. Policy, thus being reduced to 'following', tends to respond to the momentary situation because it is politically impossible to act otherwise, but at the same time is shaping the near or distant future, a future in which there will be new demands to take up.

What with the structural evolution of society, the increased complexity of the societal process, the limits imposed on the government's freedom of action by the activities of zealous groups, and, most of all, the internal dynamics of society, many measures that in short-term surveys may be presented as the application of exogenous instruments have indeed become endogenous factors, determined as they are by the dynamics of the system itself.

Conclusion

The conclusion to be drawn from what has been put forward in the previous sections is not limited to a specific government of given political composition, but apply to all governments of democratic countries. Governing has indeed become a far from enviable job. Numerous groupings, desirous of putting in their oar, make their wishes known in unmistakable terms. The problems are getting ever more complicated and the points of view ever wider apart. A political party ignoring those facts lacks the wisdom now more than ever essential to government; voters unable to recognise the problems that governments have to face, lack insight and – harsh as it might sound – have forfeited part of their right of criticism.

To give the government a fair chance it is necessary to realise how much the powers of central and local authorities are limited when it comes to practical policy measures. The criterion of good government should not be the absolute degree to which objectives have been realised, but the degree to which they have been achieved in relation to what, under the prevailing conditions, was humanly possible. On the other hand, and this may be our final conclusion, wisdom and modesty become the government as it sets out to elaborate its policy programme.

7.3 Considerations on the power of government institutions in spatial planning

Introduction

Institutions are the infrastructure of decision-making on a government level. Since institutional structures differ from country to country, a treatment of institutional factors may be expected to take these differences into account and consequently either to concentrate on one particular country or to compare and/or evaluate the different institutional structures in different countries. We will not do so here, however. However useful such studies may be, to us it seems rather more interesting to concentrate on the question to what extent government institutions, whatever their structure, are able appreciably to influence the actual spatial developments in their country. In other words, we want to investigate what the usual practice in physical planning is and how effective this practice is in reaching certain a-priori objectives. It will be shown that in trying to answer this question, we automatically arrive at the institutional structure and the degree of its efficiency.

The classical approach to planning is the one introduced by Tinbergen in his famous *Design of Economic Policy*. Since then we have more or less automatically formulated every planning problem in terms of objectives and instruments. The question may be raised whether such a procedure applies to physical planning in its present stage. Tinbergen's approach assumes the existence of a well-described model, well-defined objectives and well-defined, efficient instruments. It will be shown in the following that none of these three conditions is actually fulfilled in physical planning.

Although the words used for physical planning in other languages such as 'aménagement du territoire', 'Raumordnung', 'ruimtelijke ordening', etc. all suggest a somewhat more restricted activity than physical planning, we will start from the assumption that originally physical planning was also intended to be an activity aiming at 'arranging physical elements in an orderly way'. We will leave aside what 'orderly' is supposed to mean, and assume that there is an ideal order of the physical elements and that it is the task of the physical planning authorities to use their influence to bring the actual order of things as closely as possible to the ideal order. We will try later to get some idea of what an ideal order might be. For the moment, it suffices to assume that the authorities are aware of the direction in which the existing order has to be changed in order to bring it closer to this, as yet undefined, ideal order.

Physical planning, or the re-ordering of things, can be done in a direct way or in an indirect way. *Direct* ordering is defined as ordering performed by an authority that has both the power to create or replace the elements that have to be ordered and the power to perform the ordering itself, i.e. to locate the elements according to a pattern preferred by that authority. A simple example of direct ordering is the ordering of furniture in a room, where the family chooses the furniture *and* arranges the separate pieces according to its preference.

Direct ordering can be performed in a *negative* way or in a *positive* way. This can be shown by a simple example. Suppose three elements A, B and C have to be placed in three cells, 1, 2 and 3. The 'ideal' ordering is as shown below:

1	2	3
A	B	C

If the ordering proceeds in a positive way, the elements are placed according to the rule that A has to be placed, and thus will be placed, in cell 1, B in cell 2 and C in cell 3. Obviously, however, the same result could have been obtained if a rule had been applied that each element had to be placed in a cell, but that A must not be placed in cells 2 and 3, B not in cells 1 and 3 and C not in cells 1 and 2. The result in this case is identical to the ordering obtained by applying the first rule.

However, the latter procedure comes much closer to the one applied in practical physical planning than the first one. Direct planning is only possible for elements that are effectively in the hands of the government. For the results of such planning, it is irrelevant whether it takes place according to a positive or a negative rule.

In cases of *indirect* planning, however, the government tries to influence the spatial behaviour of others by means of certain instruments and negative rules. In this case, positive rules cannot be applied since the government lacks the power to handle the elements directly. Indirect planning, therefore, has to work with negative rules indicating the elements that are not allowed in certain places.

But if the decision to construct, or not to construct, a certain element is in the hands of others, then there is no guarantee at all that the result will be as originally planned. The previous example may be used to elucidate this point. Suppose element B is not interested in its place in cell 2; then that cell will remain empty, and the result will be:

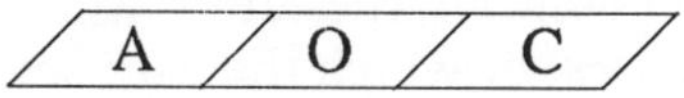

Obviously such a solution could be completely senseless. If A is a collection of houses, C is infrastructure and B represents industrial activities, the arrangement AOC is clearly sub-optimal, since A and C were placed in cells 1 and 3 under the assumption that cell 2 would be filled by B. With B lacking, A and C might not be needed at all, or, if created, would lead to commuting over enormous distances to other places, where B is also permitted and where its location might be much more attractive from a private economic point of view. Of course, the government might use other instruments to induce industries to locate in cell 2, but it is possible and even likely that given the choice between subsidising industries in cell 2 or accepting another order, e.g. ACB, the government will opt for the latter choice. However, the order that thus finally materialises will be sub-optimal from the government's original point of view because it has been adjusted to the preferences of others than the government.

The more we realise the essence of this conclusion, the more we might be inclined to believe that the actual final order is not determined by government action, but by the preferences of entrepreneurs, buyers or tenants of houses, or users of infrastructure. This becomes even clearer when we realise that many elements that are handled by the government in a direct way, such as technical and social infrastructure and housing, depend for their location upon the location of employment opportunities, if not in a micro scale, most certainly so in a wider spatial context. If industrial locations cannot be controlled, i.e. if industries cannot be induced to locate in the places preferred for them by the government, the locations of the complementary elements will have to be shifted. The result of this procedure will be that physical planning becomes a process of permanent adjustment. The more the original plans deviate from the ones actually realised, the less efficient this process will be.

Dynamic factors

In fact the foregoing has shown already that the adjustment process is characterised by dynamic elements originating from the deviations of government preferences from private preferences. One could protest that this situation could occur only in capitalist countries, since in socialist countries the government is the sole decision-maker. This is, in fact, far from true. Although the conflict has been presented as one between government and private enterprises, it is in fact much more a conflict between physical planners and industrial planners. In socialist countries the latter will try to reach optimum results for the enterprises for which they are held responsible. As such they do not in their behaviour differ basically from the entrepreneur in capitalist countries.

More important is the dynamic character of the process itself. It seems worthwhile to analyse this element somewhat more precisely.

Let us consider road construction and assume that the government has decided to change its policy in this field. Instead of using road construction as an instrument to adjust road capacity in an optimum way to the volume of traffic, as it was done in the past, the government has decided for reasons of environment and spatial planning to limit road capacity to a certain maximum level, at least in certain congested regions.

Indicate this level by r_0. Suppose further that actual plus potential traffic in the year t would require a road capacity r_t. Then the pressure on the government to expand road capacity in year t may be represented by:

$$\pi = \phi\left(\frac{r_t}{r_0}\right) \qquad (7.57)$$

in which $d\pi/(d\frac{r_t}{r_0}) > 0$ and most likely $d^2\pi/\left\{(d\frac{r_t}{r_0})^2\right\} > 0.$

As the costs of resisting this pressure are a positive function of the traffic itself, at a certain moment the ratio r_t/r_0 will reach a critical level. The usual development is that congestion will reach a point at which there is so much publicity about it that the government simply has to give in and decide to adjust the road capacity.

The only difference between this course of events and the one developing before the government changed its policy is that in the original procedure roads were constructed in advance, while now they are adjusted to the pressure of traffic afterwards. No doubt, the latter procedure is a better one if one believes that there should not be any more road construction at all, but it certainly does not reflect the policy that was originally intended. Apart from the fact that the time-lead has been replaced with a time-lag, there is little real change. In both cases, the volume of road construction is determined by the actual development of traffic.

It should be noted that a basic assumption implied in the foregoing was that developments in the volume of traffic are largely autonomous. If these developments were determined only by the developments in the available road space, things would have been different. In that case, the value of r_t could never exceed r_0 and the policy would have been completely successful. The degree to which the above argument holds is therefore determined by the degree to which developments in traffic volumes are to be considered autonomous. We will come to this point later.

Another example of the government having to adjust its policy is to be found in its dealing with a problem that is being widely discussed in the Netherlands (and in the UK). It concerns regional shopping centres outside towns, as recently have been constructed in large numbers in the USA, Western Germany, France and Belgium.

In the Netherlands the government so far has firmly resisted the applications for permits to construct such shopping centres. The reasons for this resistance were clear and reasonable. These shopping centres create traffic flows where they have not been foreseen, require space in areas which should remain open and green, and are a menace to existing shopping centres in towns and cities.

Here, too, the question arises to what extent the government will be able to resist the pressure exerted by the population. Many will argue (and in fact already are doing so) that the new shopping centres are easily accessible, particularly by car, allow for much more efficient shopping, are cheaper, etc., arguments that are all perfectly valid. Moreover, the disadvantages of these centres are not really felt by the average consumer until they have become too evident to be ignored. The consumer is not likely to realise the influence of the shopping centres on existing town centres until the latter have suffered so badly that their degeneration becomes visible. Even then he might not care too much, to realise perhaps only in the very long run what values have been lost.

How firm a stand will the government make in the face of these tendencies? Municipalities that could profit from the location of a regional shopping centre within their territory will, by promoting such a centre, compete with their urban neighbours for the buying power of the urban population. Smaller, already existing, local shopping areas might be adjusted little by little to the consumer's preferences, and gradually grow out to what is in fact a regional shopping centre. Retailers will propose further renovations, which can hardly be refused because they benefit not only the retailers themselves, but also the municipality and the consumer. In their efforts to promote their own welfare, municipal authorities will increase the accessibility of the centre, create parking places, etc.

If this process continues, not only will urban centres suffer, but the quality of life in the surrounding municipalities will degenerate. As soon as this becomes evident, it is not at all unlikely that the central government will finally accept the creation of a limited number of new well-planned shopping centres in places where it seems less harmful than in the built-up areas of smaller towns. If this actually happens, we have another case where the original policy has to be adjusted, or even reversed as a result of the pressure of autonomous developments.

Objectives and instruments

It appears from the foregoing that the procedure in conventional physical planning cannot in fact be described in terms of objectives and instruments, unless in a more or less artificial way by calling a constraint an objective, and a legal measure, taken to ensure that the constraint is met, an instrument. We will continue to speak in terms of instruments and objectives, however, as this will enable us later to shift gradually to the real meaning of these words.

Let us repeat in a formal way the foregoing arguments. Indicate the actual situation in a given region by x and the situation that would materialise if no restrictive measures were taken by x^*. Denoting the restrictive measures by Γ, we then have:

$$x = \Gamma x^* \tag{7.58}$$

The restrictive measures are taken in order to prevent that x will exceed a certain level x_0. The constraint then reads:

$$x \leqslant x_0 \tag{7.59}$$

Combining equations (7.58) and (7.59) we find:

$$\Gamma \leqslant \frac{x_0}{x^*} \tag{7.60}$$

If:

$$x^* = x^*(t) \tag{7.61}$$

and:

$$\frac{dx^*}{dt} > 0$$

we find:

$$\Gamma(t) \leqslant \frac{x_0}{x^*(t)} \tag{7.62}$$

or, in words, the restrictive measures will have to be enforced more heavily in the course of time. The more time proceeds, the larger $x^*(t)$ will become and the more difficult it will be to maintain the constraint.

In the case that x is a variable that is to be promoted (such as the centre function of a city core), the foregoing argument remains formally similar; in this case:

$$x = \Gamma x^* \tag{7.63}$$

$$x \geqslant x_0 \tag{7.64}$$

and thus:

$$\Gamma \geqslant \frac{x_0}{x^*} \tag{7.65}$$

$$\text{If } x^* = x^*(t) \text{ and } \frac{dx^*}{dt} < 0 \tag{7.66}$$

Γ will have to become larger and larger over time which, in practice, means that the subsidy to maintain the minimum level will have to be increased every year (public transport is such a case).

Since $\Gamma = 1$ represents the situation in which the government does not interfere, it follows that Γ-values much lower than unity will be as difficult to maintain as values much higher than unity. In both cases, there will be a heavy pressure on the government to give way to the development of the autonomous factors.

Otherwise than in the static case in which a given instrument is used to reach a certain value of the objective, we find here that because of the exogenous developments the instruments have to be used more and more intensively to maintain a given value of the objective. The objective itself is well defined but the force needed to maintain its value over time is variable and will eventually lead to an adjustment of the objective itself. The objective thus becomes a function of the development of the system as a whole. Its value is continuously being adjusted to the preferences of society. The process is no longer one of using instruments to reach certain well-defined objectives, but one characterised by a marked exogenous influence on objectives to which the use of the instruments is regularly adjusted and vice versa. It is marked by the search for a maintainable tension or compromise between the aims of the government and the aims of the totality of individuals, in which the behaviour of these individuals regularly compels the government to revise its objectives. It is the basic forces in society that determine the real objectives, and definitely not the objectives that determine the development of society.

If this is true, we should have to reconsider also our general approach to physical planning. It might mean that we have to shift a little back again to the procedure of forecasting instead of assuming that developments need not be forecasted since they are determined by the use of our instruments and thus by our own preferences. If exogenous forces are really that important, we should try to analyse them more properly. Only in such a way could we get a better understanding of how they work, and perhaps we should then be able to redefine real objectives and real instruments. In that case, the objectives could be reached and maintained by the use of the instruments at our disposal.

Space as an element in planning

In order to get a better insight into the role of space in the general planning process, we start from the fact that each variable in this process has a given value in a given area during a certain period of time. For instance, considering income, we always speak of income in a given region in a given period of time. The region can be the nation or a group of nations or a province, the period of time may be a month or a year or a decade, the only important thing is that each variable has these two dimensions.

Considering for a moment only the spatial element, we could write the welfare function as:

$$w_t = w_t(M) \tag{7.67}$$

where w_t represents the welfare level during the period t, and M the matrix of all relevant variables in all the regions. The general objective of government policy in the case of direct planning would be to maximise w_t over time, in other words, to determine the levels of all elements of M in each coming period such that:

$$\int_0^\infty w_t \exp(-\rho t)dt$$

reaches a maximum. Following this procedure, we find a given value for each element in each region in each period of time.

Although in this presentation we might be far out of reality, one thing is clear and important, namely that the spatial structure follows from the general optimisation process. It does not seem necessary to introduce a preference for a given spatial structure over another spatial structure. If we prefer one spatial structure to another, we do so only because the former fits into a general pattern that corresponds to a higher level of well-being or welfare, not because the structure itself would be better than another.

It might be argued that this is not wholly true and that aesthetic arguments can certainly lead to preferences for one structure to another, but that holds only in microspace and certainly not for, for example, the distribution of economic activities and population over the provinces of a country.

But if our vision is true, is it then justified to follow the conventional physical planning procedure which actually starts from a desired spatial pattern, or would general planning automatically lead to a desired spatial pattern if performed properly?

It seems that we have now arrived at the essential point in the argument. And that is whether our general planning can be so sophisticated and effective that we do not need a separate set of legal and other measures to reach a desired spatial pattern, or whether general planning is so defective that we do need that assistance in order to prevent undesirable situations from developing. Before answering this question, we should take a somewhat closer look at the planning procedure in the real world.

The structure of general planning

As soon as we start thinking about general planning, we realise that examples of veritable general, interdisciplinary planning are hard to find. General planning is at most a not-too-well-coordinated facet of planning, each facet being handled within a different institution, not seldom simultaneously and uncoordinatedly on different levels of government. Leaving the latter aspect out of consideration, we find that labour market planning takes place in the Ministry of Labour, educational planning in the Ministry of Education, transportation planning in the Ministry of Transportation, economic planning in the Ministry of Economic Affairs, spatial planning in the Ministry of Public Works or the Ministry of Housing, etc. It has been like that for ages and probably will remain so for a long time to come. Admittedly, planning in each of these fields requires special knowledge of the subject, and to this extent, it is understandable that things are as they are. Less clear, however, is who is responsible for the relationships between all these sorts of planning, or, even worse, whether or not these relationships are taken into consideration at all.

Let us give a few examples. One of the objectives of the Minister of Education is to promote education, to increase the average educational level of the population, usually by paying particular attention to the promotion of education of the less privileged social classes. It cannot be denied that so far these efforts have been crowned with success. But what exactly is success in this field? Is it education *per se* or is it the contribution that education can make to the well-being of the population? And what, then, if larger and larger numbers of the highly educated population become redundant because the increase in the demand for highly skilled workers is lower than the increase in the supply? Who can then be held responsible for the unemployment in the higher-skill levels and the open demand for lower-skilled workers that has to be filled by foreign guest workers? Is it the Ministry of Education or is it the Ministry of Labour that has failed to provide the jobs? Or both?

Obviously, in this case, one may speak of a common responsibility of the two ministries or rather of a general responsibility of the government as a whole, which has failed to provide for proper co-ordination between the educational structure and labour market developments.

We might carry the argument still further. When the disequilibrium between the skill structures of the supply of and demand for labour leads to the introduction of foreign workers, who are forced to live under inadequate housing conditions, is then the Ministry of Housing to blame for this? And the Ministry of Justice or of Social Affairs for the social troubles when the rate of admission of foreign workers exceeds the absorption rate of society?

Another example may be taken from economic policy. Suppose a government devaluates the currency of the country in order to provide for a better position of the balance of payments. The efficiency of such a policy is usually evaluated according to its influence on the balance of payments in later years. It hardly ever happens that the government before seriously considering devaluation, inquires what industries in what regions will expand, and what the consequences of such an expansion will be for the physical structure of these regions. If the effects do in fact cumulate in the congested urbanised areas, is it then the Ministry of Finance who is responsible for the additional congestion and environmental effects, or is it the Ministry of Transportation together with the Ministry of the Environment?

Who is responsible for the deficits of the public transportation system? Is it the Ministry of Housing, which permits or in many cases even promotes, suburbanisation, resulting in inefficient use of the existing infrastructure, or is it the Ministry of Transportation, which provides inadequate means of transportation that do not attract enough travellers to cover their own expenses?

The more we think about these problems, the more we realise that each ministry or, more generally, each responsible authority handles only one small, sometimes even tiny, portion of a large set of heavily interdependent models, in which every change has repercussions which reach even the furthest corners of the model. Labour market, industrial location, environmental conditions, transportation, residential location, etc. are so closely interrelated that it seems hardly possible to carry out one policy in isolation from the other. That this is still done on a large scale is probably due to tradition and stems from a period in which the government did not yet claim to control all developments. Since they started doing so, it has become more and more clear that their power is in fact extremely limited. Of the large interdisciplinary model some parts have been studied and are rather well known. The major part of it, however, must still be built. We are in the initial stage. Integrated interdisciplinary models do not yet exist and it will take a long time before they really have been evolved. In addition, we do not yet know which part of this model is autonomous and consequently will not lend itself to being influenced by government measures. It might be that the increase in the demand for education of which we spoke earlier is not due to government measures at all, but just a consequence of the rise in income which enables many more parents than before to let their children go to university. Maybe suburbanisation is not at all the result of promotion, but has just resulted from the fact that people with rising incomes preferred to live outside the towns, in green surroundings and yet not too far from the town centre. Maybe the government just responded to the currency speculations resulting from the deficit on the balance of payments when devaluating the currency.

As long as we do not actually have the model at our disposal, it is hard to find out what is really autonomous and what the result of government policy. One should not be surprised, however, if the latter influences turned out to be small compared to the autonomous ones. The similarity in actual developments in practically all developed countries, including the socialist countries, points very clearly in that direction.

But if this is true, then we should once more reach the conclusion we formulated, when discussing the power of the government in spatial planning, namely that developments in society are largely autonomous, also as far as spatial aspects are concerned. They are autonomous not only in *spatial* developments, they are so in general, and thus also in spatial developments.

But must, then, the conclusion be that institutional structures do not matter since, whatever institutions do, factual developments will take their own course? That may indeed be true, and precisely for that reason we should perhaps concentrate on trying to make at any rate the negative rules more effective. At least we can try to make clear what we do *not* want. We do not want to let the hearts of our cities die, to sell the shores of our lakes to private owners, to let our landscapes be spoiled by ugly shopping centres and cheap tourist attractions. The foregoing was meant to make clear that governments in many cases will have to give way to all kinds of pressures from outside, but the least we can expect from a government that is wont to promise so much is that it takes a firm stand when these values are threatened. It does not seem likely that we shall have a better solution than this to offer in the short or even medium term. Therefore we should ask the physical planner to continue their part of the work. They have been the first to recognise the real meaning of the word 'well-being' and should be permitted at any rate to do their utmost to prevent undesirable developments. We cannot expect their work to be effective, but at least it is appreciated widely.

7.4 Co-operation/competition between consultant and government

Introduction

In various recent documents and investigations attention has been given to the role of a consultant in preparing and execution of private and especially public investment. Execution by the government and subcontracting to private agencies have been praised, in turn, as contributing most to efficiency. Of the various reports published about the subject can be mentioned 'Hydro in Ontario, a policy for make or buy'* and the 'Gutachtliche Ausserung des Bundesrechnungshofes zur

*Committee on Government Productivity, Ontario, 1976.

verwaltungsmässigen Durchführung der bilateralen technischen Hilfe'.* In the Netherlands the Instituut voor Onderzoek van Overheidsuitgaven (Institute for the Examination of Government Expenditure) is gathering information from government agencies and business circles about the opinions on 'make or buy' prevalent there.

Part of the reports are concerned with the question to what extent the costs of government and consulting firms differ significantly. The German report concludes that it cannot be proved that consultants work more expensively than the government if similar activities are compared. Consultants have repeatedly argued that the differences in cost sometimes pointed out can often be explained as distortions due to faulty calculating methods applied by government agencies. These agencies, so the argument goes, are inclined not to compute certain overhead costs (e.g. for research) to the total costs of a certain project. Of course, consultants calculating like that would constantly lose money on all their projects.

This is an essential argument, but one that will not for the moment be used. In what follows it will be assumed that both consultants and government agencies calculate correctly, and that the resulting cost prices are comparable. There is no reason to suppose, a priori, that the government will have either a lower or a higher cost price than the consultants. There are efficient government agencies and inefficient consultants, and the other way about, and there are no indications that there is *on an average* a marked and significant difference in efficiency either way. It seems right to make that clear right at the start.

But it *is* justified to query whether or not consultants and government agencies work under the same conditions. In particular, one might wonder if the occupation rates are equal for consultants and public authorities, and if not, whether on that score the respective costs per unit of product could differ significantly. Consultants may work with the same salaries, social charges, rents for office buildings, and so on, but if their occupation patterns are inferior to those of the government agencies, the cost price of the private project could still be considerably higher than those of the government project.

To answer the question, let us look at the whole problem of 'make or buy' from a general point of view, trying to find the best way to deal with all the projects that in a certain country are waiting to be carried out. In other words, the problem to be solved is: given a certain total of projects to be realised, and given the division into small and large, routine and innovating projects, what is the optimum distribution of these projects among government agencies and

*December 1973.

consultants? That is a fundamental problem, far more essential than the question of different cost prices under equal conditions. It is precisely the different working conditions that make for different costs, rather than the situation that would occur if everybody worked under the same conditions.

An optimum division of projects

Let us start from a situation in which, in a certain country, a given number of projects varying in size need to be carried out, projects of the central government, regional governments and local governments. Furthermore, let us assume that the total amount the projects represent is 'normal', i.e. neither significantly higher nor significantly lower than the amount spent in the previous periods or expected to be spent in the coming periods.

If the approximate time for realising the various projects is given, a certain amount comes available for spending on projects, say, every month. Now the first question is what would be the apparatus needed to carry out these phased government projects as efficiently as possible.

A first possibility is for the government to man and equip its services in such a way that they are permanently occupied in full; the lowest cost price will thus be effected. In practice, that is not so simple as it looks. Projects are often indivisible and may extend over many months, so, if the staff were adjusted to the month with the fewest projects, it would mean that certain parts of projects allotted to other months would have to be contracted out. Therefore, a better approach would be to select a number of projects that keep the government's own services occupied as regularly as possible; in that way, the minimum cost price comes within reach.

If there were no other reasons than the price to grant the preparation or execution of projects to one or the other agency, there could not be, in the case of full occupancy and even spread, any optimum division between government services and consultants; every division would yield the same average price, and the price quoted by consultants would be the same as the government's.

In practice, however, the spread will not be perfect, and the government's efforts result in full occupancy of its own services and a most fortunate allocation to the consultants' services. Indeed such situations do occur, and governments cannot in such cases, in good faith, pride themselves on being cheaper than the consultants (though they have been known to do so) since they themselves have burdened consultants with the high cost of incomplete occupancy.

It would be a much more rational policy for the government to try to increase the occupancy of its services in such a way that the marginal costs of carrying out a project equals the price charged to the government by consultants. The government can achieve that by taking more projects upon itself until a rate of occupancy is reached at which the costs of the last-added project is equal to the amount involved in contracting that project out.

An extremely interesting development could theoretically occur. By proceeding to carry out more projects itself, the government renders the situation of the consultants even more unfavourable (provided the projects are selected according to rational principles of business economy). A consultant who is entirely dependent on the government will find his/her occupancy becoming even more unfavourable accordingly as the government's occupancy deteriorates, because the government will take the most regular portion of his/her turnover, so that the cost price rises, more than the government's even. The final situation would be that the government carries out all the projects.

The outcome is remarkable, in that the government, reasoning in a completely rational way from its own point of view, must come to the conclusion that the most rational behaviour is for the government itself to carry out all the projects itself. But if it does that, the final cost price will be exactly the same as the consultants would calculate if *they* carried out all the projects. It is indeed the price that is determined by the frequency distribution of the projects over the year.

However, the outlook is brighter for the following simple reason. In every country the number of consultants is far inferior to the number of public authorities, and thus the regular occupancy of a consultant is not determined by the assignment he/she gets from one particular authority, but by the sum total of the assignments given by several municipalities, regional authorities and the central government. Together they ensure him/her an average occupancy and a corresponding average cost price. If that is more or less stable (and experience tends to show it is), it is for every authority to take care that the costs of the marginal product do not justify contracting the project out. In such a fashion, a natural, optimum spread of projects among government and consultants will be achieved.

Further considerations

In the concept presented in the previous section, the size of the governmental apparatus was such that the execution of a most favourable project would involve the same costs as charged, on average, by the consultants. Because the regularity of the consultants' occupancy is determined by the projects they are carrying out for several authorities (and often business companies as well), consultants will always be able to carry out projects that to the government are infra-marginally cheaper than the government itself; the consultants function as a machinery enabling public authorities to have these infra-marginal projects executed efficiently.

Taken in a strict sense, the foregoing implies that the larger the number of authorities concerned with projects (and hence the larger the number of phased projects), and the smaller the number of consultants, the lower the average cost price of projects will become. We shall not now discuss the desirability of such a situation, which could easily interfere with healthy competition and open the way for the government to aspire to a central consultant agency of its own for all public authorities in the whole country in the shape, for instance, of a national government service. Anyhow, it is obvious that it is to the advantage of public authorities that consultants have the most favourable occupancy that can be achieved without detracting from the principles explained above.

Exportation of consultants' services is a good proposition, then. When consultants find the regularity of their occupancy enhanced by external projects, they will be able to offer a lower price to authorities at home. One might wonder whether such considerations of business economy do not play a role in countries where governments support their own consultants in securing commissions from abroad. Apart from the lower cost price foreign commissions help to achieve, service exports have a favourable effect on the balance of payments and may enhance the exporting country's fame abroad. Of course, export is also in the interest of the consultants themselves, because of the direct revenues and because the resulting lower cost price improves their position on the national market.

Of course, exportation would not be any use if attended by even larger imports. If all European consultants set out to export their know-how to other European countries, all of them in the end working abroad, the final situation would not be any better than the initial one, everybody having greater outlays because of working abroad. From the point of view of the national economy, international trade in know-how would only make sense if the export and import flows corresponded to the specific expert knowledge of individual consultants.

Perhaps even more important is the question how far governments are in a position to phase their projects in such a way as to permit consultants to work at lower tariffs. An interesting question, and a hazardous one for consultants, who often argue when negotiating with the government, is: 'If you can guarantee a continuous flow of commissions, I can supply my services cheaper. That situation would be advantageous for both of us.' Suppose the government could indeed comply, then the question immediately rises why consultants should still be enlisted at all. The question would become all the more justified if the wish to assign continuous flows of commissions would lead to several authorities to co-operate and combine their commissions.

Indeed, according as authorities manage to combine their projects, they will be in a better position to keep the projects in their own hands, so that fewer commissions will be given out to consultants. That would be a favourable evolution from a national point of view, but it could bring about a contraction of the consultancy, unless there were reasons other than cost-price technical ones to go on commissioning consultants. In what follows these reasons will be discussed more closely.

Quality differences

The foregoing argument leads logically up to the question of whether there can be other reasons than those of cost-price technique for the government to grant commissions to third parties. The question arose when it had become clear that if co-operation between authorities as well as better phasing of projects could lead to a lower cost price for projects carried out by consultants, then the same would be true with reference to execution by the authorities themselves. On the other hand, if the authorities kept most of the projects in their own hands, the (much desired) macro-economic improvement would unfortunately, and against the intention of consultants, be accompanied by a relative weakening of the consultants' position.

Consultants' best justification is in the quality of the service they can offer at a price equal to the government's cost price. On what grounds could they presume to such special expertise? First, because a consultant's research team, thanks in part to export activities, is often superior in size to that of one or even a number of co-operating authorities, it can handle those parts of a project that call for specialised knowledge far better than the government could. Owing to extreme specialisation, consultants have experts available for all kinds of sub-areas, who can be enlisted at strategic moments to guarantee the smooth and thorough execution of the project.

Secondly, most consultants' firms are big enough to have experience with the more rarely occurring projects, and for that reason, are more qualified to undertake such projects than a government service that would have to start from scratch. It cannot be denied, to be sure, that such specific knowledge can also be present with the authorities. The services in control of Rotterdam harbour, the greatest in the world, if properly organised for the purpose, would without doubt be capable of advising expertly on the equipment of ports and the handling and dispatch of goods. The Public Waterworks Department of the Ministry of Traffic and Public Works could do the same in the field of waterworks. Still, such examples are exceptions, and large private consultant firms or specialised smaller ones may, on the whole, be considered better qualified to deal with special projects than the government or the lower public authorities.

Thirdly, a very important argument is that the larger firms especially, and in times of underoccupancy, can carry out research that is fundamental – and owing to the consultants' many-sided experience and marketing insight, research that makes for more efficient working in the future. Once more, the presence of many specialists within a consultant's research team is a guarantee for an efficient and therefore relatively cheap approach.

Irrespective of the factors mentioned above, it is these qualitative differences that will in fact determine whether a certain project will be dealt with by the government apparatus or contracted out. The optimum co-operation between government and consultants will have to be worked out on that basis, with certain other factors being taken into account. Some of these factors are referred to in the next section.

Additional factors

So far, a number of more or less objective factors have been discussed. It would be wrong, however, entirely to disregard a number of other elements that play a role in the daily practice of consultancy. Here we mention a few, not aspiring to completeness.

1 Especially with investigations of a somewhat delicate nature, it is of the utmost importance that they be carried out by an independent, objective adviser, who can be relied upon to weigh all the interests concerned, one against the other, unbiased in favour of commissioner's interests. In particular, objectivity may be essential to the central government, and that can never be achieved when the authorities take on the execution themselves.

2 When an authority assigns a commission to a consultant, it wants to keep a firm grip on the work and its progress. To that effect, it is now common practice to install so-called 'guiding committees' which, as the term indicates, are charged with supervising and guiding the

project's execution. The underlying principle is sound enough: the authorities wish, through the intermediary of a group of officials detailed for the purpose, to keep in regular contact with those in charge of the execution of the product so as to ensure that the execution proceeds correctly, and be informed in good time of the difficulties that are bound to arise. Obviously such a guiding committee incurs costs, but such costs are by no means exclusive to subcontracted projects. The broad composition of many committees proves that such a body would have been required as well had the project been carried out by government agencies (e.g. within one ministry). But when it is a consultant who is guided and supervised, the authorities are fortunate, in that any criticism given by officials of one ministry will not be directed at the research team of another ministry, but rather aimed at a neutral consultant, who has already had so many committees to deal with that his back has become very broad indeed!

Good guidance and supervision, whether provided by a committee or otherwise, are of great advantage to a consultant. They add a bit of local flavour to his activities and can save him from making often costly mistakes. The knowledge that the committee members possess can represent a valuable contribution to his work. The support of a guiding committee may in fact be indispensable for adequate execution, that is one that fully corresponds with the client's requirements. On the one hand, consultants are often reproached for supplying less than had been asked for by the client according to the terms of reference; on the other hand, it cannot be denied that engineering firms from a kind of professional pride are apt to 'overdesign'. Adequate supervision can avoid both kinds of derailment.

The authorities, on their side, should develop an understanding of the consultant's precarious or dependent position, which they can only maintain as far as they manage (a) to supply work of good quality that may lead to new assignments, (b) to keep the work within such limits that the budget at their disposal suffices and (c) that they do not exceed disproportionately the time set aside for the investigation. Naturally conditions (b) and (c) can apply only as long as no special circumstances persist. The contact with the commissioner should be such (via guidance committees or otherwise) that if special circumstances do occur, the commissioner is informed in good time.

Only when a consultant has managed, by being open and sincere in his work and his calculations, to gain the government's (or any other client's) confidence, can that atmosphere of trust and mutual respect be engendered that ideally should always exist between the one who asks and the one who gives advice. Only then can a consultant work well or the principal expect the full confidence of his consultant. And that is more essential than a discussion of whatever differences over efficiency there may be.

Notes

1 By a policy should be understood here the operation of a set of policy instruments to attain a set of specific objectives.

2 By 'government' we understand the central government, unless specified otherwise.

3 That is, as the Cabinet members are less of a mind, as Parliament gives less constructive support, as the followers in society are less numerous, and as the government coalition depends more on interest groups.

References

van den Berg, L., Klaassen, L.H. and Vijverberg, C.H.T. (1975), 'Evaluation of governmental welfare policy by means of a social welfare function', unpublished ms., Netherlands Economic Institute, Rotterdam.

Graaff, J. de V. (1967), *Theoretical Welfare Economics*, London: Cambridge University Press.

Heide, H. Ter. (1965), *Binnenlandse migratie in Nederland*, 's-Gravenhage.

Hordijk, L., Mastenbroek, P. and Paelinck, J.H.P. (1974), 'Estimation of preference elasticities. A simulation approach', unpublished ms., Netherlands Economic Institute, Rotterdam.

Isard, W. (1960), *Methods of Regional Analysis*, New York: MIT Press.

Klaassen, L.H. and Drewe, P. (1973), *Migration Policy in Europe*, Saxon House: Farnborough.

Klaassen, L.H. and Verster, A.C.P. (1974), 'SPAMO I. Een Ruimtelijk Model', unpublished ms., Netherlands Economic Institute, Rotterdam.

Nijkamp, P. (1970), 'Determination of implicit social preference functions', unpublished ms., Econometric Institute, Netherlands School of Economics, Rotterdam.

Nijkamp, P. (1974), 'Theorie en toepassing van graviteits- en entropie-modellen in ruimtelijke systemen', unpublished ms., Free University, Amsterdam.

Nijkamp, P. (1975), 'Operational determination of collective preference parameters. A survey of revealed preference methods

in collective decision-making', unpublished ms., Free University, Amsterdam.
Prakke, L. (1974), *Pluralisme en staatsmacht*, Deventer: Kluwer, p. 11.
Schouten, C.W. (1975a), 'De regionale doorlichting van Nederland. Achtergronden en uitkomsten', *Economisch-Statistische Berichten*, vol. 60, pp. 52–6.
Schouten, C.W. (1975b), 'Binnenlandse migratie en regionale politiek', *Economisch-Statistische Berichten*, vol. 60, 1975, pp. 76–81.
Tinbergen, J. (1956), *Economic Policy: Principles and Design*, Amsterdam: North-Holland.
Wilson, A.G. (1971), 'A family of spatial interaction models, and associated developments', *Environment and Planning*, vol. 3, pp. 1–32.

8 Futurology

8.1 Long-term forecasting*

Introduction

Long-term forecasting is an activity at once amusing and relatively risk-free. It means, especially in economics, sketching a picture of a far-off future with the help of a set of equations that are mostly arbitrary and, in any case, difficult to understand, the picture conjured up being dependent on the figures and further assumptions fed into it.

Such forecasting is amusing because it is impressive, particularly if and to the extent that the consumer of these forecasts does not quite understand how they have been made. Many forecasters have become very apt to disguise their basic assumptions. The more because the situation which is forecast tends to deviate strongly in structure and dimensions from the present one, great authority is attributed to the forecaster: he shows himself familiar with situations the consumer has hardly dreamt of yet. There is little risk in making such forecasts because the year to which they refer lies in the very distant future. This reduces the chance of the forecaster being seriously confronted with a comparison of prognosis and reality, the more

*See L.H. Klaassen and Z. Pawlowski, 'Long-term forecasting', published in *De Economist*, Leiden: Stenfert Kroese, 1981, and *Man, Environment, Space and Time*, USA, 1982.

so as comparing forecasts with reality is far more complicated than it looks. For indeed the forecaster will make numerous explicit or implicit hedging reservations. If once in a while it should come to a confrontation, people tend to have so much understanding for 'circumstances that have greatly altered since the forecast was made', that criticism, if given at all, is mostly very mild.

Nevertheless, the authors suggest not starting at too tender an age with long-term forecasts; the chance of being confronted with one's own predictions might just be a bit too great! Especially the first author has found that out most painfully, and for that reason thinks it right and proper to give an earnest warning to young researchers. However, by labelling the forecast an opening gambit made, first and foremost, to induce other researchers to try to deepen their understanding and to improve the quality of the prognosis, the forecaster can already considerably lessen the danger of a confrontation with reality. For in this way the odium is thrown on those who have failed to introduce the necessary refinements:

> Most of the concepts in the world model reflect the attitudes and motivations of the recent past and present. Therefore the book does not incorporate the possible changes in human aspirations and values that might come from widespread recognition of the predicament facing mankind. All these and others are issues for future investigation. We hope this book contributes to the sense of urgency and also that it points to an effective direction for work by others who may choose to explore the alternatives for the future.[1]

Nevertheless there was in most cases quite a good reason to make the forecast. To decide about investments, for instance, one has to take rather a long future period into account. Likewise, for many measures such as changes in legislation, admission of foreign workers, issuance of rules of spatial planning, it is desirable to have an insight into the future, preferably on the longest possible term. Now that the forecasting profession has lost much of its glamour, a device had to be found to satisfy both the producers of forecasts – the forecasting scholars – and their consumers – the decision makers. The solution has been for the forecast maker to change the name of his activity: after an intermediary stage in which, in the Netherlands at any rate, only 'precalculations' were talked about, the term 'scenarios' has now come to be adopted as the ultimate expression. Unlike prognoses and even interval prognoses, with scenarios one has ample choice. They can be custom-made and have thus greatly enlarged the forecasters' (now scenarists') production range. On the other hand, because alternative scenarios can cover a very broad spectrum, they give consumers the feeling of having much more say in the supermarket of the future than they had in the time of simple forecasts.

The points touched upon above will be discussed in more detail in what follows, the first point covering the general pitfalls of long-term forecasting.

General pitfalls

Introduction In what follows we will assume that the long-term forecast is made with the help of a quantitative model. Such a model contains endogenous variables next to exogenous and lagged endogenous variables. Controllable variables are, traditionally, called instrument variables. The dynamics of the system together with the exogenous variables determine the development of the endogenous quantities which we want to observe. The coefficients figuring in the system are estimated, by a more or less complicated procedure, from the data available from the past. It is that procedure which will be critically discussed in the next section.

A model as a subsystem The first problem confronting us is the difference, or rather the distinction, between endogenous and exogenous variables. To explain why it is a problem we must indulge in a little side-slip, choosing as point of departure a simple shopping model. Suppose that

$$n_{ij} = a_j \phi(d_{ij}) (\pi_i)^{-1} n_{i*} \qquad (8.1)$$

where n_{ij} = number of persons living in i who go shopping in j;
d_{ij} = generalised transportation costs from i to j;
a_j = attractiveness ($\equiv$ square area) of shopping centre j;
n_{i*} = total number of persons shopping from i;
π_i = $\Sigma_j a_j \phi(d_{ij})$.

We can test this equation on the assumption that a_j, d_{ij}, π_i and n_{i*} are given; they are, then exogenous, only n_{ij} being endogenous. Many shopping models rely on this assumption; they are distribution models distributing a given number of customers among the shopping centres, the term envisaged being the ultra-short one.

If the term is made a little longer, changes will occur in n_{i*} as a result of income changes and population growth. If that assumption is introduced into the model, we arrive at an equation like the following:

$$n_{i*} = f(y_i, \pi_i, p_i) \tag{8.2}$$

in which y_i, as well as p_i and π_i, are exogenous. It has been assumed, though, that π_i exerts influence on n_{j*}. The shopping possibilities affect the total number of shoppers as well as the income level and the population size; their number has passed from exogenous to endogenous as our view of the future and of the shopping procedure has widened. In transport terminology equation (8.2) would be called the production model.

Is the model which now consists of the equations (8.1) and (8.2) a complete one? By no means! For in this model a_j is still taken as given, while presumably the shopping apparatus will also adjust to the consumer's shopping orientation. Evidently the supply element is still missing; we can add by assuming, for instance:

$$a_j = g(c_j, n_{*j}) \tag{8.3}$$

where c_j = cost of constructing a shopping unit in j, and

$$n_{*j} = \Sigma\, n_{ij}$$

Thus we have added a new 'exogenous' variable and lost another (a_j); the picture has changed once more.

Now the model seems fairly complete; we might make similar models for leisure activities, visits to friends and relations, commuting, etc. Of course, they all have their typical properties, but the main structures are comparable, such variables as a_j having specific dimensions in each model.

Still, especially in view of the last observation, the model situation is not yet quite satisfactory. Indeed, if all those traffic-generating activities take place on a given traffic network (as they are bound to), it will become difficult, certainly in the long run, to regard d_{ij} as given. Congestions may occur as time goes on, and render d_{ij} dependent on all flows n_{ij}.[2] But that means that d_{ij} has passed from exogenous to endogenous, and as a_j has already become so, π_i will follow suit. The population's access to work, leisure activities, shops, etc. has then become endogenous, and the changed situation is likely to reflect on the locational behaviour of persons, i.e. their preference for a certain residence. As a result, the distribution of people among regions will alter according to the changed accessibilities, so that p_i can no longer be considered exogenous. Moreover, the location of activities, especially in the tertiary sector, has come to depend very much on the supply of staff, especially in the higher-skilled professions, who are more mobile than others; consequently the location of activities is adjusting to the changed preference of the population, which affects the income situation by region. So y_i, too, loses its exogenous character, certainly in the long run, which is the very time horizon that interests us.

This example may suffice to demonstrate that the question as to what is endogenous and what is exogenous in a model is by no means easy to answer. In practice, it is decided as a function of the problem formulated, or even later. The model is then delimitated, severed from a 'total – general – interdisciplinary – world-model'; there are no scientific reasons to do so; the choice is purely pragmatic.

The procedure may be as follows: p_i and y_i are considered exogenous, a prognosis is made on that basis and the values of the endogenous variables derived, circular relationships being left out of account for reasons of efficiency, probably mostly unawares. The procedure really implies that the forecast relies on prognoses of exogenous variables which are actually determined also by the endogenous variables to be predicted, both kinds of variables being parts of the same interdependent system. The degree to which such a procedure is justified depends of course on the intensity of the circular relations; if it is unknown the procedure is risky and the forecast may fail.

A model as a simplification A model always describes only part of a large entity and, by the very choice of its endogenous and exogenous variables, contains an element of arbitrariness; apart from that, it always represents a simplified version of what really happens in that sub-area. Keeping to our previous example, we soon find that our model's shopping section has some serious disadvantages because it takes no account of the following factors:

1 A shopping centre cannot be measured by square area alone; qualitative elements are also important. A division by kind of shop (supermarket, general store, ordinary shop, boutique, etc.) is indispensable.
2 Shopping behaviour differs by type of merchandise, so the coefficients of the function $\phi(d_{ij})$ are activity-specific.
3 Shopping behaviour differs by socio-economic group; those with a higher education behave otherwise than those with a lower education.
4 The means of transport available plays a role; model split has to be accounted for in the model; car owners shop in a different fashion than non-owners;

5 A considerable portion of the purchases are made from the workplace and not from the residence.
6 The entrepreneurs' pricing policy does not figure in the model.
7 No account is taken of the government policy regarding the establishment of shopping centres.

And so on, and so forth; it is not difficult to lengthen the list *ad libitum* but, as it is, it suffices to demonstrate the model's serious limitations. The question is, however, whether or not these limitations are justified. The enumeration of what is lacking actually provides the answer.

If it is true that shopping behaviour varies by socio-economic group of the population and if in the course of time (long run!) the relative sizes of the groups change considerably, then the limitation was not justified. Should the structure of supply alter in the course of time, from whatever cause (for instance, rising wage costs), then the constraint was not warranted either. In short, a constraint that proves unwarranted in the long run should not be imposed in the first place. A meagre consolation, to be sure, for the fact that the constraint had been incorrectly imposed mostly does not emerge before the long term is over. Constraints occur *ex ante* and have lost their sense *ex post*. True, the present limitations will no longer be imposed in the long run, but the question of whether any new ones are meaningful can once more be answered only when the new long term has passed; they may in turn prove unwarranted.

The model's fluidity The previous section has taken us logically to a question closely related to the previous one, namely which variables are significant in the behaviour of human beings and should therefore be included in the model, and which can safely be left out. After the foregoing, we assume that at a certain moment a choice has to be made and that the model, with the chosen variables, proves reasonably satisfactory for the past. The general question is then how the coefficients will behave in the model. In principle, two situations are possible:

(a) some coefficients become significantly larger; variables left out of the system may then have come to play an important role;
(b) some coefficients become significantly smaller; this can mean that, in the extreme case, variables that used to play a role can henceforth as well be left out of account.

Both cases occur in practice; they prove that the structure of the model is constantly subject to alteration.

What all this may mean can best be understood by assuming that we would have to make a forecast for the present time on the basis of time series up to the year 1965; being allowed the latest techniques but with no information available beyond 1965. The forecasts for 1980 will then abstract from, for instance:

(a) the oil crisis and the ensuing rise of the energy price, and problems with the balance of payments in many countries;
(b) the anticonception pill and its massive impact on the volume and age composition of the population.
(c) the increased sensitivity to the environment, the corresponding preference for living in medium-sized towns, and the drastic decline of the population in the large agglomerations.

Again, it is not so very difficult to make the list longer, and it would be incredibly naïve to believe that now the 'new' variables have all become manifest and that from 1980 onward we may reckon with a stable situation. Change is inherent to the development of society, or rather, it *is* the development of society, and to deny that is simply a mistake. A model that predicts the future on the basis of the present societal structure contradicts itself. The future is the product of a changing structure that not only depends on what is important now, but also helps to determine what is going to be important and what is going to be unimportant.

Final remark In the previous sections some points have been put forward that can be categorised as general pitfalls. There are also some more specific pitfalls which econometricians have tried to overcome: they will now be reviewed. Afterward we may try to proceed to an evaluation.

Specific pitfalls

Introduction Besides the general pitfalls discussed above, there are more specific ones with which econometricians have especially concerned themselves. Though partly overlapping the general pitfalls, they deserve separate treatment, because they are approached in individual ways. Here the experiences of centrally-led economies stand us in good stead. There are, in fact, four categories of pitfalls, namely:

1 Instability of the true functional form of relations.
2 Uncertainty about constant but unknown functional forms.
3 Variability of structural parameters (in part already discussed above).

4 Unknown values of explanatory variables.

These four categories will be illustrated with the help of a model which, unlike the previous one, consists of a single equation.

Instability of the functional form of relations The first problem an econometrician is confronted with is that of instability of the functional form of the model. In most practical cases, even drastic changes are not known in advance, and therefore the logical justification of long-term forecasting depends on the validity of the basic condition of the forecasting theory,[3] namely that there will be no sharp structural changes until the end of the predicted time period. Indeed there are reports in the literature on some attempts to use the theory of catastrophes to evaluate the chance of substantial structural change and to make forecasts under the new conditions[4] but the experience gathered so far is limited and we still seem to be far from an adequate and successful use of the new theoretical concept.

It is to be noted, though, that there is a class of situations for which it is relatively easy to tell in advance whether any change in the casual mechanism is likely to occur and what its impact will be as far as the direction of induced changes is considered. Here the experience of countries with centrally planned economies can be quoted. As every five-year plan requires new estimation of relations, it is often observed that a number of economic relations exhibit a different pattern of variation within the five-year periods corresponding to different five-year plans.[5] As for every five-year plan the economic relations have to be estimated anew, it is often observed that the variation patterns of some of them differ from one five-year period to another. As far as the shifts show some simple regularity – a regular upward move of the constant in a linear relationship, for instance – they can be expected to continue so in the future. Though basically rather mechanistic, the procedure provides us with some sort of solution. Its advantage is that it can be checked every fifth year, at least in centrally-planned economies with their regular five-year plans.

Uncertainty about constant but unknown functional forms Another important problem connected with the functional form of the econometric model is the uncertainty about its true analytical form. When a long-term forecast is made, it is usually assumed that the explanatory variables will change considerably from values they had at the time of the forecast. Under such circumstances a linear approximation of the relationships involved does not do. On the other hand, little is known about the true form of the relations and, moreover, within the sample range of variation of the explanatory variables there are usually several functions which give almost the same degree of fit, and the question arises which is the right functional form of the model to be used.[6]

If no function can be eliminated from further use on priority grounds[7] the following simple approach can be tried. Let X_T be the vector of values of explanatory variables assumed for the predicted time period T and let $y_{Tp1}, y_{Tp2}, \ldots, y_{Tps}$ be the sequence of forecasts obtained by using s 'competitive' functional forms of the model. Because the numbers allotted to these functions are arbitrary, we can assume that they are ordered in such a way that:

$$y_{Tp1} \leqslant y_{Tp2} \leqslant \ldots \leqslant y_{Tps} \qquad (8.4)$$

Let now ϵ be a positive real number such that the user of the forecast does not care about errors if less (in absolute value) than 2ϵ, and hence considers two forecasts that differ less than 2ϵ as practically the same.[8] Let us construct now the sequence of intervals:

$$I^{(i)} = [y_{Tpi}-\epsilon, y_{Tpi}+\epsilon], i = 1, 2, \ldots, s \qquad (8.5)$$

and let us form the product:

$$I = I^{(1)} \cap I^{(2)} \cap \ldots \cap I^{(s)} \qquad (8.6)$$

We shall say that the forecasts forming the sequence in expression (8.4) are consistent with each other if and only if the set I is not an empty one. If all s different forecasts are consistent, one can build the final forecast for period T in the interval form as:

$$y_{Tp} \; : \; I^{(1)} \cup I^{(2)} \cup \ldots \cup I^{(s)} \qquad (8.7)$$

As can easily be verified, the length of the forecast interval (8.7) is always contained between 2ϵ and 4ϵ. The meaning of forecast (8.7) is the following: if the econometricians are not sure about the true (time-stable but unknown) functional form of the model, they can shift from point to interval prediction. The length of the interval involved can be interpreted as the 'price' paid for the insufficient knowledge about the causal mechansim of the predicted variable.[9]

If the set I proves to be empty and the individual forecasts are not consistent, there is no straightforward way to proceed towards one final prediction. In such cases, one is well advised to check again whether, on the grounds of the existing subject-matter knowledge, it is not possible to eliminate some more functions from further consideration.

Variability of structural parameters Still more delicate is the problem of stability of structural parameters.[10] As is well known, there are a number of reasons why such parameters shift their values in time. As the forecast refers to a more distant future, using a model with obsolete parameter values becomes more dangerous, because the ensuing prediction error tends to increase. For that reason, the econometrician is well advised to check the stability of structural parameters, and if they are found not to be constant, to estimate the pattern of their changes. Once such a pattern is known it becomes, at least in principlc, possible to update the parameter values for the time period T to be forecasted.

At least three main ways of time variation of structural parameters can be distinguished:

1 Structural parameters can be considered regular functions of time variable.
2 Structural parameters change because they depend on another variable (or vector) which is absent from the model used for forecasting.
3 Structural parameters exhibit random shifts.

To check if the structural parameters can be treated as regular functions of time one can proceed in a number of ways, two of which will be outlined here. If the time series of data are very long, one can divide the whole sample period into a number of disjointed sub-periods, and estimate the model separately on the basis of the data pertaining to one sub-period at a time.[11] Since there will thus be as many different estimates of each parameter as there are sub-periods, it can be inferred from the sequence of these estimates whether the results vary only at random or reflect a systematic dependence of the parameters on, for instance, time. It is to be noted that in view of the disjointed character of different sub-sample periods it is relatively easy to use statistical tests of significance when comparing the various estimates.[12]

If the estimates vary in a significant way they should be used for the estimation of trend functions.

Let us assume that the relation:

$$\beta_i = \beta_i(t) \tag{8.8}$$

has been found to represent the time pattern of β_i. For forecasting purposes the relevant parameter must then be updated for the predicted time period T. This consists in taking β_i to be equal to $\beta_i(T)$, where T now denotes the value of the time variable corresponding to the end of the forecasting period.

When the sample time series of data are relatively short, the disjointed sub-periods τ_j should rather be substituted by a sequence of overlapping sub-periods $\tau'_1, \tau'_2, \ldots, \tau'_q$. Let n be the total number of time-series observations and let m be a positive integer much smaller than n. The first sub-sample τ'_1 contains m first observations, i.e. from the first one up to the mth one. The second sub-sample contains m observations from the second up to the $(m + 1)$-th one, etc., and the last $(n - m + 1)$-st sub-sample includes all the last m observations. While the obvious advantage of this procedure is that even with a relatively small number of observations, one can get relatively many estimates of the structural parameters, there is one disadvantage as well: the consecutive estimates are not independent and the degree of their dependence increases with m.

Once the $n - m + 1$ estimates have been found, it becomes possible to estimate their trend. For forecasting purposes this trend is then used to update the parameter values.

In some cases there may be strong a-priori arguments for assuming regular or quasi-regular changes of parameter values in times. If that is so, it may be expedient to start building the model with this possible variation in mind, thus assuming explicitly that the structural parameters are some function of the time variable. If the model is linear and linear time variation of the parameters is assumed,[13] that leads to the following formal model:

$$Y_t = \Sigma_1 \beta_i(t) \cdot X_{it} + \xi_t \tag{8.9}$$

with:

$$\beta_i(t) = \beta_{i0} + \beta_{i1} t \tag{8.10}$$

Substituting expression (8.10) into (8.9) and after obvious simple transformations, one gets a new model:[14]

$$Y_t = \Sigma_1 \beta_{i0} X_{it} + \Sigma_1 \beta_{i1} t \cdot X_{it} + \xi_t \tag{8.11}$$

Thus the assumption of linear variation of parameters leads to a model which is linear with respect to structural parameters and contains, besides the original explanatory variables, their interactions with time. The estimation of model (8.11) presents no difficulties and then the classical unbiased forecast is equal to:

$$y_{Tp} = \Sigma_1 b_{i0} \cdot x_{iT} + \Sigma_1 b_{i1} \cdot T \cdot x_{iT} \tag{8.12}$$

where b_{i0} and b_{i1} are the estimates of β_{i0} and β_{i1}, while x_{iT} denotes the value of X_{it} assumed for the predicted time period.

The second typical situation mentioned at the beginning of this section, namely the structural parameters being functions of other variables, can perhaps best be treated along lines similar to those followed when presenting the model in expressions (8.9) and (8.10). For that reason, we shall not dwell longer on this problem.

We come now to the third situation, i.e. the structural parameters of the model exhibiting random fluctuations. To make forecasts under such circumstances one must have at least some notion of the probability distribution of random parameters. In recent years increasing attention has been devoted to the problem of econometric models with stochastically varying parameters and a number of methods of estimation of their distribution characteristics have been proposed.[15] While some of these methods are highly efficient, they are also rather tedious from the computational point of view, and sometimes require additional information that is difficult to get in practical situations. For that reason, it seems appropriate to suggest again the use of consecutive (preferably disjointed) sub-samples. For each sub-sample the model is estimated separately, which gives r different estimates of the average value of structural parameters within the corresponding sub-interval of time. That information, in turn, provides the basis for the estimation of at least two distribution characteristics, namely that of the expected value of the structural parameter and that of its variance.[16]

Let us assume, then, that for every structural parameter of the econometric model at least one estimate of its distribution is available and let us consider two real numbers β_i and $\overline{\beta}_i$. The first one is chosen in such a way that the probability of β_i falling in a random way below the level β_i is equal to a preassigned small *positive* number δ. Similarly, β_i is such a number that the probability of β_i assuming a greater value is also equal to δ. If there are sufficient grounds to expect the distribution of β_i's to be stationary (at least within the time interval from the sample period onwards to the end of the period T), then β_i and $\overline{\beta}_i$ can be used for making two long-term forecasts, subsequently referred to as the pessimistic and optimistic prediction with respect to random variation of structural parameters.

Let us suppose moreover that the utility derived from achieving a level of Y_t is a strictly increasing function of y_t. Furthermore, let the model be a linear one and let all the explanatory variables be positive.[17]

The pessimistic forecast is defined as:

$$y_{Tp}{}^p = \Sigma_1 \beta_i x_{iT} \tag{8.13}$$

while the optimistic one is:

$$y^o{}_{Tp} = \Sigma_i \overline{\beta}_i x_{iT} \tag{8.14}$$

The final forecast is then provided by the interval $[y_{Tp}{}^p, y_{Tp}{}^o]$, which can be called the interval of uncertainty of the forecast with respect to the random variation of the parameters. The width of this interval depends obviously on the variances of the random variables β_i's and on the assumed level of δ.[18]

The case of unknown values of explanatory variables In this section we turn to another crucial problem of long-term prediction, namely that of the values of the explanatory variables valid for the predicted time period T. Rare indeed are the situations where these values are known exactly at the time of forecasting.[19] As the classical forecast from casual models is a conditional one in the sense of inference being dependent on the assumed values of the explanatory variables, the problem is really a crucial one.

Several approaches to solve the problem are followed, in practice, such as using trends of explanatory variables or making a number of predictions, each corresponding to a different set of assumptions about the X_{iT}'s. In countries with planned economies values equal to plan targets are often used, eventually corrected by a coefficient equal to the expected level of plan fulfilment. In what follows, two special procedures will be outlined here, each assuming the explanatory variables to be random ones with known[20] distribution functions at time T.

The first approach consists in making pessimistic and optimistic forecasts, this being very similar to the procedure presented in the preceding section, where the structural parameters of the model were assumed to be random. The pessimistic and optimistic forecasts of Y_T are computed with respect to random variation of the explanatory variables, and the interval of uncertainty of prediction[21] can then be constructed.

The second approach worth mentioning is that leading to predictions averaged with respect to random variation of explanatory variables.[22] Let the model be:

$$Y_t = f(X_{1t}, X_{2t}, \ldots, X_{kt}, \xi) \tag{8.15}$$

and let $G_T(x)$ be the probability distribution function of the X_i's valid at time T. The unbiased averaged prediction $\bar{y}_{Tp}$ is then defined as follows:

$$\bar{y}_{Tp} = \int \underset{\Delta}{\cdots} \int f(x_1, x_2, \ldots, x_k) \cdot dG_T(x) \qquad (8.16)$$

where Δ stands for the region of variation of the explanatory variables. As can be easily shown, if the model is linear formula, expression (8.16) reduces to:

$$\bar{y}_{Tp} = \Sigma \beta_i \cdot E(X_{iT}) \qquad (8.17)$$

i.e. the forecast is obtained by substituting into the model the expected values of the explanatory variables. It can be shown (see Pawlowski, 1973) that the variance of the forecast in equation (8.17) is given by the following formula:

$$\begin{aligned} V^2 &= V_c^2 + \sum_i \beta_i^2 \operatorname{Var}^2(X_{iT}) \\ &\quad + 2 \sum_i \sum_{j>i} \beta_i \beta_j \operatorname{Cov}(X_{iT}, X_{jT}) \end{aligned} \qquad (8.18)$$

where V_c^2 denotes the classical variance of prediction formula when all the explanatory variables are set at their expected levels, that is:

$$\begin{aligned} V_c^2 &= \sum_i D^2(b_i) \cdot [E(X_{iT})]^2 + 2 \sum_i \sum_{j>i} Cov(b_i, b_j) E(X_{iT}) \\ &\quad E(X_{jT}) + \sigma^2_T \end{aligned} \qquad (8.19)$$

As the quadratic form in expression (8.19) is obviously positively definitc, it follows that the uncertainty about the values of the explanatory variables increases the variance of prediction. A straightforward generalisation of expression (8.17) is possible when it is assumed that both the structural parameters and the explanatory variables of the model are random.[23, 24]

When no probabilistic information about the future behaviour of the explanatory variables can be obtained, there is still one approach to be recommended, namely turning to experts. Eventually they may either come up with a definitive idea of the expectations regarding the values of X_{iT}, or formulate some alternative – in their opinion, more or less equally probable – scenarios. If the experts formulate their opinion as to the levels of the explanatory variables in a straightforward, unique way, their information suffices for building a 'classical' forecast whose reliability depends on the experts' correct judgement. If, on the other hand, the experts present a number of competitive scenarios, it is still possible to make a set of different forecasts, each corresponding to one scenario; it may then be expedient to pool these forecasts to formulate a single final one, taking the shape of the logical sum of the individual forecasts corresponding to the competing scenarios (see Pawlowski, 1978). Extrapolation results thus formulated explicitly inform the user of forecasts of the uncertainty of the future formation of Y_T he has to reckon with.

Decreasing the risk of false forecasts

In the preceding sections of this chapter and especially in the section, 'Instability of the functional form of relations', some serious pitfalls connected with long-term extrapolation into the future were presented, together with some suggestions about how to modify the classical standard rules of making forecasts (or predictions) in such a way that these pitfalls can be avoided. It follows from the argument that it is far from easy to get an insight into the distant future and that there is a good – or rather a bad – chance of the inferences proving incorrect.[25] Still, such insight is needed for the efficient management of economic, regional, and social systems and, if systems are to be changed, it must reach far enough ahead to allow for practical and adequate action.[26] Indeed no rational action is possible without a minimum of information about the future. So, to make the best of a difficult situation, a way must be sought to make extrapolations into the future at minimum risk. In particular, approaches that tend to increase forecast errors – for example because the model used is obsolete with respect to time period T, or because the knowledge of side-conditions in the forecast period is inadequate – should be avoided. Moreover, not just one forecast should be made but a sequence of them.[27] When forecasts are meant for the long run, that is, when the time horizon T lies far ahead, there is usually enough time to make a number of consecutive forecasts spread out in time.

Let y_{Th_1} denote the first forecast, made at time t_1 and referring to time horizon T, and let:

$$h_1 = T - t_1 \tag{8.20}$$

be its forecasting lead; similarly let $y_{Th_2}, y_{Th_3}, \ldots,$ denote later forecasts referring to the same future horizon $T^{\cdot}$, with respective forecasting leads $h_2, h_3, \ldots,$ and:

$$h_{i+1} < h_i, \text{ for } i = 1, 2, \ldots \quad (8.21)$$

Thus, as time goes on, a sequence of forecasts is obtained:

$$y_{Th_1}, y_{Th_2}, y_{Th_3}, \ldots \quad (8.22)$$

The number of elements of this sequence obviously increases in the course of time, as the horizon T approaches. We shall refer to forecasts in equation (8.22) as the successive forecasts for variable (or vector of variables) Y_T, later elements denoting newer forecasts, usually based on more recent, and therefore more reliable information about side-conditions at time T; the later forecasts may thus be expected to give a more reliable insight into the future.

The question arises whether all the forecasts of sequence in equation (8.22) are consistent with one another[28] or whether some of them differ from the others to a significant degree. If the former is true, the validity of the inference for the future is strengthened; indeed, if all the subsequent forecasts are much the same, one is justified in taking the average[29] of all the subsequent forecasts as the most reliable statement about the future behaviour of Y_t.

If the various forecasts do not coincide, the situation is much more complicated. An interesting case occurs when all but the last forecast are consistent while the last one differs much from the earlier ones, a case calling for much caution on the part of the user of the forecasting results. Three alternative explanations are possible: (1) the forecasts made previously were computed correctly while an error has been made with the last one, or (2) the other way round, all the previous forecasts were made incorrectly and only the last one is free from error, or (3) the discrepancy of forecasts is simply due to new data pointing to quite different values of explanatory variables, or different behaviour of actors, at time T. If (1) and (2) are excluded and (3) must therefore be accepted, the conclusion must be that conditions are highly unstable, which makes a successful inference about Y_T very difficult indeed.

It cannot be denied that in the past many wrong decisions have been made[30] because 'good' forecasts were not taken into account, 'good' forecasts were used badly, or 'bad' forecasts were used. In the last case, the numerical results of extrapolation into the future were taken for granted while the assumptions on which they were based were forgotten or neglected. In fact any forecast, and thus any long-term forecast, is conditional in the sense that its reliability depends on the fulfilment of a number of conditions and assumptions. Often there is no opportunity to check whether they are indeed fulfilled, and therefore it is difficult, if not impossible, to claim, a priori, that a given forecast will be proved right.

To conclude this section, let us point out yet another problem. When the realisation y_T of the predicted variable Y_T differs substantially from the original forecast y_{Tp}, it does not necessarily mean that the forecast was made in a wrong way. The deviation $|y_T - y_{Tp}|$ may be large not because of errors of inference or of an exceptionally large random shift of Y_T from its expected value, but simply because of some actions undertaken by the decision maker after the forecast had been made.[31] In fact, if y_{Tp} presented a very unsatisfactory outlook, it is only realistic and rational for the user of forecasts to have started an appropriate action to counteract it. If the action is successful the difference between y_T and y_{Tp} is bound to be large, the sign of this difference corresponding to the shift towards more 'acceptable' values of Y_T than y_{Tp}. On the other hand, a large value of $|y_T - y_{Tp}|$ with y_T being even 'worse' than y_{Tp} is to be considered proof of the failure of any actions undertaken, or proof that in spite of the negative outlook of forecast y_{Tp}, no action was undertaken to remedy the situation in the future.

Evaluation

In the foregoing sections a rather gloomy picture has been drawn of the multitude of pitfalls awaiting a forecaster, and the relative weakness of his defensive weapons. Indeed, forecasters used to believe that it was possible to forecast the future and that it was just a matter of finding the right method. It seems now that their belief was unfounded and that it is better to accept the idea that the future is unknown. That, however, is not the philosophy of centrally-planned economies in which many people still think that the future cannot be unknown because it is planned. Some degree of planning of many societal processes is also going on in market economies; there, too, attempts are made to steer the future towards a shape that we, at the present state of our knowledge, think desirable. Thinking in scenarios is the most recent form of shaping the future. Interfutures is a case in point. Scenarios are schematic representations consisting to some extent of future developments that can be envisaged; they are concerned mostly with certain subareas of society. Scenarios have the advantage of presenting alternative developments revealing a whole spectrum of situations for which to prepare oneself; the drawback is that, the future being unknown, the spectrum may become so broad as to make no sense. Moreover, politicians sometimes seem to think that the government can choose one from the array of scenarios and then, just by operating the right instruments, can make the future of that scenario come true. It is this apparent control of the future that makes it so difficult if not impossible to respond flexibly to other than planned developments. Of course, a government can wield certain tools and exert some influence, but it is highly doubtful that it can thus control the fundamental developments of society. Who can say how things will evolve on the political plane (perhaps the most uncontrollable)? Who knows but that the present, more and more childless society will invoke forces that lead to the return of larger families? What solutions may suddenly present themselves to the energy problem?

What medical innovations may lead to an essential prolongation of human life, resulting in the failure of all pension funds? No government can answer such questions, let alone control the events they refer to. And yet it is such developments that will shape our future, as they have done in the past.

Perhaps we had better forget about long-term forecasts, even if making them is, as remarked in the opening sections of this chapter, an amusing and relatively harmless occupation.

There seems more sense in increasing the ability to respond flexibly to developments likely to set in in the next five years or so, and of which the first signs can already be recognised. To that end four conditions must be satisfied, however:

1 The very latest figures have to become available far more quickly than at present; integral censuses whose results take years of cumbersome processing should be replaced with sample data, swiftly collected and processed.
2 Short-term analyses should be more profound: the effectiveness of instruments operated by the government should be carefully examined and new instruments developed.
3 Interdisciplinary models like Forrester's should be constructed, but especially for short-term analysis.
4 Periods for analysis and planning should be internationally harmonised.

When these conditions are met, the result will be, at any rate:

(a) that the information on which forecasts rely is recent, so that forecasts for 1995 are no longer based on statistics from 1985 but on figures of 1988; recent information and shorter forecast periods will lead to more reliable statements, which are moreover more relevant to short-term policy than long-term prognoses based on old statistical material;

(b) that the international comparability of short-term forecasts increases;
(c) that research funds hitherto spent on long-term forecasts come available for more relevant and meaningful activities, especially in the interdisciplinary field.

It may well be that activities performed in this way are less entertaining and less harmless than long-term forecasting; that is the price which must be paid for doing work that has more meaning.

8.2 Some societal trends

Introduction

The future becomes the present and then the past. In the course of time, many futures have become pasts. People had expectations of the future, and when the future had become past, they could check whether their expectations had come true. Had they? Well, if once in a while they had, mostly the reasons were not the preconceived ones. So nowadays economists tend to draw up scenarios rather than make forecasts.

Quite an impressive literature has already developed about scenarios, about as much as about jogging and aerobic dancing. What jogging and aerobic dancing do for the body, scenario-making does for the mind: keeping it supple.

Making a good scenario is not the simple job some people think it is. Most aggravatingly, a scenario has to be consistent, realistic and plausible. Obvious inconsistencies like tax returns exceeding national income are not so difficult to avoid, but the problems lie deeper and to achieve full consistency, much study is necessary.

The question what to do with a set of scenarios once it has been developed, is one the present author prefers to leave unaswered. For one thing, trying to find the answer would lead us too far away from our topic, and for another, frankly, the author is not quite sure what the answer would be, and speculations would not be of much use to the reader.

Politicians, now, they do know all the answers. Having chosen from the parcel of scenarios the one representing a future that suits them, they proclaim that to be the scenario worth realising (though lately they seem to have done so with less enthusiasm than before). Evidently the future conjured up in that way is guaranteed never to be a non-pleasing one. Unfortunately, probably many can be envisaged that are as plausible as they are unpleasant. Here we describe the main elements of one such future.

Starting-points and assumptions

A scenario, like a forecast, needs points of departure. The first is that technical development – also sometimes called technical progress – is assumed to be very fast in future, and that means that, apart from its other benefits, technology will enable us to replace human beings with machines at a faster rate than ever before.

The second point of departure is that the only variable we can compute with reasonable certainty, that is to say, if we exclude the influence of migration, is the future age distribution. We are able to calculate with reasonable accuracy what the age distribution will look like in the year 2000. Admittedly, we have to make some assumptions about the number of births, but we can at any rate approximate the magnitude of the group most relevant to our investigation. The rate of decline in the proportion of young people and the rate of increase in the proportion of older people are relatively simple to compute; by the results, drastic changes in the demographic structure are afoot.

The third, perhaps somewhat less probable, assumption is that society will accept new technology unflinchingly; in other words, its attitude towards technology will be unchanged. Any technical innovation is looked upon as an improvement – well, people do seem to shy off a little when it comes to our stupendous progress in killing techniques but the future Ministry of Economic Affairs will continue to aim at innovation as a natural objective.

Finally, of course there is the economic point of view. We are at present coming out of a period of recession. In what follows we will assume that this recession was indeed temporary, and that total production will continue to increase be it perhaps slowly. We also assume that in the long run the increase in the supply of women on the labour market will come to a stop, and that after the year 2000 the volume of the potentially active population will stabilise in some countries and decline in others. In the longer run demographic problems will not rank therefore among the most important ones.

Owing to technological advance, the recovery of the economy from the short-term recession will change the structure of employment rather than increase its volume. When the economy recovers, no doubt there will be, for example, more activity in the building trade and fewer unemployed construction workers. But people who do the kind of work that lends itself well to automation, robotisation and computerisation will lose their jobs. Will their number be larger or smaller than that of the 'cyclical' unemployed once more back in the production line? That is hard to say. In the long run the increase in structural technological unemployment may well exceed the decrease in cyclical unemployment.

In such circumstances how can we decide whether, in the long run, our economy is flourishing or declining? For example, when GNP increases but also unemployment increases, is the economy then doing well or badly? We have become accustomed to all fundamental quantities in the economy – consumption, investments, employment, etc. – running parallel, but perhaps we should look for a more subtle terminology to describe the present state and the expected development of our national economy. Current terms seem to be getting out of date.

Technology

To what extent technology develops autonomously, that is, independently of societal evolutions, is not easy to assess. A large part of the present technological development aims at lowering the cost of production by what are in fact labour-saving techniques; another part aims at finding and creating new products and improving existing ones. The two avenues are mostly indicated as process innovation and product innovation. They are normal and natural activities. Man has always tried to improve products and processes, though the technological evolution was faster in some periods than in others. But in our time, with its international interwovenness, entrepreneurs more and more feel compelled to develop new techniques just because their competitors on the world market are also at it day and night. The very existence of a company depends on holding one's own in the competitive race. On the other hand, competition is less and less among companies, and more and more among countries and even continents. The 'technological competition of the US, Western Europe and Japan' has become quite a common expression.

Is the redundancy of workers resulting from large-scale technological innovation socially justified? Economically, a technological change in a production process is justified only if it makes the product cheaper, that is, if its production costs less than labour. There is little doubt that this is the case for the individual firm. The usual consolation on the macro level is of course that every innovation opens new perspectives, because it opens new markets and creates new demands, which makes it possible for production to increase so much as to create in the end more employment than before.

The same problem has been discussed and analysed a thousand

times before. Some readers no doubt think of the English workers in the last century who destroyed the newly invented and installed steam-engine. History has very clearly put those workers in the wrong. The same thing has happened time and again, as it had before: technological evolutions have never caused permanent greater unemployment.

Nevertheless, things could be different now. Many expect from the extremely fast developments at least for a long time to come a contraction of the workforce as well as a degeneration of the quality of work for many of those who are still lucky to find a job. Three quotations may illustrate the point:

> As robotic science develops, it will progressively reduce the labor used in industrial production, ultimately to something rather close to zero.
>
> If the growth in service industries that has characterized recent US economic history proves insufficient to absorb all of those persons likely to be forced out of industry by the development and installation of robot equipment, grave social tensions may develop. Assessing these difficulties and dealing wisely with them will be important tasks for both social thinkers and national leaders. (National Science Foundation, 1983, p. 188)

> Concerns relating to structural employment, and the need for imaginative programmes to bring about effective work sharing, are mirrored by concerns about the form and nature of jobs that remain or are created. Recent and extensive surveys carried out by trade unions highlight these questions. These anxieties are not restricted to particular nation states but are found on an international level. One hundred and thirty-nine delegates from over 50 countries at the International Metalworkers' Federation Conference in 1979, set out 13 points for programmes and campaigns since they were 'deeply concerned about the consequences of modern technologies, and in particular, the rapid expansion of the use of microprocessors and robots and the effect of this on the jobs and skills of workers in production, administration and services'. They said 'the uncontrolled spread of microelectronics into all spheres of life will provoke serious disturbances with unforeseeable social consequences'. (Cooley, 1982, pp. 156–7)

> Information technologies are introduced to meet several management objectives concerning costs, productivity and system reliability . . . The two components of management thinking that appear to have the strongest influence are: (a) the desire to reduce human intervention and error, and (b) the desire to control work flow and operators more closely . . . The residual role of the operator in a nearly automated system can be a 'distanced' one in which: (a) the operator has no understanding of the equipment and machinery; (b) the operator cannot assist with repairs or give manual backup; and (c) operators become apathetic, deskilled and unpromotable. (Boddy and Buchanan, 1983)

A third point of view is possible, however. Suppose, we would define unemployment as the hours we *could* work but do not. That somewhat unorthodox definition makes us realise how much the number of hours worked has diminished *for all* of us in the course of the years. Indeed, if it were not for the general decline of the number of working hours, one part of the working population would have gone on working 12 hours a day, while others were out of work. But that is exactly the great threat of the present hour. We can shorten the working hours of all workers alike only as long as the work they do is interchangeable. If for reasons we shall go into later that is no longer true, the success of worktime contraction as a solution for unemployment becomes doubtful. Equal contraction for all might well cause shortages in one group and surpluses in another, non-competitive group. And that is the central problem in the future we are trying to sketch, selective unemployment.

Selective unemployment

Workers employed in activities that can be computerised (to include henceforth automatisable robotisable activities) are in grave danger of losing their jobs as a result of technical advance. The employment of super brains (including those engaged in medical research) is not in jeopardy, for they are the ones that keep technological development going. People doing the kind of basic jobs that computers cannot take over – most constructive workers, waiters in restaurants other than self-service ones, people engaged in the maintenance and cleaning of buildings and streets, in parks, car maintenance, hospitals and sanatoria, policemen and watchmen, etc. – can be reasonably sure of finding work. There will be fewer of them about than there used to be, with obvious consequences, but they will never disappear completely from the picture. The greatest threat, then, is to the large category of jobs that fall in between, for they contain elements of simple or complicated routine which can be performed better, faster and with fewer mistakes by machines:

> Automation may be the ultimate solution to the inroads of foreign competition on American markets, and to the loss of American plants to poorer countries. As more efficient machines replace human workers, smarter capital equipment matters more than cheaper labor. But for automation truly to serve as a remedy of this country's economic ailments, society must become far more explicit about how the benefits of automation are distributed. Leontief's idea – automation combined with redistribution – would require an even greater role for trade unions and for the state than they now play . . . With jobs being created at the top and at the bottom of

> the ladder, America may have difficulty remaining a middle-class society. (Kuttner, 1983, p. 72)

In a recent article in *Au Courant*, the journal of the Economic Council of Canada, it was said:

> Using its microelectronic simulation model in a number of scenarios, the Council finds the impact of tech change to be highly uneven across occupation. While it has the potential to cause considerable worker displacement, tech change can also produce large productivity payoffs, resulting in new jobs or 're-employment'. In fact, such re-employment must more than offset the displacement effect in sales; professional occupations; product fabrication; assembly and repair; processing; and managerial, administrative, and related occupations. Certain other occupations may, however, experience considerable job losses, most notably machining and related occupations, and clerical jobs. Materials handling, equipment-operating, and craft occupations are effected negatively as well.
>
> Major debates rage over whether tech change is eroding the size of the middle class by creating high-skilled and low-skilled jobs, but few in between. New technologies are also said to contribute to the shift in jobs from goods production to service industries, many of which offer low-paying and part-time work only. While the council did not find any conclusive evidence, it points to a number of possible warning signs of middle-class decline.
>
> First, in many respects, Canada is still only at the early stage of technological advance. As the new technologies evolve and spread, shifts in the distribution of income may yet occur. Indeed, in the United States, where tech change has progressed more rapidly, indications of a middle-class erosion do exist. Second, there are disquieting signs that changes in the composition of the middle class are taking place. The council emphasizes that such changes 'must be reflected in the policies that are put into place to facilitate adjustment'. (Council of Canada, 1987, p. 5)

Leaving aside for the moment the consequences just referred to, we may say that process innovation is societally justified – performances being equal – only if the costs of the innovation equipment plus the benefits to be paid to redundant workers amount to less than the wages paid before plus the costs of the old equipment. Should redundant workers receive a benefit of 60 per cent of their former wages, then by the societal account the new equipment must not cost more than 40 per cent of the original wage sum plus the costs of the original equipment.

The question is, who pays the 60 per cent benefit. The present system of unemployment benefit is in fact based on solidarity, that is, on the fiction that the chance of unemployment is the same for everybody and that, therefore, the premiums should be proportionate, and paid by all for the sake of all. But will that system still work if activities are divided into two classes, namely activities that can and that cannot be taken over by computers, with a far greater chance of redundancy for the former category? If the premium is to be deducted from the wages, the burden could eventually become too heavy. Another system will have to be introduced, companies paying premiums that are no longer based on the wages they pay out, but on the value added of their production. In that way a situation can be avoided in which – to take an extreme case – unmanned factories would not contribute at all towards the living of the people they themselves have helped to make redundant.

Let us assume for a moment that in such a way, at least to a certain extent, the present social system can be upheld, but that we are still confronted with massive and lasting unemployment. A number of questions arise. The first is: is it possible for people's ethical feelings about work to change to the effect that not going out to work becomes acceptable? In their present way of thinking, people are apt to be enormously frustrated if they feel they have no job because they are neither intelligent enough to work in 'the higher professions', nor fitted for the arts and crafts at the base. Perhaps the evolution itself will gradually reconcile people to the idea of 'not working for the market', but the process will not be easy.

The second question refers to the social behaviour of the non-working. Working to most people means not just being occupied, it generally implies being creatively engaged, and especially being active away from one's home. What will happen when such distinctions disappear? Will being at home with one's spouse or partner permanently become the normal situation? Will it be easy to stand such a life? Will there still be something to talk about with one's partner when they share what happens during the day? Will there still be any point in living together, or would it be better to live apart and go see each other in the evening? Or will the incomes of the non-working have dropped so low that even that is no longer possible?

The third question is: where will people be doing their non-working? With no workplace to go to (and thus less restricted as to their place of living), people are apt to put more weight on such factors as living environment, scenery and the price of housing. Quite probably, many of those joining the ranks of the non-workers will quit the cities, thus further weakening the economic and financial position of towns, in particular, large towns, which after the recent population and job losses is already precarious.

Demography

The technological developments sketched above take place in a certain socio-economic setting. Let us see whether demographic developments may compensate for the social damage due to technology, or on the contrary, aggravate the damaging effects.

In the past much of the increase in unemployment was in many countries due to large numbers of young people entering the labour market. The number of young people is now declining rapidly, however. Recent low birth figures will cause a progressive decline of the number of young people presenting themselves for the first time on the labour market.

In the recent past, and even in the present time, however, there are still a lot of youngsters who are applying for a job in vain. One result is that the wages for young people have dropped considerably in relation to other wages.

At the other end of the age scale we have the aged people, or rather the pensioners. For several reasons, the category of pensioners is growing considerably. First, owing to the technological evolution in medical science, people live longer. Secondly, well-filled age categories gradually reach the age of pensioning. Thirdly, the tendency to retire or be pensioned off early also adds to the number of pensioners. Now pensioners' incomes usually are not insignificant, and if paid out by reliable pension funds, relatively safe from downward pressures. The pensions of civil servants and those strongly dependent on the general state pension may be under some pressure, but the groups involved are becoming so numerous as to make too much pressure fraught with political risk.

Figures for the Netherlands (CBS, 1984) indicate that in families where the head of the family is in the fifties, as well as in families where the head is over 65 years of age, the net income per capita is about 40 per cent above the per capita incomes in families where the heads of family are in their thirties and forties.

For the future we cannot exclude the possibility of a population in which a small and declining group of young people have relatively low incomes, at least in the medium term, while a larger and increasing group of pensioners have relatively satisfactory income prospects.

How will these developments work out on the structure of the demand for goods and services and, in particular, how much and in what sense will the spending patterns of young and older people differ? And what are the consequences for employment? Perhaps the older people tend to ask for the more labour-intensive products, such as services of hotels, restaurants and other catering establishments, leisure services and other facilities, while the younger people's demand is for new, innovated products: video recorders, home computers, etc., a demand that automatically initiates further innovation. Would the conclusion be warranted that the developments sketched above will increase the demand for non-innovated products at the expense of that for innovated products? And would that counterbalance the innovation urge mentioned earlier?

Let us allow our imagination to run on a little further. Should – as some people foresee – the old-age pensioners together with the non-working go and live the rest of their lives in pleasant and cheaper residential areas, then a spatial separation threatens to develop between the working and the non-working, or better formulated, between income makers and income spenders. Of course, the separation cannot be strict because also in the spending areas there must be people who work to satisfy the needs of those not-working-for-the-market, the spenders.

Social innovation

The philosophy evolved in the previous section, superficial though it may seem, does hold some elements which are not only liable to quantitative research, but whose study might give us some insight into the social tensions to which our urban society will be, and in fact already is, exposed. The crucial question is how to keep going an economy in which a large and possibly growing number of people is ranged out. How can a society keep going when vast categories of people, laid off or pensioned off, no longer have jobs? (By the way, the difference between the two categories is becoming more and more diffuse and perhaps not even relevant any more.) What matters are the social relations between the progressively smaller groups who have to provide the funds, and the non-active.

Spatial separation would tend to make the problem even more acute. To ensure a peaceful coexistence, a heavy claim is laid on both the afflicted and the non-afflicted as well as the government and many societal groupings to work towards social innovation. Trade unions, too, have an enormous task before them in a society in which the role of labour gradually dwindles simply because a growing portion is becoming redundant.

Epilogue

This section, begun so lightly, has gradually assumed a rather grim undertone. The scenario we have sketched is singularly unattractive for society as a whole, and particularly for cities; societal pathology means urban pathology. Of course, there may be other scenarios less repugnant. But are there?

A model that shows a rapidly increasing labour productivity due to innovation, automatically creating an increasing demand for labour-intensive products and thus removing all threats of selective urban unemployment, would be somewhat unrealistic unless we assume at the same time the disappearance of the existing rigidities on the labour market. On the other hand, a scenario in which the non-working are massively being creative in and outside their homes, and at the same time building up an informal, labour-intensive sector specialised in arts and crafts, enjoying the benefit pay made available to them by the exertions of our permanently innovating master brains being indeed happier than when they were still slaving away at work – such a scenario seems more than a little artificial.

Even harder to make would be a scenario by which the very technological development is slowed down and, for instance, advanced armament technologies will no longer diffuse spatially.

Whatever the scenario or model, the march of technology will always be a central element. The future will be determined by technology and by society's response to it.

The optimists among us will believe that a wiser society will overcome the negative aspects of technology. Things are – as always – harder for pessimists.

Reverting to the idea implicit in the opening sentence, I tend to agree with the people of Vienna who, assembled in the wine cellars of their remarkable city, after the fall of the Austrian-Hungarian monarchy, declared that the situation of their country was hopeless but not serious.

Notes

1 Jay W. Forrester, *World Dynamics*, Cambridge, Mass.: Wright-Allen Press, p. IX.

2 Naturally, there is no direct relation between x_{ij} and d_{ij} if other traffic than x_{ij} passes along the connection *ij*, as will happen in most cases.

3 About the basic preconditions of the theory of forecasting see, for instance, Pawlowski (1973).

4 For reference to the concepts and methods of the theory of catastrophes, see Thom (1972). An interesting example of using this theory for the forecast of an economic phenomenon is provided by Pietrabissa (1979).

5 Such changes can either affect the rate of growth (or of decline)

of the variable involved or result in reversing the previous trend (decline instead of growth, say).

6 Note that as economic variables usually exhibit monotonic trends, long-term forecasting usually means using the models well outside the observed range of their variation. This, in turn, means that the standard measures of fit of sample data with the model are of little use for discrimination among the various admissible functional forms.

7 For instance, if it is known that the predicted variable has an imminent 'saturation level', one can eliminate all such functions which are not bound.

8 Obviously the choice of ϵ lies with the user of forecasts and not with the econometrician to find out the correct analytical form of the model.

9 Let us add here that the same approach is possible when a forecast of the Y_T variable is sought and there are doubts about the correct form of the trend function.

10 The problem dealt with in this section implicitly assumes that the functional form of the model remains constant while there are changes of the structural parameters the chosen family of functions depends on. Moreover, it is assumed throughout this section that the correct functional form is not only constant but also known.

11 This explains the assumption about the large number of observations. Should it be otherwise, then the consecutive estimates would be used on too small samples and might vary wildly because of large random errors.

12 Such tests can, for instance, be found in Chow (1960) or Brown, Durbin and Evans (1975).

13 The assumption of linearity is not essential and could be replaced with another, namely that the trend of the parameters is described by a higher-order polynomial.

14 Formula (8.11) shows, however, one disadvantage of the approach being discussed, namely that it increases the number of parameters which must finally be estimated. As can be verified, assuming β_i's to be an hth-order polynomial of the t-variable increases the number of parameters to be estimated h times in respect of the case of the original model in (8.9) with constant structural parameters.

15 See, for instance, A. Pagan (1978), P. Weamy (1971) or Singh *et al.* (1976).

16 For lack of space we omit details about how such estimation can be done.

17 The assumption of linearity is again not essential, although it

simplifies somewhat the procedure of building pessimistic and optimistic forecasts.

18 Note that from the theoretical point of view it would be more appropriate to determine the numbers β_i and $\overline{\beta}_i$ using the joint multivariate distribution of all the structural parameters. The estimation of such distribution, however, is very complicated, so one must use the marginal distributions instead.

19 This problem does not arise when one is forecasting using trend models as the value of the t-variable for the predicted time period is automatically known.

20 In practice this distribution is known only approximately. The minimum requirement is that the range of possible variation of the X_i's be known. In such a case, one can assume that all values within such intervals are equally likely.

21 For a more detailed exposition of this approach see Pawlowski (1978).

22 See Pawlowski (1968).

23 See Pawlowski (1980).

24 The difficulty connected with the construction of such long-run econometric models is mainly the fact that it involves a very large number of explanatory variables, jeopardising an efficient estimation of the model.

25 The main causes of large errors have already been enumerated in the section 'Instability of the functional form of relations' of this chapter.

26 This is so because usually such actions take time, especially investment activities aimed at creating new production capacity or infrastructure facilities, which moreover tend to have very long life cycles. On the other hand, when a system is not supposed to undergo major changes, short-term forecasting will be used to assess its future state.

27 That is, of the values of the explanatory variables of the model used for forecasting.

28 Forecasts are said to be consistent if the maximum absolute value of the difference between two of them does not exceed a preassigned level, σ.

29 Usually this will be some weighted average of individual forecasts, the weights being some function of the chosen measure of accuracy of these forecasts.

30 On the other hand, let us not forget that some correct forecasts have also been made.

31 Observe that in the case of long-term forecasting there is always a lot of time before the horizon T is reached, which makes it

possible, physically and otherwise, to get some activity started towards a specific goal.

References

Boddy, David and Buchanan, David A. (1983), 'Information technology and the experience of work' in *Information Technology, Fast Programme Commission of the European Committee National Board for Science and Technology*, Brussels: EC, pp. 156–7.

Brown, R.L., Durbin, J. and Evans, J.M. (1975), 'Techniques for testing the constancy of regression relationships over time', *Journal of Royal Statistical Society B*, vol. 37, pp. 149–92.

Centraal Bureau voor de Statistiek, Heerlen, The Netherlands: Budgetonderzoek, 1984.

Chow, G.C. (1960), 'Tests of equality between sets of coefficients in two linear regressions', *Econometrica*, vol. 28, no. 3, pp. 591–605.

Cooley, M. (1982), 'New technologies – some trade union concerns and possible solutions' in *Information Society*, Amsterdam: North-Holland, p. 194.

Economic Council of Canada (1987), 'Tech change and the job market', *Au Courant* (Journal of the Economic Council of Canada), vol. 8, no. 1.

Forrester, Jay W. (1971), *World Dynamics*, Cambridge, Mass.: Wright-Allen Press.

Koyck, L.M. (1954), *An Econometric Study of the Time-Shape of Economic Reactions*, Amsterdam: North-Holland.

Kuttner, Bob (1983), 'The declining middle', *Atlantic Monthly*, July, p. 60ff.

Outlook for Science and Technology: The Next Five Years, Report for the National Science Foundation, Washington, 1983, vol. III, p. 188.

Pagan, A. (1978), *An Unified Approach to Estimation and Influence for Stochastically Varying Coefficient Regression Models*, CORE Discussion Paper no. 7814, Louvain, Belgium.

Pietrabissa, E. (1979), 'Un possibile utilizzo della teoria della catastrofe nella costruzione di modelli econometri', *Rivista di Statistica Applicata*, pp. 171–84.

Pawlowski, Z. (1968), *Theory of Econometric Prediction in the Socialist Economy* (in Polish), Warsaw: PWN.

Pawlowski, Z. (1973), *Econometric Predictions* (in Polish), Warsaw: PWN.

Pawlowski, Z. (1978), *The Use of Alternative Predictions in Long-Term Inference into the Future*, Research Report RR-78-15,

International Institute for Applied Systems Analysis, Laxenburg, Austria.
Pawlowski, Z. (1980), *Basic Problems of Long-Term Inference into the Future*, Working Paper WP-80-18, International Institute for Applied Systems Analysis, Laxenburg, Austria.
Pawlowski, Z., Barczak, A., Fijalkowska, Cz., Stolarska, E. and Zadora, H. (1979), *Econometric Method of Prediction of Fulfilment of Econometric Plans* (in Polish), Warsaw: PWN.
Singh, A., Nagar, A.L., Choudhry, N.K. and Raj, B. (1976), 'On the estimation of structural change: a generalisation of the random coefficient regression', *International Economic Review*, vol. 17, no. 2, pp. 340–61.
Swamy, P.A.V.B. (1971), *Statistical Inference in Random Coefficient Models*, Berlin: Springer Verlag.
Thom, R. (1972), *Stabilité structurelle et morphogénèse*, Reading.

Index